JOURNAL FOR THE STUDY OF THE OLD TESTAMENT SUPPLEMENT SERIES

262

Sheffield Academic Press

Gender and Law in the Hebrew Bible and the Ancient Near East

edited by
Victor H. Matthews,
Bernard M. Levinson
and Tikva Frymer-Kensky

Journal for the Study of the Old Testament
Supplement Series 262

Published by
Sheffield Academic Press Ltd
Mansion House
19 Kingfield Road
Sheffield S11 9AS
England

Typeset by Sheffield Academic Press
and
Printed on acid-free paper in Great Britain
by Bookcraft Ltd
Midsomer Norton, Bath

British Library Cataloguing in Publication Data

A catalogue record for this book is available
from the British Library

ISBN 1-85075-886-7

CONTENTS

PREFACE: FROM *THE WOMAN'S BIBLE* TO *GENDER AND LAW*

In November, 1995, the Biblical Law Group of the Society of Biblical Literature held a special session to commemorate the centennial of the publication of *The Woman's Bible*, edited by Elizabeth Cady Stanton.[1] Four papers were presented: those by Tikva Frymer-Kensky, Carolyn Pressler, Martha T. Roth, and Harold Washington. That session generated strong interest and a very lively debate. Consequently, the Biblical Law Group decided to solicit additional papers, from members and non-members alike, and to publish a volume on gender and law in the Bible and the ancient Near East. A substantive introduction by Tikva Frymer-Kensky follows. This preface, in the spirit of the original session, commemorates the neglected accomplishment of the editor of *The Woman's Bible*.

Elizabeth Cady Stanton, who lived 1815–1902, organized a group of women scholars to comment upon Scripture from a feminist perspective. These women systematically went through the Bible, marking passages where women were prominent either for the inferior status accorded them or for their absence altogether. The feminist editors then cut these passages out, pasting them onto blank pages, on which they wrote their own commentary. This new version of R^P, the final redactor of the Pentateuch, is often full of understandable outrage.[2] Moreover, the women responsible for the project undertook the work at great personal and professional cost. They were alienated both from the church of their day, for their feminist claims to equality, and from the

1. *The Woman's Bible* (ed. Elizabeth Cady Stanton; 2 vols.; New York: European Publishing Company, 1895–98; repr.; New York: Arno Press, 1972). Valuable information on Stanton's life and work is provided by Jeanne Stevenson-Moessner, 'Elizabeth Cady Stanton, Reformer to Revolutionary: A Theological Trajectory', *JAAR* 62 (1994), pp. 673-97.

2. Stanton's project actually includes the whole Old Testament as well as the New Testament.

Women's Movement of their day, for embracing a liberal, historical-critical approach to Scripture.[3]

The 1972 photo-reprint of *The Woman's Bible* is made from an original that contains the handwritten notes of Stanton herself. On the dedication page of volume II, she wrote, in large and vigorous hand:

> A Merry Christmas & Happy New Year
> compliments of Elizabeth Cady Stanton
> Genesis Chap I says Man & Woman were a simultaneous creation
> Chap II says Woman was an afterthought
> Which is true?

That question—which is true?—was central to her project and to the concerns of the contributors to this volume. Stanton's book pulls no punches. She saw biblical law as enforcing the degradation of women and inscribing male power. She saw it as denying women a point of view because of the seemingly overwhelming orientation of biblical law to a male addressee conceived of as a legal person. She stressed the near absence of woman as legal subject and insisted: 'We cannot accept any code or creed that uniformly defrauds woman of all her natural rights' (p. 127). At the same time, the question has to be raised, are either man or woman by 'nature' legal persons—or is nature not the realm of brute power rather than a model of equality? Is it not Scripture itself, both in the creation story and in the laws, that offers an emancipatory vision of man and woman alike conceived as 'person'—independent of gender? Were this the case, Scripture would provide its own critique and itself be the ultimate source of Stanton's trenchant demands for equality.

These are among the issues that will be addressed, pro and con, by the contributors to this volume, all of whom probe how biblical and cuneiform law constructs and represents matters of gender.

Bernard M. Levinson
Chair, Biblical Law Section
Society of Biblical Literature

3. For a valuable exposition of the continuing marginalization of Stanton, Irene Makarushka, 'Elizabeth Cady Stanton and *The Woman's Bible*', *Biblicon* 1 (1997), pp. 43-60.

ABBREVIATIONS

AB	Anchor Bible
ABD	David Noel Freedman (ed.), *The Anchor Bible Dictionary* (New York: Doubleday, 1992)
AfO	*Archiv für Orientforschung*
AfO.B	Archiv für Orientforschung Beiheft
AJS	Association for Jewish Studies
ANET	James B. Pritchard (ed.), *Ancient Near Eastern Texts Relating to the Old Testament* (Princeton: Princeton University Press, 1950)
AOAT	Alter Orient und Altes Testament
AOS	American Oriental Series
ArOr	*Archiv orientálni*
ASOR	American Schools of Oriental Research
BASOR	*Bulletin of the American Schools of Oriental Research*
BBB	Bonner biblische Beiträge
BDB	Francis Brown, S.R. Driver and Charles A. Briggs, *A Hebrew and English Lexicon of the Old Testament* (Oxford: Clarendon Press, 1907)
BETL	Bibliotheca ephemeridum theologicarum lovaniensium
BFCT	Beiträge zur Förderung christlicher Theologie
Bib	*Biblica*
BibInt	*Biblical Interpretation: A Journal of Contemporary Approaches*
BJS	Brown Judaic Studies
BTB	*Biblical Theology Bulletin*
BWANT	Beiträge zur Wissenschaft vom Alten und Neuen Testament
BZ	*Biblische Zeitschrift*
BZAW	Beihefte zur *ZAW*
CAD	Ignace I. Gelb *et al.* (eds.), *The Assyrian Dictionary of the Oriental Institute of the University of Chicago* (Chicago: Oriental Institute, 1964–)
CBQ	*Catholic Biblical Quarterly*
CBS	Tablets in the collections of the University Museum of the University of Pennsylvania, Philadelphia
CH	Code of Hammurabi (older term for LH)
ConBOT	Coniectanea biblica, Old Testament
CT	Cuneiform Tablets
EncJud	*Encyclopaedia Judaica*

ErF	Erträge der Forschung
FAT	Forschungen zum Alten Testament
FOTL	The Forms of the Old Testament Literature
FRLANT	Forschungen zur Religion und Literatur des Alten und Neuen Testaments
HALAT	Ludwig Koehler *et al.* (eds.), *Hebräisches und aramäisches Lexikon zum Alten Testament* (5 vols.; Leiden: E.J. Brill, 1967–1995)
HAT	Handbuch zum Alten Testament
HKAT	Handkommentar zum Alten Testament
HL	Hittite Laws (ca. 1650–1500 BCE) (Roth, *Law Collections*, pp. 213-37)
HSM	Harvard Semitic Monographs
HTR	*Harvard Theological Review*
HUCA	*Hebrew Union College Annual*
ICC	International Critical Commentary
ICK	Inscriptions cunéiformes du Kultépé
IEJ	*Israel Exploration Journal*
IKZ	Internationale katholische Zeitschrift
JAAR	*Journal of the American Academy of Religion*
JANESCU	Journal of Ancient Near Eastern Society of Columbia University
JAOS	*Journal of the American Oriental Society*
JBL	*Journal of Biblical Literature*
JBTh	Jahrbuch für biblische Theologie
JCS	*Journal of Cuneiform Studies*
JEN	Joint Expedition with the Iraq Museum at Nuzi
JFSR	*Journal of Feminist Studies in Religion*
JJS	*Journal of Jewish Studies*
JNES	*Journal of Near Eastern Studies*
JSOT	*Journal for the Study of the Old Testament*
JSOTSup	*Journal for the Study of the Old Testament*, Supplement Series
JSS	*Journal of Semitic Studies*
KAJ	Keilsschrifttexte aus Assur juristischen Inhalts
KTS	J. Lewy, *Die altassyrischen Texte vom Kültepe bei Kaisarije*
KTU	M. Dietrich, O. Loretz, J. Sanmartín, *Die keilalphabetischen Texte aus Ugarit* (Neukirchen–Vluyn: Neukirchener Verlag, 1976)
LE	Laws of Eshnunna (ca. 1770 BCE) (Roth, *Law Collections*, pp. 57-70)
LH	Laws of Hammurabi (ca. 1750 BCE) (Roth, *Law Collections*, pp. 71-142)
LL	Laws of Lipit-Ishtar (ca. 1930 BCE) (Roth, *Law Collections*, pp. 24-35)
LNB	Neo-Babylonian Laws (ca. 700 BCE) (Roth, *Law Collections*, pp. 143-49)

LU	Laws of Ur-Namma (ca. 2100 BCE) (Roth, *Law Collections*, pp. 15-22)
MAL	Middle Assyrian Laws (ca. 1076 BCE) (Roth, *Law Collections*, pp. 155-94)
MVAG	Mitteilungen der vorderasiatisch-ägyptischen Gesellschaft
NAB	*New American Bible*
NCB	New Century Bible
NICOT	New International Commentary on the Old Testament
NRSV	New Revised Standard Version
OBO	Orbis biblicus et orientalis
OIP	Oriental Institute Publications, Oriental Institute, University of Chicago
Or	*Orientalia*
OTL	Old Testament Library
PBS	Publications of the Babylonian Section, University Museum, University of Pennsylvania
QD	Quaestiones disputatae
RB	*Revue biblique*
REB	Revised English Bible
RIDA	*Revue internationale des droits de l'antiquité*
Roth, *Law Collections*	Martha T. Roth, *Law Collections from Mesopotamia and Asia Minor*. With a contribution by Harry A. Hoffer, Jr (SBL Writings from the Ancient World Series, 6; Atlanta: Scholars Press, 2nd edn, 1997).
SBAB	Stuttgarter biblische Aufsatzbände
SBL	Society of Biblical Literature
SBLDS	SBL Dissertation Series
SBLMS	SBL Monograph Series
ScrHie	Scripta Hierosolymitana
SDIC	Studia et documenta ad iura Orientis
SESJ	Schriften der Finnischen Exegetischer Gesellschaft
SFSHJ	South Florida Studies in the History of Judaism
TBT	*The Bible Today*
TDOT	G.J. Botterweck and H. Ringgren (eds.), *Theological Dictionary of the Old Testament*
TIM	Texts in the Iraq Museum
TLZ	*Theologische Literaturzeitung*
TOTC	Tyndale Old Testament Commentaries
TRev	*Theologische Revue*
TuM	Texte und Materialen der Frau Professor Hilprecht Collection of Babylonian Antiquities im Eigentum der Universität Jena
UF	*Ugarit-Forschungen*
USQR	*Union Seminary Quarterly Review*
UT	Cyrus H. Gordon, *Ugaritic Textbook* (Analecta orientalia, 38; Rome: Pontifical Biblical Institute Press, 1965)
VT	*Vetus Testamentum*
VTSup	*Vetus Testamentum*, Supplements
WBC	Word Biblical Commentary

WO	*Die Welt des Orients*
ZA	*Zeitschrift für Assyriologie*
ZAH	*Zeitschrift für Althebraistik*
ZAR	*Zeitschrift für Altorientalische und Biblische Rechtsgeschichte*
ZAW	*Zeitschrift für die alttestamentliche Wissenschaft*
ZBK	*Zürcher Bibelkommentar*
ZTK	*Zeitschrift für Theologie und Kirche*

LIST OF CONTRIBUTORS

Marc Brettler is an Associate Professor of Hebrew Bible at Brandeis University. He has published widely on metaphor and the Bible, the nature of biblical historical texts, and gender issues and the Bible. He has written *God is King: Understanding and Israelite Metaphor* (Sheffield: JSOT Press, 1989) and *The Creation of History in Ancient Israel* (London: Routledge, 1995). He is also committed to applying innovative methods to classroom teaching and is the recipient of the Michael A. Walzer Award for Excellence in Teaching.

Carol J. Dempsey is Assistant Professor of Biblical Studies and Theology at the University of Portland. Most recently, she has published a series of articles related to biblical theology for the *New Pastoral Dictionary of Biblical Theology* (Collegeville: Liturgical Press, 1996), and is currently working on a book, *Paradigm Shifts for a New Creation: A Liberationist-Critical Reading of the Prophets* (forthcoming from Fortress Press).

Tikva Frymer-Kensky is Professor of Hebrew Bible and Jewish Theology at the Divinity School of the University of Chicago. She draws on the fields of Bible, the ancient Near East, feminist criticism and contemporary Jewish theology in her books, *In the Wake of the Goddess: Women, Culture and the Biblical Transformation of Pagan Myth*
(New York: The Free Press, 1992) and *Motherprayer: The Pregnant Woman's Spiritual Companion* (New York: Putnam–Riverhead, 1995). She is currently working on *Victims, Vivtors and Virgins: Reading the Women of the Bible* (Schocken Books) and *The Judicial Ordeal of the Ancient Near East* (Styx).

Bernard M. Levinson holds the Berman Family Chair of Jewish Studies and Hebrew Bible at the University of Minnesota, where he is an Associate Professor in the Department of Classical and Near Eastern Studies. He is the author of *Deuteronomy and the Hermeneutics of Legal Innovation* (New York: Oxford University Press, 1997), and the editor of *Theory and Method in Biblical and Cuneiform Law* (JSOTSup,181; Sheffield: Sheffield Academic Press, 1994). He is currently a member of the Institute for Advanced Study in Princeton, NJ (with support from the National Endowment for the Humanities), an honorary Fellow at the Center for Judaic Studies at the University of Pennsylvania, and Chair of the SBL Biblical Law Section.

Victor H. Matthews is Professor of Religious Studies at Southwest Missouri State University, where he has served since 1984. He is currently the editor of the ASOR Book Series, Convener of the Conference of SBL Regional Secretaries, and Secretary of the Biblical Law Group. His most recent publications include with Don C. Benjamin a second, revised edition of *Old Testament Parallels: Laws and Stories in the Ancient Near East* (Mahwah, NJ: Paulist Press, 1997) and with James C. Moyer, *The Old Testament: Text and Context* (Peabody, MA: Hendrickson, 1997).

Geoffrey P. Miller is Professor of Law and Director of the Center for the Study of Central Banks at New York University. A former law clerk to Supreme Court Justice Byron R. White, Miller has written widely on a number of topics in legal studies, including a series of articles on Hebrew Bible topics.

Eckart Otto is Professor of Old Testament and Biblical Archaeology at the Institut für Alttestamentliche Theologie, Ludwig-Maximilians-Universität, Munich, Germany. He is the founder and editor of the annual *Zeitschrift für die Altorientalische und Biblische Rechtsgeschichte* and is co-editor of *Studia et Documenta ad Iura Orientis antiqui pertinentia* (Leiden: E.J. Brill). Among his most recent publications are *Theologische Ethik des Alten Testaments* (Stuttgart: W. Kohlhammer, 1994; English translation forthcoming) and *Kontinuum und Proprium: Studien zur Soziel und Rechtsgeschichte des Alten Orients und des Alten Testaments* (Wiesbaden: Otto Harrassowitz, 1996).

Carolyn J. Pressler is Associate Professor of Old Testament Theology at the United Theological Seminary of the Twin Cities. She is the author of *The View of Women Found in the Deuteronomic Family Laws*

(BZAW, 216; Berlin: W. de Gruyter, 1993) as well as a number of articles and papers on gender and pentateuchal law. She is currently working on a book on women and the family in pentateuchal law.

Martha T. Roth is Professor of Assyriology at the University of Chicago in the Oriental Institute, the Department of Near Eastern Languages and Civilizations, the Committee on the Ancient Mediterranean World, the Committee on Jewish Studies, and the College, and Lecturer at the Law School. She is the Editor-in-Charge of the Chicago Assyrian Dictionary.

Raymond Westbrook is Professor of Ancient Law at the Johns Hopkins University, where he teaches in the departments of Near Eastern Studies (cuneiform law and diplomacy, biblical law) and Classics (Roman law). He is a member of the bar of England and Wales and holds degrees in law from the University of Oxford and the Hebrew University of Jerusalem, and a PhD in Assyriology from Yale University.

Harold C. Washington is Associate Professor of Hebrew Bible at Saint Paul School of Theology, Kansas City, Missouri. His publications include *Wealth and Poverty in the Instruction of Amenemope and the Hebrew Proverbs* (Atlanta: Scholars Press, 1994) and 'The "Strange Woman" of Proverbs 1–9 and Post-Exilic Judaean Society', in T. Eskenazi and K. Richards (eds.), *Second Temple Studies*. II. *Temple and Community in the Persian Period* (Sheffield: Sheffield Academic Press, 1994). The present essay is a preliminary version of a chapter in a forthcoming book on violence and the construction of gender in the Hebrew Bible.

Gender and Law: An Introduction

Tikva Frymer-Kensky

The ten articles in this book draw upon a very great variety of techniques, methodologies and disciplines to study the many ways in which gender impacts on biblical institutions. This book provides a perspective that emphasizes how gender can illuminate aspects of biblical texts that would otherwise stay buried or unnoticed. Biblical laws, narratives, songs and psalms are investigated for diverse questions relating to life, image, status and behavior. Brettler presents an important aspect of the lives of women: how and what do they pray? Miller, Dempsey and Roth consider the stereotypical images of women; Pressler and Westbrook discuss the varying social statuses of women, slave and free; Frymer-Kensky and Matthews look at the connection between gender and laws of honor and shame, and Frymer-Kensky, Matthews, Otto and Washington analyze the prescriptive laws about women's sexuality.

There is great diversity in the methodologies employed to answer these questions. All the articles build on fine techniques of close reading and philological analysis. In addition, Otto relies on two traditional European disciplines: *Rechtsgeschichte* (the classic history of law approach) and redaction criticism of the Bible. Washington draws upon one of the Critical Legal Studies movements in the study and philosophy of law, Frymer-Kensky and Matthews build on the work of social and legal anthropologists, and Frymer-Kensky, Roth and Westbrook concentrate on Mesopotamian law.

Gender Studies

Several of the articles remind us that gender counts also in non-legal arenas. Marc Brettler's article on women's prayer ranges far beyond the Hebrew Bible—both before and after—to look at the role of prayer in women's lives and at the role of women in Israelite prayer life. Starting with Psalm 128, Brettler notes that כל יוא יהוה, *'all* the fearers of Yhwh' are rewarded with fruitful wives. Israelite women are peripheralized, both in the mind of the Psalmist and physically in the corner of the house. Brettler suggests that this psalm was influenced by the misogynist wisdom tradition. The late date of this Psalm and of the wisdom texts may be as decisive as genre in marginalizing women.

Women are rarely specifically mentioned in the Psalms, except in the second halves of parallel lines, which, Brettler argues, have no independent semantic weight. Even compassion is illustrated in Psalm 103 by the image of a compassionate father. Truly gender-inclusive psalms like Psalm 65 are a very small minority, and some of these may not be intentionally so.

Brettler rejects עלמות of Psalm 46, or משררות in Ezra and Nehemiah as evidence for women cultic composers or singers. On the other hand, even P lets women be Nazirites, and women clearly participated in the cult and are reckoned as part of the congregation in Deuteronomy 31. Like Phyllis Bird, Brettler concludes that the primary cultic distinction in the Bible is between priest and laity rather than male and female.

Brettler asks: if women were part of the active laity, what Psalms did they say? Quoting a Jewish love-charm from the Cairo Genizah translated by Schiffman and Swartz and birth incantations from Babylonia that Frymer-Kensky has translated in *Motherprayer*, Brettler suggests that Israelite women probably also had rituals and prayers not recorded by the Biblical authors. For the Biblical record, Hannah could recite the Song of Hannah because its theme of reversal of fortune and of barren women giving birth would be appropriate to her situation. Brettler introduces the concept of 'secondary use' of the Psalms: whatever their original *Sitz im Leben* was, they could be appropriated by women.

A second non-legal article, by Carol Dempsey, deals with the now familiar problem of the once-beloved metaphor of Israel as wife of God. Previous studies have concentrated on Hosea's development of this image. Dempsey analyzes Ezekiel's presentation of this image in Ezekiel 16 and looks to the legal and social realities that underlie the details of Ezekiel's presentation. Jerusalem begins as an exposed and abandoned daughter, reminding us how vulnerable infant daughters often are. Like other foundlings, she is seen by a passer-by, Yhwh, who adopts her as a ward and ultimately marries her. Dempsey reacts to the 'adornment' of Jerusalem with splendor as to the adornment of other women: women are adorned because their natural beauty is not valued and moreover, because the woman becomes a reflection of the man's care. But the moment God makes Jerusalem beautiful, he accuses her of trusting in her beauty and playing the whore with Egyptians, Assyrians and Babylonians and still being lustful. God accuses Israel of adultery, idolatry, child sacrifice and forgetfulness of Yhwh. Through these accusations Yhwh is revealed as verbally and physically abusive even though justly angry, a God who will bring punishment until his fury is abated. Moreover, three of these misdeeds are punishable by death. And so Yhwh was sentencing and handing over his wife to the death penalty. The law is on the side of the men, but the sentence goes even farther than the law, for instead of being sentenced themselves, the lovers will humiliate her as she stands naked. God then heaps scorn upon Jerusalem. When the evil of Jerusalem and her sisters Samaria and Sodom is attributed to their evil mother, Dempsey asks if this does not induce the readers to form assumptions about the evilness of women. The very use of the metaphor of husband and wife for God and Jerusalem, she concludes, is fraught with theological problems.

A third non-legal article also deals with a question about stereotypical images of women. Geoffrey Miller offers an analysis of the Song of Deborah as a riposte. A riposte, explains Miller is a response to a verbal insult that accepts part of the insult as true, but claims it as a point of pride. Miller reconstructs the original insult from the Song: 'the Israelites are backward hill people who lack culture, refinement and sophistication, who adhere to absurd norms of hospitality and whose men are dominated by masculine women' (p. 119). The Song mocks the uselessness of the sophisticated chariotry of the Canaanites, lauds Yael's use of hospitality to defeat Sisera and revels in the strength of Deborah and Yael.

Legal Texts

The premise of the insult against the Israelites is that women are not fighters. This was a common belief in the ancient Near East, and shows up as part of the defense's argument in the Nippur homicide trial that Martha Roth analyzes. The text is a summation of court proceedings, real or imagined, that was studied in the schools of Mesopotamia. In telling about the case, it reveals assumptions about women's roles and fears about what dissatisfied women might do. Nin-dada was accused of keeping mum about the murder of her husband. The woman's defenders played what we might call the 'misogyny card': 'given even that

Nin-Dada, daughter of Lu-Ninurta might have killed her husband—but a woman, what can she do, to warrant that she be killed'? Roth rightly labels this a plea of 'diminished capacity', but we can see operating behind it the familiar stereotype: women are weaker and easily intimidated into collusion. The court in its decision operates on a different assumption about women, applying a harsh standard, and 'proceeds to spin what might appear to be a paranoid and prejudicial series of escalating offenses' (p. 179). A woman does not value her husband: this could bring her to know his enemy (lover) and from there she might ask to kill her husband, and then be also an accessory after the fact. Because she violates the trust, says the court, 'her guilt exceeds even that of those who kill a man'. This harsh standard is a fear of the 'slippery slope'—even a minor infraction will lead to adultery and then murder. Clearly, Roth concludes, the law assumes its subject to be an adult male of the established class. But, Roth cautions, another factor is also at work: the woman has violated a contractual obligation.

Two sets of contradictory stereotypes operate in the Nippur homicide trial: one, that women are weak and easily intimidated, and the other, that women are inherently dangerous and wives are suspect. These are the same assumptions that we have encountered before. The court in its sentencing has much the same set of assumptions that inform Ezekiel as he depicts God's judgment on Jerusalem. The defense argument, that woman are weak, is the flip side of the belief that men are naturally warriors, women are not, and that ferocity in battle is a mark of manhood or (in Miller's reconstructed taunt) of unnatural, manly women. In his article on violence and gender, Harold Washington also brings examples of this belief. He cites the oaths of Hittite soldiers: 'whoever breaks these oaths...let these oaths change him from a man to a woman' (p. 197). The stereotype persists in Israel even though the Song of Deborah is one of Israel's oldest poems, despite the memory of Yael. Biblical prophets taunt their enemies in the old stereotypical language. 'Look to your troops', says Nahum: 'they are women in your midst'! (Nah. 3.13, sentiments expressed also by Jeremiah and Isaiah, for which see p. 197.)

Washington argues that this stereotype is actually part of a basic belief that violent power belongs to men and women are its victims. Warfare itself is imaged as rape and the cities attacked are its victims. Washington turns to Deuteronomy to see how this concept is embedded in the legal system. He starts with the basic realization that Deuteronomy is framed by military orations. They may seem gender-inclusive, but the war code itself in Deut. 20.1-20 is addressed to the army, which is male. The female reader is gender-identified with the victim: the city. The feminine grammatical gender of 'city' adds to the force of the imagery: you attack *her*, *she* opens and you seize *her*. Addressing the commonly held belief that the law code is 'humane' and restrains violence, Washington argues that no text that calls for destruction is humane, and that violence is only constrained with the aim of more efficient exploitation.

To Washington, the purpose of the law of the war-captive woman in Deut. 21.10-14 is not to prevent battlefield rape (for the law takes effect after capture) but to 'assure a man's prerogative to abduct a woman through violence, keep her indefinitely if he wishes or discard her if she is deemed unsatisfactory' (p. 207). Prior claims on the woman by the men in her life disappear with their defeat. The captive woman waits a month for a liminal transition to the captor's community. A whole month ensures paternity, and the rituals performed during the month are the typical degrading elements of transition rituals. Even after a month, sex with her might still be rape, for 'to assume the consent of the woman is to erase her personhood'. Washington notes that there is no biblical Hebrew word for 'rape', and that the laws of sexual assault in Deut. 22.23-29 are really a subset of the general laws of adultery, 'which is defined as one male's violation of another man's right to possess a woman' (p. 208). These laws secure men's property interests. Deuteronomy accepts the prerogative of males to use force, and does not assume that women have bodily integrity. As a result, these rules silence women's experience of violence. Washington draws on Foucault's insight that the ostensible regulation of power can legitimate the effective exercise of domination and violence. In their regulation of sexual access to women, the laws authorize male force if certain conditions and criteria are met. As a result, the laws contribute to constructing male gender as licitly violent and have helped maintain the institutions of warfare and rape.

The assault and adultery laws of Deut. 22.20-29 are also the subject of Otto's study. Otto also realizes that the law protects the privileges of the male. But he compares Deuteronomy to Exodus and notes that in Exod. 22.15-16, the father could deny the marriage of his daughter. In Deuteronomy the culprit was forced to marry her and not divorce her.

To Washington, this provision seals the rapist's rights over the woman. To Otto, it is a fundamental improvement in the status of women. He believes that the woman is treated as her own legal subject, not an appendage of her father's will. Otto also examines the slandered bride in Deut. 22.13-21. He interprets the bridegroom's accusation as an attempt to divorce his bride without giving her her dowry and divorce money. If the malicious rumors are proved, she will die and he will suffer no financial loss. But if the charge could be refuted, he could no longer divorce her. Otto argues that this protects women from unfair divorce. Using the same kind of analysis for Deuteronomy's law against remarriage and the provision of the levirate, Otto concludes that the Deuteronomic laws had a protective attitude towards the legal status of women and were deeply concerned with the restriction of male predominance. I wonder, however, whether Deuteronomy's restriction of the dominance of one male (husband or father) over a woman really restricts male predominance when power is vested in a council of males or in a patriarchal state.

Matthews also studies the law of the slandered bride. Like Otto, Matthews believes that the bridegroom's accusations are a ploy to divorce the girl without financial loss. But Matthews concentrates on the damage that the accusation can do to the girl's family, on the shame that this accusation brings and the danger of the family's loss of social status. He interprets the execution of the girl (if she is proved guilty) at her father's tent door as a mark of shame for the household for the fraud they perpetrated when they passed their daughter off as a virgin. The honor of the household, in this case of the husband, is also the underlying issue in the trial of the suspected adulteress in Num. 5.11-21 Here, the husband's suspicions are not a ploy, and in some instances may result from someone's accusation. But since there is no direct evidence and she has not been caught *in flagrante delicto*, the matter cannot be resolved. The legal remedy, argues Matthews, is a trial by ordeal. It should be noted that even though Matthews calls the procedure an ordeal, his description of the ritual, in which the potion is not life-threatening and is really a prop for the execration, is more the profile of a solemn purgatory oath. By this act, the community is 'restrained from direct action since her punishment will come directly from God' (p. 108), and the honor of the household is reaffirmed.

Frymer-Kensky also studies the laws about sleeping with an unwed virgin and the case of the slandered bride. To her, the diminution of the rights of the paterfamilias may enable girls to force their fathers' hands by elopement; at the same time, it could also empower a rape–capture marriage. Like Matthews, Frymer-Kensky sees the case of the slandered bride as an issue of the honor of the family. She accepts the possibility that the bridegroom's accusation is honest, and focuses on a strange peculiarity of this law, the method of proof by which the girl will be exonerated or condemned. The proof is by bloody sheets, a common procedure throughout the world. But they are collected and displayed, not by the bridegroom and his parents, but by the father of the girl. The reason for this anomaly is that even though the girl's father in Deuteronomy does not have the authority summarily to execute his daughter for faithlessness (an authority that Judah demonstrates in Genesis 38), the law restores actual power to his hands. If he forgives his daughter for being unchaste, or if he has known and colluded in defrauding the bridegroom, he has the opportunity to bloody the sheets before he brings them out for display. But if he is angry that she was not chaste, he will bring out clean sheets and she will be executed at her father's door *because she committed an outrage by being faithless towards her father's house*. Frymer-Kensky looks at the same connection of virgin daughters with honor and shame as it plays out in the story of Dinah in Genesis 34, and then looks to anthropological theories to understand why the honor of men should depend on the chastity of their women. Not finding satisfactory answers, she suggests that part of the answer may be the relationship of control and chastity. We may have to turn our assumptions around: rather than needing control to guard chastity, families may need chastity to provide grounds for and proof of control.

No matter how subordinate wives and daughters were to the men of the household, there is a difference in their subordination from the position of slaves. Two of our articles explore the status of slave women. Pressler considers the slave laws of Exodus 21 and argues that the אמה who does not go free at the seventh year is only one type of female slave, one given in concubinage. An unbetrothed female would most likely have been purchased for sex and reproductive purposes. These would be frustrated if the girl were later released. Other types of woman slaves could be included in the generic term 'Hebrew slave', עבד עברי, much as slave women are included in the term עבד in the law of the fugitive slave. These women would be released in the seventh year. Deuteronomy does not innovate the sabbatical release of female slaves. Rather, Deuteronomy is unwilling to use slave language for concubines and therefore only deals with those non-sexual slaves who have always been released.

Westbrook's focus is on the way slaves have a split legal category: family law applied to slaves as persons, and property law applied to slaves as chattels. Westbrook explores the evidence from Mesopotamia, operating with a central principle: contract clauses are not typical—they modify social justice principles, such as those laid down by the law codes. He explores the status of slaves and their children and the marriage of slaves, recognized in Near Eastern law even though not in Roman law. He illuminates the difficulties with the surrogate-womb slaves of Genesis. They are elevated to the status of wives (אשה) because the purpose for which they are taken is to produce legitimate offspring. They become non-slaves with regard to the husband, since marriage and slavery are incompatible. But they remain the wife's slave. But the wife has limited jurisdiction and Sarah has to get authority from Abraham to chastise Hagar.

Westbrook explores the differing status of the women in Exod. 21.7-11 and Deut. 21.1-14. In Exodus, a man who has acquired a girl for concubinage cannot make her into an ordinary slave. In Deuteronomy, the captive woman is initially a slave, but marriage makes her a free person. A later divorce revives her slave status and the man might think that he could sell her. This the law forbids him to do.

Many of these articles build on the growing body of literature in gender-focused studies of the Bible and the ancient Near East. Looking at status, image and regulation, they continue the discussion of issues raised in the past ten years and, in turn, lay the groundwork for much further study and analysis of these crucial biblical passages and the principles upon which they depend.

WOMEN AND PSALMS: TOWARD AN UNDERSTANDING OF THE ROLE OF WOMEN'S PRAYER IN THE ISRAELITE CULT*

Marc Zvi Brettler

The analysis of biblical texts from a feminist perspective has been applied to a variety of books in the Hebrew Bible, most especially Genesis, Judges, Proverbs, Song of Songs, Esther and Ruth, books in which women play a prominent, and sometimes problematic role.[1] The book of Psalms, however, has been largely ignored in this context; the bibliography of the chapter on Psalms in *The Women's Bible Commentary* shows no synthetic article on women in Psalms,[2] and Alice L. Laffey's *An Introduction to the Old Testament: A Feminist Perspective* discusses Psalms only in a general chapter on 'The Writings'.[3] A search of the American Theological Library Association CD-ROM under 'women and Psalms' resulted in seven citations, only one of which concerned women in biblical psalms,[4] in contrast to, for example, 'women and

* Earlier versions of this paper were delivered at the 1995 Annual Meeting of the Society of Biblical Literature, a seminar of the Hebrew Bible group of the Boston Theological Institute, and a colloquium for the study of Jewish feminist texts at Brandeis University; I benefited from the comments and suggestions of the participants at these conferences.

1. These four books are especially highlighted in the Feminist Companion to the Bible series, edited by Athalya Brenner (Sheffield: Sheffield Academic Press, 1993–).

2. Kathleen A. Farmer, 'Psalms', in Carol A. Newsom and Sharon H. Ringe (eds.), *The Women's Bible Commentary* (Louisville, KY: Westminster/John Knox Press, 1992), pp. 137-44.

3. Philadelphia: Fortress Press, 1988.

4. The CD-ROM index is ATLA Religion Database on CD-Rom, March 1996 version; the only article that was cited was Erhard S. Gerstenberger, 'Weibliche Spiritualität in Psalmen und Hauskult', in Walter Dietrich and Martin A. Klopfenste (eds.), *Ein Gott allein? JHWH-Verehrung und biblischer Monotheismus im Kontext der israelitischen und altorientalischen Religionsgeschicte* (OBO, 139; Freiburg: Universitätsverlage Schweiz, 1994), pp. 349-63. Though this article con-

Genesis', which resulted in 100 citations. This lack of treatment of women in Psalms is quite unfortunate; Psalms is obviously a very important, but clearly under-utilized source for understanding biblical attitudes to gender, and the relation of women to the cult.[5]

Rather than surveying the entirety of the Book of Psalms, I will focus on selected texts, and will make several different types of observations concerning women, Psalms and prayer in ancient Israel.[6] These

tains much useful material, a comparison between the way we each analyze Pss. 127 and 128 (see his p. 356 and my treatment of these psalms below) makes it quite clear why I do not rely more fully on his treatment of the issue. To Gerstenberger's article should now be added Patrick D. Miller, *They Cried to the LORD: The Form and Theology of Biblical Prayer* (Minneapolis: Fortress Press, 1994), pp. 233-43 ('"Things Too Wonderful": Prayers Women Prayed'). Thornen Wittstruck, *The Book of Psalms: An Annotated Bibliography* (2 vols.; New York: Garland, 1994), also has no references to this issue.

5. The most important works on this topic are by Phyllis A. Bird; see her 'The Place of Women in the Israelite Cultus', in Paul Hanson *et al.* (eds.), *Ancient Israelite Religion: Essays in Honor of Frank Moore Cross* (Philadelphia: Fortress Press, 1987), pp. 397-419; 'Women's Religion in Ancient Israel', in Barbara S. Lesko (ed.), *Women's Earliest Records From Ancient Egypt and Western Asia* (BJS, 166; Atlanta: Scholars Press, 1989), pp. 283-302; and 'Israelite Religion and the Faith of Israel's Daughters: Reflections on Gender and Religious Definition', in David Jobling *et al.* (eds.), *The Bible and the Politics of Exegesis: Essays in Honor of Norman K. Gottwald on His Sixty-Fifth Birthday* (Cleveland: Pilgrim Press, 1991), pp. 97-108. Some of these essays are now collected in her *Missing Persons and Mistaken Identities: Women and Gender in Ancient Israel* (OBT; Minneapolis: Fortress Press, 1997). In addition, see Mayer I. Gruber, 'Women in the Cult According to the Priestly Code', in Jacob Neusner *et al.* (eds.), *Judaic Perspectives on Ancient Israel* (Philadelphia: Fortress Press, 1987), pp. 35-48, reprinted in Gruber's *The Motherhood of God and Other Studies* (SFSHJ, 57; Atlanta: Scholars Press, 1992), pp. 49-68. Gruber's study is extremely important for showing cases where women *are* included in the cult and offers a view that is significantly different than the one taken by the psalmist. See more recently Richard A. Henshaw, *Female and Male. The Cultic Personnel: The Bible and the Rest of the Ancient Near East* (Allison Park, PA: Pickwick, 1994), pp. 26-28 and Marie-Theres Wacker, '"Religionsgeschichte Israel" oder "Theologie des Alten Testaments"—(K)eine Alternative? Anmerkungen aus feministisch-exegetische Sicht', *Jahrbuch für Biblische Theologie* 10 (1995), pp. 142-54.

6. My article is thus complementary to the (still unpublished) study of David Clines on Women and Psalms, also presented at the 1995 meeting of the Society of Biblical Literature, in that he surveys the entirety of Psalms using broad categories of analysis, while I explore a small number of texts in depth and adduce comparative material. The conclusions that we reach are similar and mutually reinforcing.

observations should be viewed like experimental cuts or trenches dug by archeologists in their first season of excavation, which are usually modified and refined through more detailed and comprehensive exploration.

I begin with a discussion of Ps. 128.1-4.[7] A careful reading of the psalm with gender issues in mind brings out points that are relevant to both traditional interpretation and feminist interests. After the superscription שיר המעלות,[8] the psalm opens: אשרי כל ירא יהוה ההלך בדרכיו, 'O for the happiness[9] of everyone who fears Yhwh, who walks in his ways'.[10] This would initially seem to be a gender-neutral sentence, where ירא and הלך appear in the masculine singular as 'prior gender'.[11] Proverbs 31.30, אשה יראת יהוה היא תתהלל, 'A woman who fears Yhwh—she shall be praised', indicates that fearing Yhwh may be attributed to women as well as men. However, the context of Psalm 128 indicates that this כל, 'every[one]' is every male. This is clear from v. 3, where the wife 'of everyone who fears Yhwh' is mentioned. Furthermore, v. 4, which parallels v. 1, reads: הנה כי כן יברך גבר ירא יהוה, 'Note: that is how a man who fears Yhwh is blessed'; the use of the gender specific term גבר, 'man', shows that the psalm is explicitly addressing men only.

Although Ps. 45.11-13 is specifically addressed to a woman, the context of that psalm is so narrow (a royal wedding) that it provides little evidence concerning women and psalms, so it has been excluded from this study.

7. My focus on these verses does not suggest that I follow the position of several scholars that this is a composite psalm. Rather, the gender issues are no longer significant after v. 4. For the position that the psalm is composite, see most recently Loren D. Crow, *The Songs of Ascents (Psalms 120–134): Their Place in Israelite History and Religion* (SBLDS, 148; Atlanta: Scholars Press, 1996), pp. 141-42.

8. The focus of this article is on gender issues, and will not address, for instance, the meaning of phrases such as שיר המעלות, or technical philological issues, unless they bear directly on the issues I am attempting to explore.

9. I am not convinced by the recent suggestion of K. C. Hanson, 'How Honorable! How Shameful! A Cultural Analysis of Matthew's Makarisms and Reproaches', *Semeia* 68 (1994), pp. 85-93, that אשרי should be translated as 'how honorable'.

10. The translations of this psalm are my own.

11. See the standard grammars for this term, e.g. Gesenius §122g, esp. n. 2, and more recently, Bruce K. Waltke and M. O'Connor, *An Introduction to Biblical Hebrew Syntax* (Winona Lake, IN: Eisenbrauns, 1990) §6.5.3, p. 108, 'The priority of the masculine gender is due in part to the intensely androcentric character of the world of the Hebrew Bible'.

The use of כל ירא יהוה, 'everyone who fears Yhwh' by the psalmist to refer specifically to men should not be surprising, since many gender studies have noted that concepts such as 'everyone', 'we' or 'all' are often much less inclusive than they would seem.[12] This is obvious in the preamble of the US Constitution, which opens: 'We, the people of the United States'; 'the people' is certainly not an all-inclusive term, but refers to upper-class, land-owning, white, Protestant men.[13] A biblical example from Exodus 19 is similarly instructive. That chapter is quite central within the Torah, offering the narrative introduction to the decalogue. Verse 15 reads: ויאמר אל העם היו נכנים לשלשת ימים אל תגשו אל אשה, '[Moses] said to the people, "Be prepared for the third day; do not approach a woman"'. Here, as noted most forcefully by the feminist Jewish theologian Judith Plaskow, העם, 'the people', the recipients of the decalogue, are defined as the male Israelites.[14] As in Ps. 128.1, the language is only apparently inclusive.

Verse 2 of the psalm introduces the agricultural imagery that will continue through v. 3 as well: יגיע כפיך כי תאכל אשריך וטוב לך, 'You will indeed eat the fruits of your labor; you will be happy and all will go well for you'. This verse too is likely specifically addressed to men. Though we do not know much about the distribution of labor in ancient Israel, the term יגיע כפיך, 'toil of your hands', most likely refers to the intensive male agricultural labor, which is noted, for example, in Gen. 3.17-19, especially in the final verse, בזעת אפיך תאכל לחם, 'with the sweat of your brow you shall eat food'. The evidence from Ruth, where

12. See e.g. Deborah Cameron, *Feminism and Linguistic Theory* (New York: St Martin's Press, 2nd edn, 1992).

13. For a survey of the gradual inclusion of women in Supreme Court interpretations of the constitution, see Sandra Day O'Connor, 'Women and the Constitution: A Bicentennial Perspective', *Women and Politics* 10.2 (1990), pp. 5-16.

14. The last law of the decalogue, which prohibits coveting a neighbor's wife, but not husband, confirms this reading. On Exod. 19.15, see Judith Plaskow, *Standing Again at Sinai: Judaism from a Feminist Perspective* (San Francisco: Harper & Row, 1990), pp. 25-28. This point was already made in the first (and still the finest) modern synthetic article concerning women in the Hebrew Bible: Phyllis Bird, 'Images of Women in the Old Testament', in *Religion and Sexism: Images of Women in the Jewish and Christian Traditions* (New York: Simon & Shuster, 1974), pp. 41-88 (49-50). Most recently, see Athalya Brenner, 'An Afterword: The Decalogue—Am I an Addressee?', in *idem* (ed.), *A Feminist Companion to Exodus to Deuteronomy* (Sheffield: Sheffield Academic Press, 1994), pp. 255-58.

a predominantly male force gathers the crops,[15] as well as from various Egyptian tomb paintings, which typically show men involved in agriculture,[16] corroborate Gen. 3.17-19, suggesting that men rather than women were typically involved in all stages of agriculture, from plowing to winnowing.[17]

Verse 3 is the most important verse of the psalm in terms of gender issues. It reads: אשתך כגפן פריה בירכתי ביתך בניך כשתלי זיתים סביב לשלחנך, 'your wife will be like a fertile[18] vineyard in the corner of your house; your children will be like olive suckers[19] [= young olive trees] around your table'. Given the importance of the vineyard, grapes and wine within ancient Israelite society,[20] this verse might seem to present a positive image of the wife. However, it is immediately evident that the woman is contrasted to the children; she is peripheralized, in the corner (בירכתי[21]) of the house, while the *man's* children are with their father around *his* table.[22] Furthermore, the agricultural imagery used of the woman follows clearly from that used in v. 2; in the same way that the man owns fields, which he tends with the hope that they will

15. See Ruth 2.5-9, especially the last verse, which suggests that Ruth was subject to harassment as one of the few females in the field. (On this, see Michael Carasik, 'Ruth 2,7: Why the Overseer was Embarrassed', *ZAW* 107 [1995], pp. 493-94.)

16. See the various plates in Oded Borowski, *Agriculture in Iron Age Israel* (Winona Lake, IN: Eisenbrauns, 1987), esp. fig. 10 on p. 60, which shows many stages of agricultural production performed by men.

17. Prov. 31.16b depicts a woman planting a vineyard, but the context makes it quite clear that this is an exceptional woman (cf. vv. 10 and 29b). On the work of women in biblical Israel, see Carol Meyers, *Discovering Eve: Ancient Israelite Women in Context* (Oxford: Oxford University Press, 1988), pp. 139-64 ('Household Functions and Female Roles'), esp. p. 146 on women providing some agricultural tasks, with the heavy agricultural labor (Ps. 128's יגיע כפיך) left for men.

18. Alternately, 'branching out'; see H. L. Ginsberg, '"Roots Below and Fruit Above" and Related Matters', in D. Winton Thomas and W.D. McHardy (eds.), *Hebrew and Semitic Studies Presented to Godfrey Rolles Driver* (Oxford: Clarendon Press, 1963), pp. 72-76 (75).

19. On the botanical meaning of this image, see Borowski, *Agriculture in Iron Age Israel*, p. 119.

20. On the importance of the grape and its products, see Borowski, *Agriculture in Iron Age Israel*, p. 103.

21. I will deal with this word in detail below.

22. This contrast is noted by Daniel Grossberg, *Centripetal and Centrifugal Structures in Biblical Poetry* (SBLMS, 39; Atlanta: Scholars Press, 1989), p. 44.

produce food for consumption (כי תאכל), he also owns a wife, here represented by simile as a vineyard; he hopes she too will be fertile. The image of the wife as the husband's fertile vineyard fits a predominant biblical view of a man's wife, who is a chattel when it comes to the issue of the husband's ownership of his wife's sexuality.[23] Phrased differently, for our psalmist, just as the husband is the בעל of his fields in v. 2, in v. 3 he is the בעל of his wife. Thus, the main role of the woman here is consistent with a role that we find elsewhere in the Bible—to produce children for her husband.[24] This idea is also reflected in the final verse of the psalm, where the male reciting the psalm will live to see his grandchildren (or grandsons)—וראה בנים לבניך.

The woman in this verse is in some sense dehumanized through the simile of the fertile vineyard. A vineyard, of course, can be a positive image for female sexuality, as seen most clearly in the Song of Songs, where for example, the female lover observes coyly (1.6): כרמי שלי לא נטרתי, 'I have not guarded my own vineyard'.[25] Psalm 128, however, takes a quite different perspective: the women as גפן is an object, significant for what she produces, but not valued here for her intrinsic human qualities. In Ps. 128.3, the male values the wife's importance for procreation, in contrast to the Song of Song's perspective, which highlights the female's evaluation of her own sexuality. Finally, the vine *itself* is not considered useful within the Hebrew Bible, as is made very clear in the extended image of Ezekiel 15,[26] where the prophet

23. This is clearest for the rabbinic period; see Judith Romney Wegner, *Chattel or Person? The Status of Women in the Mishnah* (New York: Oxford University Press, 1988), pp. 12-14. For the Bible, see Bird, 'Images', p. 51 and Anthony Phillips, 'Some Aspects of Family Law in Pre-exilic Israel', *VT* 23 (1973), pp. 349-56.

24. On the centrality of the maternal role for biblical women, see Karel van der Toorn, *From her Cradle to her Grave: The Role of Religion in the Life of the Israelite and the Babylonian Woman* (trans. Sara J. Denning-Bolle; The Biblical Seminar, 23; Sheffield: JSOT Press, 1994), pp. 77-92 ('The Prestige of Motherhood: Pregnancy and Birth') and Tikva Frymer-Kensky, *In the Wake of the Goddesses: Women, Culture, and the Biblical Transformation of Pagan Myth* (New York: Free Press, 1992), pp. 121-22.

25. Cf. e.g. Marcia Falk, *Love Lyrics from the Bible: A Translation and Literary Study of The Song of Songs* (Sheffield: Almond Press, 1982), pp. 100-105.

26. On the imagery of this chapter, see Moshe Greenberg, *Ezekiel, 1–20* (AB; New York: Doubleday, 1983), pp. 264-69 and Horacio Simian-Yofre, 'La Métaphore d'Ezékiel 15', in J. Lust *et al.* (eds.), *Ezekiel and His Book: Textual and*

compares the destiny of the inhabitants of Jerusalem to the vine itself, which is worthless, and easily consumed; it is only the product of the vine, the grapes that symbolize the children, that are desirable. This should be contrasted to the children/sons at the end of the verse who are like young olive trees—these are valuable for the olives and oil that they will produce, but are much more substantial and yield useful wood.

Finally, it is worth emphasizing that the wife of this psalm is not evaluated based on her own meritorious behavior, but because she is married to a man who fears Yhwh—according to vv. 1-3, the 'fruitful wife' is a gift to the God-fearing man. This is similar to Gen. 25.21, where Isaac prays for Rebecca's fertility, and his prayer is heeded—Rebecca bears children because of her husband's prayer.[27] This view of female fertility as the main concern of men, or reward to husbands, is not the only biblical view; Hannah, for example, becomes fertile after she prays and Ruth's pregnancy and progeny are more important to Naomi and Ruth than to Boaz.

Psalm 128 represents the husband as raising crops, and the children around the table, most likely eating; what then is the meaning of the place of the wife בירכתי ביתך, 'in the corner of your house'? Traditional archaeology, which concentrated on public buildings, was not interested in such issues, and even with the rise of the new archaeology, this question has not been adequately resolved; this issue is further complicated by the likelihood that the structure of lower-class and upper-class houses differed in ancient Israel, and we have no way of determining the social class of our psalmist.[28]

Literary Criticism and their Interpretation (BETL, 74; Leuven: Leuven University Press, 1986), pp. 234-47.

27. Verse 21 should be contrasted to vv. 22-23, where Rebecca is more active. These verses may derive from different sources; see Claus Westermann, *Genesis 12–36* (trans. John J. Scullion, SJ; Minneapolis: Augsburg, 1985), pp. 411-12. In some midrashic traditions, the odd phrase נכח אשתו of Gen. 25.21 is understood to suggest that Rebecca was actively praying as well; see the traditions cited in Menahem Kasher, *Torah Shelemah*, IV (New York: Shulzinger Brothers, 1952), p. 1011 n. 74.

28. For summaries of domestic Israelite architecture in the Iron Age, see Lawrence E. Stager, 'The Archaeology of the Family in Ancient Israel', *BASOR* 260 (1985), pp. 11-17; Amihai Mazar, *Archaeology of the Land of the Bible 10,000-586 B.C.E.* (AB; New York: Doubleday, 1990), pp. 485-89; Gabriel Barkay, 'The Iron Age II–II', in Amnon Ben-Tor (ed.), *The Archaeology of Ancient*

A sense of the problems involved may be gleaned from Ehud Netzer's survey of Israelite architecture,[29] which offers many possible reconstructions that depend on whether or not we assume four room houses had a second floor. Quite enlightening as well is P.M. Michèle Daviau's monograph on houses and their furnishings,[30] which attempts to understand Middle and Late Bronze room function based on the distribution of artifacts. Despite the massive amount of evidence that she surveys, she reaches no firm conclusion concerning standard room function.

Though no clear conclusion may be reached about typical structures of Israelite houses and the functions of their rooms, three possibilities should be considered for ירכתי. Some have suggested that the kitchen of the house was located in the corner of (ירכתי) the first floor.[31] This would then suggest that the imagery of vv. 2-3 describes the stages of agricultural production: the husband toils in the field (v. 2) and the wife toils in the kitchen (v. 3a) in order to sustain the children at the table (v. 3b). Alternatively, a sleeping room might be intended,[32] as suggested by some older commentaries.[33] In this case, the verses refer to sexual activity; they begin with the 'toiling' of the husband, continue with the fertile wife in the bedroom, and conclude with the birth of children, who surround the table. In this context, it is worth recalling that sexual activity may be expressed metaphorically through some

Israel (New Haven: Yale University Press, 1992), p. 332; John S. Holladay, Jr, 'House, Israelite', *ABD*, III, pp. 308-18; and Ehud Netzer, 'Domestic Architecture in the Iron Age', in Aharon Kempinski and Ronny Reich (eds.), *The Architecture of Ancient Israel from Prehistoric Times to the Persian Periods* (Jerusalem: Israel Exploration Society, 1992), pp. 193-201. I would like to thank Professor Philip J. King of Boston College for calling this last item to my attention and for discussing these issues of architecture with me.

29. Netzer, 'Domestic Architecture in the Iron Age', esp. p. 199.

30. P.M. Michèle Daviau, *Houses and their Furnishings in Bronze Age Palestine: Domestic Activity Areas and Artifact Distribution in the Middle and Late Bronze Ages* (JSOT/ASOR Monograph Series, 8; Sheffield: JSOT Press, 1993).

31. Holladay, 'House, Israelite', pp. 313-14, and illustration Hou, 03b.

32. Barkay, 'The Iron Age II–II', p. 332, suggests that in the four-room house, the central area was the 'work area', while '[t]he rear room served as living quarters'. See similarly, Mazar, *Archaeology of the Land of the Bible*, p. 488.

33. So, e.g., A. F. Kirkpatrick, *Psalms* (Cambridge Bible Commentary; Cambridge: Cambridge University Press, 1910), p. 755, though his suggestion that this refers specifically to 'the women's apartments' is not compelling, since we do not know that they had separate 'apartments'.

types of agricultural activity, for example in Judg. 14.18, where Samson notes: לולא חרשתם בעגלתי לא מצאתם חידתי, 'Had you not plowed with my heifer, you would not have solved my riddle'.[34] For this reading, we must recall the sexual use of כרם, 'vine(yard)'. On some level, then, vv. 2-3 deal with the man's sexual gratification, which ultimately results in the bearing of many בנים. It is then possible that the psalmist chose the word ירכתי not only to reflect the peripheral place of the woman, but because it plays on ירך, which is used in the sense of female genitalia in the Sotah ritual in Num. 5.21, בתת יהוה את ירכך נפלת, 'as Yhwh makes your ירך fall'.[35] The use of ירך as male genitalia is well known,[36] and it would not be surprising if the corresponding feminine ירכה referred to the female genitalia in ancient Israelite Hebrew, though this use is not attested in biblical Hebrew. If this observation is reasonable, the psalmist is then saying that the woman is totally peripheral: she is appreciated for her recesses and what issues from them, and belongs in the recesses of her house.

A final possibility is that ירכתי הבית refers to the first-floor rooms on the sides of the central pillars of the house; those rooms were sometimes used to stable animals.[37] This would yield an image of the man in the fields, the woman tending the domestic animals, and the children safely inside. This image of the wife with the cattle also reminds us of Judg. 14.18, where Samson calls the woman he was about to marry his עגלה, 'heifer'.

According to all of these readings, the wife is peripheral; she is not included in those who fear Yhwh; she is in the corner, and to varying extents, dehumanized. In his description of women, the psalmist is mirroring one well-known set of gender roles within ancient Israel, but is also perpetuating them through the cult.

34. Note especially James L. Crenshaw, *Samson: A Secret Betrayed, A Vow Ignored* (Atlanta: John Knox Press, 1978), p. 119, 'One would be hard put to discover a more apt description of the sexual act'.

35. The sexual nuance is also appreciated by Crow, *Songs of Ascents*, p. 72 n. e, following Grossberg, *Centripetal and Centrifugal*, p. 44. The rabbis already understood ירך in this way; see Jacob Milgrom, *Numbers* (The Jewish Publication Society Torah Commentary; Philadelphia: Jewish Publication Society, 1990), p. 303 n. 64.

36. See Meir Malul, 'More on *paḥad yiṣḥaq* (Genesis XXXI 42, 53) and the Oath by the Thigh', *VT* 35 (1985), pp. 192-202 (196-98) and 'Touching the Sexual Organs as an Oath Ceremony in an Akkadian Letter', *VT* 37 (1987), pp. 491-92.

37. Stager, 'The Archaeology of the Family in Ancient Israel', pp. 11-15.

Some scholars have discovered wisdom elements in Psalm 128, and it is possible that this wisdom influence may account for the psalm's attitude toward women.[38] As is well known, much of wisdom literature is highly misogynistic; this includes the majority of Proverbs, which opens with the image of the dangerous foreign woman and contains several misogynistic proverbs, as well as Job, with its depiction of Mrs Job. Qohelet, with its statement (7.26) that 'woman is more bitter than death: she is traps, her inside is snares and her hands are fetters; he who is good before God will flee from her, but the sinner will be trapped by her' is highly misogynistic.[39] However, wisdom elements are not really

38. Hermann Gunkel and Joachim Begrich, *Einleitung in die Psalmen* (Göttingen: Vandenhoeck & Ruprecht, 1985 [1933]), p. 385. This position has been followed by many commentators on the psalms, including Hans-Joachin Kraus, *Psalms 60–150* (trans. Hilton C. Oswald; Minneapolis: Augsburg, 1989), p. 458, and most recently, Crow, *Songs*, p. 142. For additional support for this position, see Roland E. Murphy, 'A Consideration of the Classification "Wisdom Psalms"', *SVT* 9 (1962), pp. 156-67, reprinted in James L. Crenshaw (ed.), *Studies in Ancient Israelite Wisdom* (New York: Ktav, 1976), pp. 456-67, and J. Kenneth Kuntz, 'The Retribution Motif in Psalmic Wisdom', *ZAW* 89 (1977), pp. 223-33. However, according to the more stringent linguistic criteria of Avi Hurvitz, *Wisdom Language in Biblical Psalmody* (Jerusalem: Magnes Press, 1991) (Hebrew), this should not be considered a wisdom psalm. One must, however, question whether linguistic markers alone may be used to determine whether a Psalm has been influenced by the wisdom tradition.

39. For a survey of women in all wisdom literature, see Athalya Brenner (ed.), *A Feminist Companion to Wisdom Literature* (The Feminist Companion to the Bible, 9; Sheffield: Sheffield Academic Press, 1995). Much of this material is on Proverbs 1–9; see Claudia Camp, *Wisdom and the Feminine in the Book of Proverbs* (Sheffield: Almond Press, 1985); Camp, 'Woman Wisdom as Root Metaphor: A Theological Consideration', in Kenneth G. Hoglund *et al.* (eds.), *The Listening Heart: Essays in Wisdom and the Psalms in Honor of Roland E. Murphy, O. Carm.* (JSOTSup, 58; Sheffield: JSOT Press, 1987), pp. 45-76; Camp, 'What's So Strange About the Strange Woman?', in Jobling *et al.* (eds.), *The Bible and the Politics of Exegesis*, pp. 17-31; Carol A. Newsom, 'Woman and the Discourse of Patriarchal Wisdom: A Study of Proverbs 1–9', in Peggy L. Day (ed.), *Gender and Difference* (Minneapolis: Fortress Press, 1989), pp. 142-60; and Christl Maier, *Die 'fremde Frau' in Proverbien 1–9: Eine exegetische und sozialgeschichtliche Studie* (OBO, 144; Freiburg: Universitätsverlag Freiburg, 1995). On Proverbs in general, see Carole R. Fontaine, 'Proverbs', in Newsom and Ringe (eds.), *The Women's Bible Commentary*, pp. 145-52, and on Ecclesiastes, see Carole R. Fontaine, 'Ecclesiastes', in Newsom and Ringe (eds.), *The Women's Bible Commentary*, pp. 153-55.

that significant within the psalm, nor is the attitude reflected in the psalm only found in wisdom literature, so the role of possible wisdom influence should not be exaggerated. Thus, Psalm 128 may be viewed as typical of the attitude toward women found in Psalms.

In sum, this psalm is a previously unexplored, but useful piece of evidence concerning the attitude toward women. Scholars either do not comment on these gender issues, or try to deproblematicize the text. One way this is typically done is by interpreting 'ירכתי' in some way other than 'corner'.[40] Among the newer translations, the NRSV, REB and NAB all translate our psalm's בירכתי ביתך, as 'within your house/ home'. Yet, in all cases in the Hebrew Bible ירכה suggests an extremity, far away from the speaker;[41] this is clear, for example, from the nation who comes מירכתי ארץ in Jer. 6.22 and elsewhere, which is to be identified with the nation from the faraway north, or from Jon. 1.5, where the reluctant prophet, trying to remove himself from the scene, descends to ירכתי הספינה, 'the inner recesses of the boat'.

In addition to Psalm 128, the phrase ירכתי הבית is also found in Amos 6.10, in a context that clearly suggests a place deep inside the house. There, the correct understanding of ירכתי הבית is picked up by most commentators and translators; for example, the NRSV translates 'in the innermost points of the house' and the REB reads 'in the corner of the house'. The older NEB offers a particularly 'interesting' distinction in its translation of ירכתי הבית; in Amos it means 'in a corner of the house', while in Psalm 128 it is rendered 'in the heart of your house'! The translators' inconsistency is quite surprising, and seems to result from their unwillingness to admit the psalm's peripheralization of women. The English Bible reader is thus protected from yet another problematic biblical text.

Though modern scholars have not appreciated the peripheral sense of בירכתי, it is recognized, for example, by the medieval Jewish exegete RaDaK or David Kimhi, who glosses the verse in Psalms:

40. This is contrary not only to the biblical uses, adduced below, but to the Akkadian cognate *(w)arkatu*, used in the sense of the 'rear side (of a building)'; see *CAD A*, II, pp. 274-75.

41. This is recognized in the standard lexica; cf. *BDB*, p. 438; *HALAT*, p. 419 and *Wilhelm Gesenius Hebräisches und Aramäisches Handwörterbuch über das Alte Testament*, II (ed. D. Rudolf Meyer, Udo Rüterswörden and Herbert Donner; Heidelberg: Springer, 18th edn, 1995), p. 498.

> he compares her to a vine, which some people plant inside their house. As it begins to grow, it is led through an aperture in the house into the sunlight so that its root is inside the house, whilst the branches are outside. So should a woman be chaste (צנועה), remaining within the house and not going forth from the home. For such is the way of a lewd woman, just as Solomon said of her 'Now she is in the street, now in the market' (Prov. vii 12). He states (specifically) *within*: that is, even in her home she is to be chaste and is not to sit at the door of her house to be seen by those who pass to and fro. For such is the way of the evil woman, just as it says of her 'she sits at the door of her house' (Prov. ix 14). She should always be *within* the house so that none may see her except her husband and the members of the household. But her children should go forth into the world to their work and for the necessities of the home, just as the branches of the vine shoot forth fruitful and numerous 'with the choicest fruits of the sun' (Deut. xxxiii 14). And if your wife is of this disposition, then *your children will be like olive shoots*... Such plants are goodly, being the legitimate offspring of the parent plant.[42]

The opposite position is taken, for example, by the turn of the century critical scholar, Briggs, who suggests that the inner room is 'where the table was placed', thereby bringing the wife back into the center, with the children.[43] This assumption, however, is not backed up with any evidence. More recently, Mitchell Dahood, has suggested that בירכתי should be understood here as a 'within' rather than the more literal 'within the penetralia', but the evidence he adduces is not compelling.[44] Artur Weiser considers the image in v. 3 to be 'charming',[45] though he (thankfully) does not elaborate. In contrast, A.A. Anderson is among the few who correctly note that the referent in 3b is 'most likely, to a room, or a corner of a room, set apart for the wife's use',[46] though he brings no archeological evidence to bear on the issue, nor does he note how the term בירכתי explicitly peripheralizes the woman.

42. Joshua Baker and Ernest W. Nicholson, *The Commentary of Rabbi David Kimḥi on Psalms CXX–CL* (Cambridge: Cambridge University Press, 1973), p. 30 (Hebrew text) and p. 31 (English translation).

43. Charles Augustus Briggs and Emilie Grace Briggs, *Psalms*, II (ICC; Edinburgh: T. & T. Clark, 1907), p. 460.

44. Mitchell Dahood, *Psalms*. III. *101–150* (AB; New York: Doubleday, 1970), p. 228.

45. Artur Weiser, *Psalms* (OTL; London: SCM Press, 1962), p. 768.

46. A.A. Anderson, *Psalms (73–150)* (NCB; Grand Rapids: Eerdmans, 1981 [1972]), II, p. 870. Crow, *Songs of Ascents*, also notes that the image is negative, but even he, in a work that studies many themes of the שיר המעלות collection, does not systematically collect the attitude of these psalms toward women.

Yet, lest one contend that these issues concerning the status of women in this Psalm are peripheral to Psalms exegesis, it is of more than historical curiosity that Hermann Gunkel, in his masterful Psalms commentary, written over sixty-five years ago, is aware of some of these issues, noting quite straightforwardly that for the author of Psalm 128, 'Träger der Religion ist der Hausvater'[47]—'the one who upholds the religion is the father of the family'. In the case of Psalm 128, the questions raised by a feminist study of the Bible help to return us to the insights of Gunkel. As a close interpreter of the psalms living decades before the rise of the academic study of feminism, he observed the importance of this psalm for understanding gender relations in ancient Israel. With the greater sophistication that the tools of women's studies have given us, we should follow in his footsteps.

To what extent may we generalize from this psalm to the Psalter as a whole? And—as a separate question—to what extent may we adduce from this psalm the role of women as 'pray-ers', and especially as pray-ers of psalms, in ancient Israel?

While Psalm 128 might be unusual in its *explicit* peripheralization of women, it is in no way exceptional. One can search the psalms high and low for the inclusion of women—and with the exception of one or two psalms, most notably Ps. 148.12 where בתולות 'young women'—are mentioned alongside בחורים—'young men'—within the groups of those who should praise Yhwh, women are strikingly missing.[48] In contrast to the mention of Abraham, Isaac, Jacob and Moses in the Psalms, and the mention of Sarah, Rebecca, Rachel, Leah and Miriam in non-Torah material, not a single one of these women is mentioned in the Psalter. In contrast to Deutero-Isaiah, I know of no case where Psalms, which uses a wide variety of rich imagery to describe Yhwh, invokes imagery that must be seen as feminine.[49] In fact, though some scholars, including Phyllis Trible, attempt to see רחמים as a specifically

47. H. Gunkel, *Die Psalmen* (HKAT; Göttingen: Vandenhoeck & Ruprecht, 1968 [1929]), p. 557.

48. This psalm is mentioned in Farmer, 'Psalms', p. 138; she also mentions the very difficult Ps. 68.26.

49. Mayer I. Gruber, 'The Motherhood of God in Second Isaiah', *RB* 90 (1983), pp. 351-59 (reprinted in Gruber, *The Motherhood of God and Other Studies*, pp. 3-15) and the somewhat expanded Hebrew version, 'Feminine Similes Applied to God in Deutero-Isaiah', *Beer Sheba* 2 (1985), pp. 75-84; see also Katheryn Pfisterer Darr, 'Like Warrior, Like Woman: Destruction and Deliverance in Isaiah 42:10-17', *CBQ* 49 (1987), pp. 560-71.

feminine attribute in the Hebrew Bible,[50] the following from Ps. 103.13 is instructive: כרחם אב על בנים רחם יהוה על יראיו, 'just as a father has compassion on children, so Yhwh has had compassion on those who fear him'. There are four psalms that contain the gender specific phrase, אשרי הגבר, 'O for the happiness of the man' (34.9; 40.5; 94.12; 127.5); none contains the corresponding phrase אשרי האשה. Most significantly, there is not a single psalm that specifically concerns life-cycle events or other issues that would have been unique to the Israelite woman rather than the man.

There are several psalms that do mention women.[51] For example, Ps. 123.2 contains the image, 'just like a maidservant looks up to her mistress'. Psalm 109, which mentions (v. 14) וחטאת אמו, 'the sin of his mother', is similar. However, it is worth looking at the entire verse in which these phrases are found. Psalm 123.2 reads: הנה כעיני עבדים אל יד אדוניהם כעיני שפחה אל יד גברתה כן עינינו אל יהוה אלהינו עד שיחננו, 'Look: just like slaves look to their masters' hand, and maidservants look to their mistresses' hand, so our eyes are to Yhwh until he favors us', while 109.14 reads יזכר עון אבתיו אל יהוה וחטאת אמו אל תמח, 'May the iniquity of his fathers be remembered to Yhwh, and the sin of his mother not be blotted out'. In both of these cases, women are mentioned in the second or B part of the verse, parallel to the men who are mentioned first, in the A part. Though the structure of Hebrew poetry continues to be debated, a strong argument can be made, especially for several psalms, that the A section carries the semantic weight of the verse, while the B part is largely a filler, formally seconding the first part, but not imparting new meaning to the psalm as a whole. This is perhaps clearest from Ps. 121.6, which appears immediately after a verse which says that Yhwh is the psalmist's shade (צלך): יומם השמש לא יככה וירח בלילה, 'By day the sun will not smite you, nor the moon by night'. Certainly one can succumb to sunstroke, but is moonstroke a common ancient Near Eastern disease? Rather, the B part of this verse seems to be a filler, which merely formally seconds the A part, and imparts no new meaning: בלילה is a formal (antithetical) parallel to יומם, and וירח to השמש, but these words in the B part impart no new semantic value to the verse. This phenomenon is called 'automatism' in

50. *God and the Rhetoric of Sexuality* (Overtures to Biblical Theology; Philadelphia: Fortress Press, 1978), pp. 31-59, but see the critique of Gruber, 'The Motherhood of God in Second Isaiah', pp. 352-53.

51. See Gerstenberger, 'Weibliche', p. 355.

parallelism by Menahem Haran,[52] and is quite prevalent in ancient Near Eastern poetry. This phenomenon has been incorrectly ignored as a result of the understandings of biblical poetry developed by Kugel and Alter, which have predominated in the field.[53] Thus, as we return to Psalms 123 and 109, the mention of women may be seen as relatively inconsequential, since they are found in the B part of the verse, and may be fillers, just like Psalm 121's וירח בלילה. That Psalm 109 is specifically addressed to men is made clear in v. 9, יהיו בניו יתומים ואשתו אלמנה, 'may his children be orphans, his wife a widow'. This substantiates the idea that the specific references to women in the B part of these verses is likely the result of automatism.

Psalm 131 (v. 2) does contain an image that has a woman in the primary position, as the psalmist sees himself contented כגמל עלי אמו, 'like a weaned child with its mother'.[54] The verse which contains this image is relatively difficult;[55] in any case, the weaning of babies seems to have been a period of general family rejoicing, and according to Gen. 21.8, it was Abraham who gave Isaac a party when he was weaned.[56] Thus, although this psalm uses a formerly nursing mother as its central image, the image would have been well-known to males in ancient Israel, and there is little to suggest that this psalm was composed for or by a woman.

Some have argued for the inclusion of women in the composition or the singing of Psalms based on the term עלמות, which appears in the superscription of Psalm 46 (cf. 1 Chron. 15.20 and עלמות in Psalm 9 and possibly 48.14); these scholars have connected עלמות to biblical

52. M. Haran, 'The Graded Numerical Sequence and the Phenomenon of "Automatism" in Biblical Poetry', *SVT* 22 (1972), pp. 238-67. Wilfred G.E. Watson, *Classical Hebrew Poetry: A Guide to its Techniques* (JSOTSup, 26; Sheffield: JSOT Press, 1986), p. 148 concurs.

53. James L. Kugel, *The Idea of Biblical Poetry: Parallelism and Its History* (New Haven: Yale University Press, 1981) and Robert Alter, *The Art of Biblical Poetry* (New York: Basic Books, 1985). Both emphasize that the entire verse carries semantic content and the B part often extends the A part. Neither engages Haran's article.

54. This psalm is discussed by Miller, *They Cried to the LORD*, pp. 239-43, in the context of women's prayer.

55. See Crow, *Songs of Ascents*, pp. 92-98.

56. For a reconstruction of this weaning party and its significance, see Gerhard Pfeifer, 'Entwöhnung und Entwöhnungsfest im Alten Testament: Der Schlüssel zu Jesaja 28$_{7-13}$?' *ZAW* 84 (1972), pp. 341-47.

עלמה, 'a young woman of marriageable age'.[57] However, the technical terms in these superscriptions are unusually obscure, and most scholars would agree that it is dangerous to use them to reconstruct social or musical institutions in ancient Israel.[58]

Some have suggested, in a tentative fashion, that women played a role in the cult in the postexilic period, citing, for example, the list of those who returned from exile in Ezra 2.65 and Neh. 7.67, which includes משררים ומשררות, 'male and female singers'.[59] However, there is no reason to assume that these are cultic singers.[60] The evidence of postexilic 1 Chron. 25.5-6 is even more confusing; it seems to mention the three daughters of Heiman, the king's seer, along with their fourteen brothers, as part of those who are involved in the production of Temple music (v. 6a כל אלה על ידי אביהם בשיר בית יהוה), but the verses that follow probably do not leave room for the daughters' participation in the Temple cult.[61] Thus, there is no positive evidence, from pre-exilic or postexilic sources, for the participation of women in the cult in some role connected to the singing of psalms.

On the more positive side, however, I would observe that there are several gender neutral psalms. These include Psalm 65, which notes (v. 3), עדיך כל בשר יבאו, 'all people may come to you', and rather than having the expected אשרי הגבר, has simply אשרי, 'O for the happiness' (v. 5), and Psalm 142, in which the psalmist only speaks in the first person common singular, and no masculine pronouns are used in relation to the psalmist. It is impossible, however, to show that these psalms are intentionally 'gender neutral' or 'inclusive', in other words, that they

57. See for example A. F. Kirkpatrick, *The Book of Psalms* (CBC; Cambridge: Cambridge University Press, 1902), p. 255.

58. See Hans-Joachin Kraus, *Psalms 1–59* (trans. Hilton C. Oswald; Minneapolis: Augsburg, 1988), p. 31. For a more detailed discussion of עלמות and related issues, see my forthcoming article, 'Alamoth', in Carol Meyers (ed.), *Women in Scripture: A Dictionary of Named and Unnamed Women in the Hebrew Bible, Apocrypha, and New Testament* (Boston: Houghton Mifflin).

59. See e.g. Susan Grossman, 'Women and the Jerusalem Temple', in Susan Grossman and Rivka Haut (eds.), *Daughters of the King: Women and the Synagogue* (Philadelphia: Jewish Publication Society, 1992), pp. 15-37 (19).

60. Joseph Blenkinsopp, *Ezra–Nehemiah* (OTL; Philadelphia: Westminster Press, 1988), p. 93.

61. Sara Japhet, *I and II Chronicles* (OTL; Louisville, KY: Westminster/John Knox, 1993), p. 445.

were composed so that women would feel more comfortable reciting them.[62]

In any case, these possibly intentional gender neutral psalms are a small minority, and must be contrasted to Psalm 128, or to images such as Ps. 127.3-5a. This Psalm begins in a promising fashion, mentioning the importance of children, which are a primary concern of women throughout the Hebrew Bible. Verse 3 is totally gender neutral: הנה נחלת יהוה בנים שׂכר פרי הבטן, 'Children/sons are the provision of Yhwh; a reward is the fruit of the womb'. In the next verse, however, the imagery becomes much more masculine and phallic: כחצים ביד גבור כן בני הנעורים 'Just like arrows in the hand of a warrior, so are children/sons of youth'.[63] The following verse goes beyond masculine imagery; it begins: אשׁרי הגבר אשׁר מלא את אשׁפתו מהם, 'Happy is *the man* who fills his quiver with them', making it quite clear that this psalmist is specifically concerned only with the importance of children/sons to their father. It is possible that אשׁפתו, 'his quiver', reflects vaginal imagery, in which case the male is the only person considered here, having incorporated male and female genitalia—metaphorically, אשׁפה and חצים, leaving the women with no sexual identity.[64] These implements are used, for example, metaphorically in a similar way in a list of the divine prerogatives (*ME*s) that the goddess Inanna received from Enki.[65] Thus, from the construction of Psalm 127 as a whole, we see that it is quite coincidental that v. 3 is gender neutral, and we may at least wonder if the longer gender neutral sections in other psalms are really intentionally gender neutral, that is whether any psalm was specifically composed to enfranchise women.

This should not imply that women did not participate in the cult in

62. It is impossible to list such gender neutral psalms until we answer some fundamental questions, such as what was the nature of the חסידים פֹּעלי און or ענוים and how such groups may have come into contact with women. Note how Gerstenberger, 'Weibliche', p. 356, inquires about women reciting various types of laments; see now Ulrike Bail, 'Vernimm, Gott, Mein Gebet: Psalm 55 und Gewalt gegen Frauen', in Hedwig Jahnow *et al.* (eds.), *Feministische Hermeneutik und Erstes Testament* (Stuttgart: W. Kohlhammer, 1994), pp. 67-84.

63. On men and arrows, see Harry A. Hoffner, Jr, 'Symbols for Masculinity and Femininity: Their Use in Ancient Near Eastern Magic Rituals', *JBL* 85 (1966), pp. 326-34.

64. This was suggested to me by Dr Bonna Haberman.

65. Gwendolyn Leick, *Sex and Eroticism in Mesopotamian Literature* (London: Routledge, 1994), p. 151.

ancient Israel. It is very difficult to reconstruct institutions related to the cult in ancient Israel; most of what we do know comes from the Priestly source(s), which presents a particular, perhaps ideal viewpoint.[66] In any case, that legislation does not match various narrative texts or even the psalms, so we certainly may not generalize from P to the larger construct 'ancient Israel'. Yet even in P women are not excluded; as noted by Mayer I. Gruber,[67] the priestly text explicitly mentions the possibility of women becoming Nazirites, which involved not only a particularly close relationship to Yhwh, but access to the Temple for sacrifices. Gruber also calls attention to non-priestly material, especially Deuteronomy's legislation of הקהל in Deuteronomy 31, where once every seven years, at the main fall festival of Sukkot, העם, 'the people or nation', here (v. 12, contrast Exod. 19.15) defined explicitly as האנשים והנשים והטף וגרך אשר בשעריך, 'men, women and children, along with the stranger who lives among you', must come to the place that Yhwh will choose in order to hear a public reading of the law, women are explicitly included. I also concur with Phyllis Bird, who, in analyzing the place of women in the cult, concerning the place of women in the Israelite cult distinguishes between women in the religious hierarchy and female lay participation.[68] Her conclusions are significant enough to quote at length:

> During the period reflected in the Old Testament sources there appear to have been a number of changes within the cultus and in its relationship to the population as a whole that had significance for women's participation. The progressive movement from multiple cultic centers to a central site that finally claimed sole legitimacy and control over certain ritual events necessarily restricted the participation of women in pilgrim feasts and limited opportunities for women to seek guidance, release and consolation at local shrines, which were declared illegitimate or demolished. At the same time, increased specialization and hierarchical ordering of priestly/levitical ranks within the royal/national cultus deprived males in general (as well as Levites) of earlier priestly prerogatives, increasing

66. For one aspect of the disparity between P and other conceptions of the cult, see Israel Knohl, 'Between Voice and Silence: The Relationship between Prayer and Temple Cult', *JBL* 115 (1996), pp. 17-30.

67. Mayer I. Gruber, 'Women in the Cult According to the Priestly Code', in Jacob Neusner, Baruch Levine, and Ernest A. Frereichs (eds.), '*Judaic Perspectives on Ancient Israel* (Philadelphia: Fortress Press, 1987), pp. 35-48, reprinted in his *The Motherhood of God*, pp. 49-68.

68. Bird, 'The Place of Women in the Israelite Cultus'.

> the distance or sharpening the boundary between the professional guardians of the cultus and the larger circle of male Israelites who comprised the religious assembly. Reorganization of the cultus under the monarchy and again in the postexilic period appears to have limited or eliminated roles earlier assigned to women. On the other hand, there appears to have been a move (most clearly evident in the Deuteronomic legislation) to bring women more fully and directly into the religious assembly, so that the congregation is redefined as a body of lay men and women. As the priesthood becomes more powerful and specialized, the primary cultic distinction or boundary within the community becomes between priest and laity rather than between male and female.[69]

Bird's observations may be extended chronologically into the period of the early synagogue as well, though there is some evidence for women in leadership positions there.[70]

It is quite possible that in all periods of biblical Israel, women's rituals that paralleled those of men existed, but by its very nature, the Bible tells us quite little about these. It is likely, for example, that the very difficult text in Judges 11 concerning Jephthah's vow, which notes a ritual in which Jephthah and her women friends go to the mountains and bewail the daughter of Jephthah's maidenhood, reflects such a ritual.[71] I sense that the male author of this chapter, who elsewhere shows some signs of confusion,[72] had no real idea of what this ritual was about, though he was fascinated by it; he created a rather bizarre and awful story to explain and to justify it. In any case, the story does reflect women functioning religiously within their own world, far from 'official' religion.[73]

69. Bird, 'The Place of Women in the Israelite Cultus', p. 411.

70. Hannah Safrai, 'Women and the Ancient Synagogue', in Grossman and Haut (eds.), *Daughters of the King*, pp. 39-49. The classic treatment of this topic is Bernadette Brooten, *Women Leaders in the Ancient Synagogue: Inscriptional Evidence and Background Issues* (BJS, 36; Chico, CA: Scholars Press, 1982); see for example p. 129, 'Women's attendance at synagogue worship services is taken for granted in the ancient sources'.

71. For various suggestions about the nature of this ritual, see Athalya Brenner and Fokkelien van Dijk-Hemmes, *On Gendering Texts: Female and Male Voices in the Hebrew Bible* (Leiden: E.J. Brill, 1993), pp. 86-90.

72. Note that in 11.24, the author incorrectly considers Kemosh to be the god of the Ammonites.

73. The terms 'popular' and 'official religion' must be used with caution; see J. Berlinerblau, 'The "Popular Religion" Paradigm in Old Testament Research: A Sociological Critique', *JSOT* 60 (1993), pp. 3-26.

The evidence that I have set out so far concerning women in the psalms and women's participation does not quite seem to fit: if women participated in the cult as laity, in other words as worshippers, why are there no prayers in Psalms that are especially appropriate to women? For example, what did the ancient Israelite woman do when she, for example, wanted to pray for children or thank God for their birth? The model of Gen. 25.21, where, as we saw earlier, Isaac prays for Rebecca, is certainly not the only model—indeed, in that same chapter, Rebecca directly consults Yhwh and is answered (vv. 22-23). The first two chapters of Samuel offer two important examples of a woman praying that help to clarify the nature of female prayer in ancient Israel.

These chapters have a long history, and are not a unified text, and are certainly not a text which comes from the period of Samuel.[74] Instead, like much biblical 'historical' literature, they are an imaginative construction of the past meant to convey various ideologies. In constructing these ideologies, biblical authors either aim at verisimilitude, that is, they attempt to reconstruct earlier institutions as they believe they might have existed, or they are anachronistic, assuming that institutions have not fundamentally changed, and retrojecting contemporaneous institutions back into the past. This means that the social institutions found in 1 Sam. 1-2 might not be representative of the period of the rise of the monarchy, when they supposedly transpire, but might be representative of some later reality in ancient Israel. The period that they reflect is unimportant for what follows; what is crucial is that the institutions depicted in the text likely reflect some reality. The author or editor, who depicted Hannah as praying in a certain way, would have created a scene which was consistent with the practices that he knew or imagined on some basis.

In 1 Sam. 1.11, Hannah first prays to Yhwh. That verse reads: ותדר נדר ותאמר יהוה צבאות אם ראה תראה בעני אמתך וזכרתני ולא תשכח את אמתך ונתתה לאמתך זרע אנשים ונתתיו ליהוה כל ימי חייו ומורה לא יעלה על ראשו, 'She vowed, "Yhwh of Hosts, if you truly see the

74. On the pre-history of the text, see the commentaries and my, 'The Composition of 1 Samuel 1–2', *JBL* 116 (1997), pp. 601-12. For my view of material like this as history, see Brettler, *The Creation of History in Ancient Israel*. For a feminist analysis of the chapters, see now Carol Meyers, 'The Hannah Narrative in Feminist Perspective', in Joseph E. Coleson and Victor H. Matthews (eds.), *'Go to the Land I Will Show You': Studies in Honor of Dwight W. Young* (Winona Lake, IN: Eisenbrauns, 1996), pp. 117-26.

affliction of your maidservant and remember me, and do not forget your maidservant, giving your maidservant a male child, then I will give him to Yhwh for his whole life, and a razor shall not go up on his head"'. This prayer is in prose, using the form of a vow, a genre that we know from Num. 30.4-16 women might use. Eli's reaction to this prayer is well known; he thinks this pray-er is drunk. This is because Hannah prayed silently—silent reading after all was quite unusual until the modern period,[75] and one opinion in the Mishnah, for example, states that certain prayers must be said audibly so that the pray-er can hear them (*m. Ber.* 2.3). There is nothing in the text to suggest that Eli had a problem with a woman praying.[76]

Hannah's prayer of thanksgiving in ch. 2 is even more significant.[77] As is well known, it is very far indeed from what a woman blessed with a child might be expected to pray. Why then did the editor put it in Hannah's mouth? Certainly, as several recent literary interpreters have noted, it is no accident that a psalm concerning the monarchy is placed at the beginning of a book that deals with the rise of the monarchy,[78] but it is doubtful if that is a sufficient reason for this psalm's placement. Even if one sides with these interpreters, the question must still be asked: 'Why this particular psalm?'

Following Yehezkel Kaufman and Moshe Greenberg, I would suggest that there is a fundamental difference between prose and poetic prayer in ancient Israel.[79] Prose prayer, which any individual could

75. See Paul J. Achtemeier, '*Omne verbum sonat*: The New Testament and the Oral Environment of Late Western Antiquity', *JBL* 109 (1990), pp. 3-27 (15-19); Michael Slusser, 'Reading Silently in Antiquity', *JBL* 111 (1992), p. 499; and Frank D. Gilliard, 'More Silent Reading in Antiquity *Non Omne Verbum Sonabat*', *JBL* 112 (1993), pp. 689-94.

76. Incidentally, Solomon Schechter, *Studies in Judaism* (Philadelphia: Jewish Publication Society, 1896), p. 318, noted a full century ago that such prose prayers were recited by women in the Talmudic period as well.

77. On the various functions of this poem, see Lyle Eslinger, *Kingship of God in Crisis: A Close Reading of 1 Samuel 1–12* (Bible and Literature Series, 10; Sheffield: Almond Press, 1985), pp. 99-102; Robert Polzin, *Samuel and the Deuteronomist: A Literary Study of the Deuteronomic History*. I. *1 Samuel* (San Francisco: Harper & Row, 1989), pp. 30-36; and Randall C. Bailey, 'The Redemption of Yhwh: A Literary Critical Function of the Songs of Hannah and David', *BibInt* 3 (1995), pp. 213-31.

78. See the extensive royal connections developed in Polzin, *Samuel and the Deuteronomist*, pp. 31-36.

79. Yehezkel Kaufman, *The History of Israelite Religion*, II (Jerusalem and Tel

compose, expressed the person's individual predicament, while individuals also had recourse to poetic prayer because it was poetic and 'official' and put them in continuity with other worshippers, past, present, and future. Thus, from the editor's perspective, Hannah could recite the prayer in ch. 2 because of its theme of reversal of fortune, as a result of victory over an adversary, and because it contains a brief reference to (2.5) עד עקרה ילדה שבעה ורבת בנים אמללה, 'until the barren gives birth to seven, while the one with many children languishes'.[80] It is thus 'embedded in an utterly credible way'.[81] 'Hannah'[82] would probably be deeply moved by this part of the psalm, which would be focal for her, rather than the psalm's climactic, concluding words of ויתן עז למלכו וירם קרן משיחו, 'may he give strength to his king and raise the horn of his anointed one'.

The difference between Hannah's spontaneous prose prayer in ch. 1 and her highly formulaic, poetic prayer in ch. 2 was keenly appreciated by Kaufmann, who noted:

> When we compare the [prose] prayers in the Bible to the psalms we see that in the prayers, there is not even a single word which is inappropriate to the given situation, in contrast to the psalms. The prayer of Hannah (1 Sam. 1.11) fits its context, but the psalm of thanksgiving that she recited, according to 1 Sam. 2.1-10, when fulfilling her vow, is formulaic, and does not fit the context. A hint to the context may be found only in v. 5 ('until the barren one gives birth to seven'), which is really only a general rhetorical trope praising God. This verse served as the basis for

Aviv: Bialik & Dvir, 1972), pp. 504-506 (Hebrew) and Moshe Greenberg, *Biblical Prose Prayer as a Window to the Popular Religion of Ancient Israel* (Berkeley: University of California Press, 1983). The issue of free versus fixed prayer is a major theme of the classic work by Friedrich Heiler, *Prayer: A Study in the History and Psychology of Religion* (trans. Samuel McComb; New York: Oxford University Press, 1932).

80. Cf. e.g. P. Kyle McCarter, *I Samuel* (AB; Garden City, NY: Doubleday, 1980), p. 76 and Polzin, *Samuel and the Deuteronomist*, pp. 31 and 36.

81. J. P. Fokkelman, *Narrative Art and Poetry in the Books of Samuel: A Full Interpretation Based on Stylistic and Structural Analysis*. IV. *Vow and Desire (I Sam. 1–2)* (Assen: Van Gorcum, 1993), p. 107. See also Clarence J. Vos, *Women in Old Testament Worship* (Delft: Judels & Brinkman, 1968), p. 155: 'It is, however, unlikely that such a "song" would be inserted if women were not wont to use such songs at the sanctuary'.

82. I use quotation marks to make it clear that I am referring to the literary Hannah rather than the historical Hannah; see my comments above about the historicity of this pericope.

> the narrator to put this psalm in Hannah's mouth, but it is really a royal psalm of thanksgiving, as we learn from v. 10.[83]

This observation concerning the way in which a woman might meaningfully recite a royal psalm that is largely inappropriate for her is central to my understanding of the Psalter. It suggests that psalms *could accommodate* women and their experiences, though there is no evidence for even a single psalm specifically tailored to them. No psalm singles out women's experiences, though a woman might find many ways to connect to specific aspects of certain psalms, just as Hannah is connected to only a small part of 1 Samuel 2. Thus, one could imagine many situations in which a woman might have wanted to recite an 'official', ready-made psalm rather than composing her own prayer, and in certain circumstances, would have had to settle for a psalm that dealt with her situation in a most minor or indirect fashion.

As suggested by the example of 1 Samuel 2, the recitation of particular psalms by women might have involved saying sections that were irrelevant or inappropriate. This is not at all unusual in the course of prayer—how often is the entirety of a statutory prayer relevant to a particular situation? The pray-er effectively brackets the irrelevant or even the offensive sections, while concentrating on the part that is appropriate to the issue at hand, no matter how small the reference to that issue might be within the larger prayer. To give an example from traditional Judaism: the first paragraph of the Jewish grace after meals, which is obligatory for men and women,[84] contains a reference to בריתך שחתמת בבשרנו, 'your covenant that you stamped on *our* flesh', namely circumcision. Though there has been some discussion in the halakhic literature concerning whether women should say this phrase,[85] it is typically said by women, though I doubt that it is at the center of their thoughts as they recite the grace. One can even wonder if a woman could recite Psalm 127 as either a prayer for fertility or as a prayer of thanksgiving after giving birth, concentrating on v. 3, הנה נחלת יהוה בנים שכר פרי הבטן, while bracketing, mumbling through, or not thinking about v. 5, which makes it so clear that the psalm has men as its intended audience.

This model of secondary usage of psalms, where a particular psalm is

83. Kaufman, *The History of Israelite Religion*, II, pp. 503-504 (Hebrew); the translation is my own.

84. See already *m. Ber.* 3.3.

85. See *Oraḥ Ḥayyim* 187.3.

used for some purpose other than that for which it was composed, has been largely ignored because of scholars' continued obsession with *Sitz im Leben*.[86] As noted by Childs and Slomovic, the Psalms superscriptions in Hebrew and Greek reflect how various editors imagined a Psalm was used in David's life on the basis of *quite limited* thematic or linguistic evidence.[87] This reflects an *ancient, secondary* use of psalms, far-removed from their *Sitz im Leben*. Especially apt to our context is Childs's observation that the superscriptions show the text's ability 'to address the changing context of the community'.[88] The superscriptions and the use of an originally royal psalm in 1 Samuel 2 by a woman who has just borne a child thus highlight the same phenomenon—the use of particular psalms outside of their original *Sitz im Leben*, often in ways that would have surprised, perhaps even upset, the original psalmist!

In closing this exploration of Hannah's prayer, I would note that the case of Hannah, a woman, praying, is not totally isolated. There are over ten cases where women pray; for example, in Ruth 4.14, the women's comments to Naomi begin with ברוך יהוה.[89] Given the lack of representation of women within the biblical canon, the lack of numerous female prose prayers is not surprising, and in no way suggests that women did not pray. Thus, to fill in the picture, it is important to turn to analogies from extra-biblical sources which represent women's voices in a clearer fashion.

Analogies are fundamentally useful, but fundamentally dangerous.[90] How much, and with what degree of confidence may we analogize either from later Judaism or from ancient Near Eastern societies that were contemporaneous to Israel? To what extent may we construct an ideal or typical pattern of female prayer or spirituality, and assume that ancient Israel fitted this pattern? I certainly recognize the dangers of the analogies I am about to propose; given the paucity of the biblical evidence, I feel that they are worth pursuing, though caution must be used.

86. See the many works cited in Erhard S. Gerstenberger, *Psalms: Part 1 with an Introduction to Cultic Poetry* (FOTL, 14; Grand Rapids: Eerdmans, 1988).

87. Brevard Childs, 'Psalms Titles and Midrashic Exegesis', *JSS* 16 (1971), pp. 137-50 and Elieser Slomovic, 'Toward an Understanding of the Historical Titles in the Book of Psalms', *ZAW* 91 (1979), pp. 350-80.

88. Childs, 'Psalms Titles and Midrashic Exegesis', p. 150.

89. See the list in Miller, *They Cried to the LORD*, p. 413 n. 2.

90. On the dangers of such comparisons, see Meir Malul, *The Comparative Method in Ancient Near Eastern and Biblical Legal Studies* (AOAT, 227; Kevelaer: Butzon & Bercker, 1990).

My initial analogy is from a much later period in Judaism (the sixteenth through nineteenth centuries), where there is an entire genre of Yiddish prayers called *tkhines*[91] recited (primarily) by women, and in some cases, written by women as well.[92] In their style and content they are quite different from the standard statutory prayers. In content, they include prayers that 'hallow women's biological lives and social roles'.[93] For example, *tkhines* for the childless wife, for a woman so she should not miscarry, for a woman to recite while her husband is away on business, and prayers that express a woman's perspective at the birth of a child, a son's circumcision, or even a child's first day at school.[94]

91. This is a borrowing from the Hebrew תחינות, 'supplications'.

92. See the collections of Tracy Guren Klirs, *The Merit of Our Mother: A Bilingual Anthology of Jewish Women's Prayers* (Cincinnati: Hebrew Union College Press, 1992) and Norman Tarnor, *A Book of Jewish Women's Prayers: Translations from the Yiddish* (Northvale, NJ: Jason Aronson, 1995). The most important studies of *tkhines* are by Chava Weissler; see her, 'The Traditional Piety of Ashkenazic Women', in *Jewish Spirituality form the Sixteenth Century to the Present* (ed. Arthur Green; New York: Crossroad, 1987), pp. 245-75, and 'The Religion of Traditional Ashkenazic Women: Some Methodological Issues', *AJS Review* 12 (1987), pp. 73-94; 'Traditional Yiddish Literature: A Source for the Study of Women's Religious Lives', The Jacob Pat Memorial Lecture, February 26, 1987 (Cambridge, MA: Harvard University Press, 1988), '"For Women and For Men Who are Like Women": The Construction of Gender in Yiddish Devotional Literature', *JFSR* 5.2 (1989), pp. 3-24; 'Prayers in Yiddish and the Religious World of Ashkenazic Women', in Judith Baskin (ed.), *Jewish Women in Historical Perspective* (Detroit: Wayne State University Press, 1991), pp. 159-81; 'Woman as High Priest: A Kabbalistic Prayer in Yiddish for Lighting Sabbath Candles', *Jewish History* 5 (1991), pp. 9-26; '*Mitzvot* Built into the Body: *Tkhines* for *Niddah*, Pregnancy, and Childbirth', in Howard Eilberg-Schwartz (ed.), *People of the Body: Jews and Judaism from an Embodies Perspective* (Albany, NY: State University of New York Press, 1992), pp. 101-15; 'The *Tkhines* and Women's Prayer', *CCAR Journal: A Reform Jewish Quarterly* 40 (Fall 1993), pp. 75-88; and 'Women's Studies and Women's Prayers: Reconstructing the Religious History of Ashkenazic Women', *Jewish Social Studies* NS 1.2 (Winter 1995), pp. 27-47. I would like to thank Professor Weissler for sending me offprints of these articles. Jewish woman's prayer in the vernacular was also discussed by an earlier generation of scholarship; see especially Schechter, 'Woman in Temple and Synagogue', pp. 321-22.

93. Weissler, The *Tkhines* and Women's Prayer', p. 78.

94. Klirs, *The Merit of Our Mother*, pp. 114-39 and Tarnor, *A Book of Jewish Women's Prayers*, pp. 16, 20-23, 57-58. For *tkhines* from the Western European for special occasions connected to women's lives, see Weissler, 'Traditional Yiddish Literature', pp. 8-13. On *tkhines* related to commandments connected to women's

These prayers express a wide variety of ways in which a woman might express herself; Chava Weissler has found in them 'a complicated web of resistance and accommodation, valorization and abnegation'.[95] In general, it is not unusual for religious communities to have a special genre of vernacular female prayer that parallels the official male world.[96] Given the nature of the compilation of the Hebrew Bible, such prayers from ancient Israel would not have survived.

Especially useful in this context is the 1786 Women's prayerbook from Italy edited by Rabbi Nina Beth Cardin as *Out of the Depths I Call to You*,[97] a prayerbook that is representative of other contemporaneous siddurim. Reading through the siddur, one immediately feels the pull between a pray-er's desire to find a new spirituality that fits women's needs, and the counter-desire to be anchored in traditional, authoritative (male), texts. The result is that in the midst of quite creative liturgy, biblical verses or chapters are appropriated in the most unexpected ways. For example, while separating out Hallah, a woman is to recite Psalm 130. The major connection between separating out the Hallah, dough which is burnt in lieu of being given to the priest,[98] and Psalm 130, as noted by Cardin, is the Psalm's use of the verbs הוחלתי (v. 5) and יחל (v. 7), which pun on the term חלה.[99] Psalm 67 is read after returning from the Mikveh (ritual bath), before going to bed with her husband:[100] it is a general request for blessing and for the nations to acknowledge Yhwh, and it has no reference to either water or children. It becomes appropriate because it contains mention of (v. 7) ארץ נתנה יבולה, 'the earth gave forth its produce', where earth is being read metaphorically as 'wife', and especially because v. 3 contains the word לדעת, 'to know', often 'to know' in the biblical sense, and the rest of the psalm has several references to יודוך, which plays on that verb. It might also not be too far-fetched to imagine that since the term דרך in

bodies, see Weissler, '*Mitzvot* Built into the Body: *Tkhines* for *Niddah*, Pregnancy, and Childbirth'.

95. Weissler, 'Women's Studies and Women's Prayers', p. 31.

96. Tikva Frymer-Kensky, *Motherprayer: The Pregnant Woman's Spiritual Companion* (New York: Riverhead Books, 1995) contains citations of many such prayers and perpetuates this genre of prayer for women.

97. Nina Beth Cardin, *Out of the Depths I Call to You: A Book of Prayers for the Married Jewish Woman* (Northvale, NJ: Jason Aronson, 1995).

98. See Num. 15.17-21 and *EncJud*, VII, pp. 1193-95.

99. Cardin, *Out of the Depths*, pp. 2-3.

100. Cardin, *Out of the Depths*, pp. 56-57.

rabbinic parlance is a euphemism for intercourse,[101] the reference in v. 3 to דרכך also helped to make the psalm appropriate to this context. Thus, a combination of evocative terms, which in their 'original' context had nothing to do with ritual baths or intercourse, allowed the psalm to be recast for a new context. This is quite similar to an editor finding the royal psalm appropriate to Hannah, largely because of the reference to the barren woman giving birth to seven children. In this context, it is noteworthy that royal psalms play an especially important role in this prayerbook. For example, Psalm 20, which states 'now I know that the LORD has saved his anointed one (משיחו)' is used in the ritual before going to the Mikveh[102] and at the onset of labor.[103] This supports the position that Hannah's prayer was originally a royal psalm that was reappropriated by an editor and put into Hannah's mouth as an official prayer that a women might recite.

In addition to these Yiddish and Italian prayers for women, there are several Aramaic prayers that take the form of magical incantations. These typically derive from the Cairo Genizah, and reflect 'the magical traditions of eighth- to thirteenth-century Mediterranean Jewry'.[104] Much of this material has been summarized by Peter Schäfer,[105] who notes the centrality of magic in relation to 'the fears and needs of Jews (and particularly those of the often quoted simple folk) of late antiquity and the Middle ages'.[106] The following observations concerning what Schäfer calls 'books of magic' are especially pertinent:

> The spectrum of themes and corresponding magical acts contained in the books of magic is, as might be expected, very broad. If my preliminary

101. See Marcus Jastrow, *A Dictionary of the Targumim, the Talmud Babli and Yerushalmi, and the Midrashic Literature* (New York: Jastrow, 1967), p. 323 דרך c and the discussion of ביאה שלא כדרכה in Michael L. Satlow, *Turning the Dish: Rabbinic Rhetorics of Sexuality* (BJS, 303; Atlanta: Scholars Press, 1995), pp. 238-43.

102. Cardin, *Out of the Depths*, pp. 38-39.

103. Cardin, *Out of the Depths*, pp. 90-91.

104. Lawrence H. Schiffman and Michael D. Swartz, *Hebrew and Aramaic Incantations from the Cairo Genizah: Selected Texts from Taylor-Schechter Box K1* (Semitic Texts and Studies, 1; Sheffield: Sheffield Academic Press, 1992), p. 7. This practice still continues; see Eli Davis, 'The Psalms in Hebrew Medical Amulets', *VT* 42 (1992), pp. 173-78.

105. Peter Schäfer, 'Jewish Magic Literature in Late Antiquity and Early Middle Ages', *JJS* 41 (1990), pp. 75-91.

106. Schäfer, 'Jewish Magic Literature', p. 91.

> impression is correct, the dominant themes are those connected with a woman's pregnancy: the barren woman (לעקרה דלא ילדה); the danger of losing the child (לאיתתא דלא תפיל); difficulties when giving birth (לאשה המקשה לילד); the child dying in the womb (לאתתא דמית עולה במעה) and even abortion (להפיל האובר). An important role is also played by themes connected with the relationship between man and woman, thus all possible sorts of love charms.[107]

The following is from an amulet found in the Cairo Genizah, published in the recent collection of Schiffman and Swartz:

> In the name of HYH, HWH, and YHYH, I have adjured and decreed upon you, O zodiacal sign Leo, to arise with all might and strength, force and power, to prevail against all harmful spirits and those which cause pain and sickness to the woman Ḥabibah bint Zuhra; to represent her in prayer and petition before the King of kings and angels, the Holy One, blessed be he; to drive away all kings of demons and demonesses, lilis and liliths, evil diseases, harmful male spirits and harmful female spirits, and evil spirits, male and female; and every sort of fear and trembling, faintheartedness and feebleness of the heart, and heart seizure, and any kind of pain in her limbs or her sinews so that she be healthy and protected from any harm for all time. Specifically, if there be within her any of the seven spirits which enter the wombs of women and deform their offspring, that she will not abort the fruit of her womb... And furthermore, I adjure and decree upon you, all sorts of evil diseases, and evil pains, every kind of nausea and dysentery, indisposition, pain and infirmity within the body of the woman Ḥabibah bint Zuhra, in the name of...to get going, flee and leave this...so that she may experience no pain during the period of her menstrual impurity or when she is ritually pure, so that she may be healthy for all time. Amen. But if you abrogate this, my adjuration, I will beat you with the iron rods of those four holy matriarchs, BILHAH, RACHEL, ZILPAH, LEAH. Therefore, fulfill this adjuration so that a blessing of goodness may befall you. Amen.[108]

We have entered a new world here, the realm of popular religion and magic, worlds that are not well represented within the biblical canon. This brings me to my second area of analogy, which is chronologically more satisfactory, namely ancient Mesopotamia, where many of the prayers connected to women are considered 'incantations', connected to the world of magic. The following incantation is used to introduce Tikva Frymer-Kensky's new book, *Motherprayer*:

107. Schäfer, 'Jewish Magic Literature', p. 88.

108. Schiffman and Swartz, *Hebrew and Aramaic Incantations from the Cairo Genizah*, pp. 69-82.

In the waters of intercourse,
bones were created.
With tissue of muscle,
the birthling was formed.

In the waters of the turbulent and fearful sea,
In the waters of the distant sea,
where the child's limbs are ties,
into the midst of which
the eye of the sun does not shine—
there the god Asarluhi saw him.
He opened the bonds
by which he was bound.
He prepared the road for him,
opened the route.

The way is open for you,
the way is clear.
She will assist you,
She the creator,
She who created us all.

To the locks she will say,
"Be loosened",
the door sills are apart,
the door is raised.

As a desired child,
bring yourself forth.[109]

Many of these incantations are associated with Lamashtu, a goddess, the daughter of Anu, who enjoys killing babies and causing mothers to miscarry.[110] Fear of Lamashtu was rampant in the ancient Near Eastern world, as reflected in the approximately seventy anti-Lamashtu amulets found, mostly from the first millennium, from an area extending from Syro-Palestine to Susa.[111] A typical amulet reads:

109. Frymer-Kensky, *Motherprayer*, p. xxvii.

110. On Lamashtu, see Jeremy Black and Anthony Green, *Gods, Demons and Symbols of Ancient Mesopotamia: An Illustrated Dictionary* (Austin: University of Texas Press, 1992), pp. 115-16. Lamashtu appears in post-biblical Jewish tradition as Lilith.

111. Mordechai Cogan, 'A Lamashtu Plaque from the Judaean Shephelah', *IEJ* 45 (1995), pp. 155-61 (161).

Lamashtu, daughter of An
whom the gods call by name,
Inanna, the heroine of the mistresses,
she who fetters the dangerous asakku,
important alu-demon of humanity.
Exceedingly great lamashtu,
do not approach this person!
Be adjured by heaven,
be adjured by earth![112]

A similar amulet, written in Akkadian and found in Israel in the Shephelah at Bet Guvrin, has been recently published and discussed by Mordechai Cogan, who suggests very tentatively that it is a remnant from an Assyrian who participated in the siege of Lachish.[113] It seems at least equally feasible that a Judean woman might have used such an amulet, even if, or especially if, it was written in cuneiform, the funny looking language of the imperial power.[114]

Many other Mesopotamian texts could be cited—especially relevant are the texts connected to the Cow of Sîn ritual,[115] some of which have a combination of ritual words and ritual action, a combination that the Hebrew Bible generally eschews, though one may wonder how many ancient Israelites avoided this combination. The prevalence of such material outside of Israel reinforces the distinction that must be made between ancient Israel and biblical Israel: ancient Israel reflects far more than is found in the canon, and includes those who for example composed the Kuntillet Ajrud inscriptions and drew the lovely pictures that accompany them,[116] while biblical Israel reflects a much narrower band of elites.

112. Frymer-Kensky, *Motherprayer*, p. 104.

113. Cogan, 'A Lamashtu Plaque from the Judaean Shephelah', p. 161.

114. I would wonder in this case if Cogan is sharing a tendency which Frederick H. Cryer, *Divination in Ancient Israel and Its Near Eastern Environment: A Socio-Historical Investigation* (JSOTSup, 142; Sheffield: Sheffield Academic Press, 1994) properly points to—minimizing the influence of magic on ancient Israel. While I think that Cryer overstates the case for magic in the Hebrew Bible, it is very likely that magic played a major role in ancient Israel, as it did elsewhere in the ancient Near Eastern world.

115. Niek Veldhuis, *A Cow of Sîn* (Groningen: Styx, 1991).

116. The meaning of the inscription and the pictures continues to be debated; for one reconstruction, see William G. Dever, 'Asherah, Consort of Yahweh? New Evidence from Kuntillet 'Ajrûd', *BASOR* 255 (1984), pp. 21-37. For a summary of various viewpoints, see Steve A. Wiggins, *A Reassessment of 'Asherah': A Study*

This survey of Mesopotamian material suggests that women's prayers were often performed at times of great danger to women, and not surprisingly, like the amulet from the Genizah, combined magic and religion to accomplish their results. This possibility certainly would have existed in ancient Israel, but would have not been tolerated by biblical authors, most of whom are drastically anti-magic. This is especially true of the authors of legal sections, where we find catalogues of prohibited magical practices (e.g. Deut. 18.10-11). Yet such practices certainly did exist, as is seen from the story of Saul visiting the (woman!) necromancer at En-Dor (1 Sam. 28). Women are also depicted in the Bible as centrally involved in several of the rituals described in Susan Ackerman's study of late Judaean popular religion.[117] Thus, it is not simply that the biblical authors were blind to women's rituals or thought that they were irrelevant; as noted above, there was likely a substantial body of ritual, including incantation prayers, which was simply abhorrent to them, and was not recorded for that reason. Finally, one must also consider the possibility that various types of ancient Israelite female piety were not expressed in words; here I think of the rituals described in detail in Susan Starr Sered's *Women as Ritual Experts: The Religious Lives of Elderly Jewish Women in Jerusalem.*[118] Much earlier, Schechter had noted the importance of women as ritual weepers at funerals in biblical and Talmudic times.[119] Such female rituals too would barely be reflected in the Bible, just as they were hardly noted by previous generations of anthropologists.[120]

As I conclude, it is possible to return to one of the questions that I

According to the Textual Sources of the First Two Millenia BCE (AOAT, 235; Kevelaer: Butzon & Bercker, 1993), pp. 171-81. For a detailed analysis of the iconography, see Pirhiya Beck, 'The Drawings from Ḥorvat Teiman (Kuntillet 'Ajrud)', *Tel Aviv* 9 (1982), pp. 3-68 and Brian B. Schmidt, 'The Aniconic Tradition: On Reading Images and Viewing Texts', in Diana Vikander Edelman (ed.), *The Triumph of Elohim: From Yahwisms to Judaisms* (Grand Rapids, MI: Eerdmans, 1995), pp. 75-105.

117. Susan Ackerman, *Under Every Green Tree: Popular Religion in Sixth Century Judah* (HSM, 46; Atlanta: Scholars Press, 1992).

118. New York: Oxford University Press, 1992. For a summary, see her 'The Synagogue as a Sacred Space for the Elderly Oriental Women of Jerusalem', in Grossman and Haupt (eds.), *Daughters of the King*, pp. 205-16.

119. Schechter, 'Woman in Temple and Synagogue', pp. 320-21.

120. In this context, it is worth considering whether 2 Kgs 4.23 reflects a ritual of women visiting the holy man on the new moon or Sabbath.

raised earlier concerning the use of psalms for our understanding of women as reciters of prayers in ancient Israel. The previous comments suggest great caution in deriving implications concerning women praying in the cult from the male-centered nature of Psalms 128, 127, or for that matter, from the majority of psalms. 1 Samuel 2 and its later Jewish analogues suggest surprising ways in which women could use quite masculine prayers, while the Bible itself offers examples of female prose prayer, some of which do take place at the major cult site. Finally, analogies suggest the possible existence of a whole type of specifically female prayer or ritual, which the Bible, due to its nature and ideology, would not reflect. Thus, the material suggests that although women might have been largely excluded *in* the psalms, most likely because psalms were composed by male elites and reflect male ideologies, this would not exclude women from reciting the psalms or from participating in various forms of Israelite prayer.

THE 'WHORE' OF EZEKIEL 16: THE IMPACT AND RAMIFICATIONS OF GENDER-SPECIFIC METAPHORS IN LIGHT OF BIBLICAL LAW AND DIVINE JUDGMENT

Carol J. Dempsey

Introduction

In recent years, Ezekiel 16 has become a popular text for study, and its metaphorical language continues to stimulate lively discussions and heated debates. But few studies, discussions, and debates have focused on the text's gender-specific imagery[1] and the impact that it has on the text's theological message when such imagery is viewed in conjunction with certain biblical laws inherent in Ezekiel 16 that come to the fore as the text's storyline is unraveled.

For the (re)readers[2] of the text, Ezekiel 16 not only contains some startling theological assertions but also raises some pertinent questions as to whether or not Ezekiel's prophetic message is truly revelatory with respect to who God is, the manner in which God interacts with

1. M.G. Swanepoel ('Ezekiel 16: Abandoned Child, Bride Adorned or Unfaithful Wife?', in P.R. Davies and D.J.A. Clines [eds.] *Among the Prophets: Language, Image and Structure in the Prophetic Writings* [JSOTSup, 144; Sheffield: JSOT Press, 1993], pp. 84-104) examines the metaphorical language of Ezekiel 16, but her analysis is for the purpose of a 'new understanding and appreciation of Yahweh' (p. 85). On the other hand, R. J. Weems ('The Lady Is a Tramp: Rhetoric and Audience in Ezekiel', in *Battered Love: Marriage, Sex, and Violence in the Hebrew Prophets* [Minneapolis: Fortress Press, 1995], pp. 58-67) focuses on the images and metaphors in Ezekiel 16 and 23 and points out how these images and metaphors are not only offensive to Ezekiel's audience but also gender-specific. Weems's study is an overview and not a detailed analysis of chs. 16 and 23.

2. One can assume that the text of Ezekiel, and most probably the other prophetic books, was read and reread repeatedly by editors, redactors, copyists, the communit(ies) for which it was written, and people today. Thus, '(re)readers' includes all people who have read and continue to read the text throughout time.

people, and what is socially and ethically acceptable within a theological framework.

Using a synchronic approach, this study examines Ezekiel 16 from both a historical and literary perspective. However, its specific focus is on metaphor and related imagery and those passages where biblical law and divine judgment have an impact on one gender and vice versa, on account of the text's pervading gender-specific imagery.

The study also looks at how various metaphors and images work within the 'conversation' between the speaking characters, namely, Ezekiel and Yhwh, and their audience within the world of the text, namely Jerusalem, and the 'conversation' between the implied author of the text and the text's actual readership. Finally, the study draws some literary, ethical, and theological conclusions.

Ezekiel 16: Some Literary Considerations

Ezekiel 16 is a 'divine' oracle that contains 'a lengthy accusation couched in allegorical terms' (vv. 3-52)[3] with only a hint of future restoration (vv. 53-58) and forgiveness (vv. 59-63). In general the oracle conveys, because of its metaphors and imagery, a most disconcerting message, one that is, for the most part, derogatory, discriminatory, harsh, and violent.[4] Even the promise of future restoration has a tone of 'verbal ridicule' and 'contempt'.[5]

3. A. Cody, *Ezekiel* (Old Testament Message, 11; Wilmington, DE: Michael Glazier, 1984), p. 76. For further discussion of Ezek. 16.3-63 as an allegory, see R. Clements, *Ezekiel* (Louisville, KY: Westminster/John Knox, 1996), pp. 69-74. On pp. 71-74, Clements critiques Ezekiel's allegory in Ezekiel 16 and concludes that the allegory 'draws particular attention to the vulnerability of women in ancient Israel', and that 'Ezekiel seems to endorse and accept patriarchal attitudes' (p. 74).

4. L. Allen (*Ezekiel 1–19* [WBC, 28; Dallas: Word Books], 1994, p. 247) comments that 'in the present climate of thought, its [Ezekiel 16's] disparaging depiction of the female as victim of social violence is particularly upsetting (cf. K.P. Darr, 'Ezekiel's Justifications of God: Teaching Troubling Texts', *JSOT* 55 [1992], pp. 97-117 (114-16). To appreciate the prophetic agenda, we must distinguish between ancient norms of handling marital infidelity and the shocking use to which Ezekiel put them. It was a vehement ploy to communicate the necessity of the fall of Jerusalem, dragging Judah down with it'. I agree, in part, with Allen's remarks, but whether or not one can 'appreciate the prophetic agenda' with its 'disparaging depiction of the female . . .' remains to be seen in the course of this discussion.

5. For further discussion, see Allen, *Ezekiel 1–19*, pp. 245-46.

The passage as a whole can be divided into three parts.[6] Part 1, vv. 3-43bα is a judgment speech that can be subdivided into three smaller units: vv. 3-14, a description of Jerusalem's origin and growth; vv. 15-34, a series of accusations; vv. 35-43bα, a proclamation of intended chastisement. Part 2, a diatribe (vv. 43bβ-58),[7] consists of: a comparison (vv. 43bβ-52) and a promise of restoration (vv. 53-58). Part 3, vv. 59-63, is a salvation oracle.

Verses 1-2, a message-reception formula (v. 1)[8] and a command (v. 2), begin Ezekiel's lengthy address to Jerusalem. With these verses, the implied author of the text makes clear to the (re)readers (1) that what follows is indeed a word from Yhwh; (2) that Ezekiel is the recipient of Yhwh's word, one that he is divinely charged to proclaim; and (3) that Jerusalem is a city—a people—that stands accused before Yhwh.[9] Together, vv. 1-2 set the stage for what is to follow (vv. 3-63),

6. Various scholars have proposed a variety of divisions for Ezekiel 16; see, e.g., W. Zimmerli, *Ezekiel 1–24* (Hermeneia; Philadelphia: Fortress Press, 1979), p. 143; M. Greenberg, 'Ezekiel 16: A Panorama of Passions', in J.H. Marks and R.M. Good (eds.), *Love and Death in the Ancient Near East* (Guilford: Four Quarters, 1987), pp. 143-50; Allen, *Ezekiel 1–19*, p. 235; and L. E. Cooper, *Ezekiel* (New American Commentary, 17; Nashville: Broadman & Holman, 1994), p. 168.

7. For further discussion of vv. 43bβ-58 as a diatribe, see T. Craven, 'Ezekiel', in *Collegeville Bible Commentary* (Collegeville, MN: Liturgical Press, 1986), p. 545. To be noted is that Craven begins the unit at v. 44.

8. See Allen, *Ezekiel 1–19*, p. 232.

9. With respect to Ezekiel 16 in general and vv. 1-14 in particular, Clements (*Ezekiel*, p.74) points out that 'it is important to take note of the extent to which Ezekiel's allegory draws particular attention to the vulnerability of women in ancient Israel. He assumes as widespread the cruel but often regrettably practised offense of leaving an infant girl to die at birth, because families preferred boys. He takes for granted the degree of women's dependence on the masculine elements of society, fathers and husbands. To pursue this theme further, however, would require a more extensive discussion concerning the patriarchal structure of the biblical social world, a feature that is widely evident in the Old Testament. Ezekiel certainly appears to accept, if not especially to endorse, such attitudes, and it is certainly open to discussion whether his priestly upbringing may have further encouraged them.'

While I agree with Clements, that the allegory does point up the vulnerability of women and their dependence on the 'masculine elements of society', and that the text does contain patriarchal attitudes, I would add further that Clements's observation seems to be based on the assumption that the text at hand was written solely by Ezekiel. Ezekiel may have accepted and endorsed patriarchal attitudes but so did the final redactors and editors who shaped Ezekiel 16 into its present form.

while communicating to Ezekiel's audience and (re)readers an authoritative tone and spirit of divine displeasure. Furthermore, Ezekiel's audience and (re)readers are presented with an image of a male prophet proclaiming to female Jerusalem what 'her' abominations are. It is very clear from the imagery that a woman, portrayed and symbolized by Jerusalem, is a sinner in need of redemption and restoration.

Before condemning Jerusalem (vv. 30-52), Yhwh confronts Jerusalem by rehearsing her past (vv. 3-29). Ezekiel's audience and (re)readers are now presented with a series of other metaphors ascribed to Jerusalem. As Yhwh rehearses Jerusalem's past in allegorical language, Ezekiel's audience and (re)readers learn that Jerusalem was once a 'foundling child' (vv. 3-5)—a little baby girl abandoned at birth by her parents—whom Yhwh cared for (vv. 6-7). Responsive to Yhwh's expressed desire that she should live (v. 6), Jerusalem blossomed into a woman whom Yhwh espoused, possessed, and adorned (vv. 8-14).

However, beginning with v. 15, the tone of the allegory shifts from seeming benevolence to one of anger (vv. 15-29). In vv. 15-29, Yhwh accuses Jerusalem of having trusted in her beauty (v. 15) and of having played the harlot among many nations who were her so-called 'lovers' (vv. 16-29). Yhwh also describes Jerusalem as an idolater (vv. 16-19) and a murderous mother who sacrificed to her idols her children whom she had borne for Yhwh (vv. 20-21).

In his confrontation with his wife Jerusalem (vv. 30-52), husband Yhwh is portrayed as an angry husband who calls Jerusalem not only *hā'iššâ hammᵉnā'āpet*, an 'adulterous wife' (v. 32) but also a *zônâ*, 'whore' (v. 35). Yhwh then says she is like her mother, a Hittite woman who abhorred her husband and children; she is the 'daughter of her mother' (vv. 44-45)! And, as if that were not a pointed enough statement, Yhwh verbally jabs Jerusalem again by reminding her that she is also the 'sister' of her sisters, namely Samaria, her older sister and Sodom, her younger sister, both of whom Yhwh says loathed their husbands and children (vv. 45-46) just as their mother did. Jerusalem, the middle child in the family of, presumably, three daughters, is then accused of having followed the bad examples of her sisters, which led

Furthermore, those who, for whatever reason—be it conscious or unconscious—choose not to comment on the offensive use of female imagery and patriarchal attitudes that underlie Ezekiel 16 are, in their own way, also accepting and endorsing patriarchal attitudes.

her to becoming more corrupt than her sisters, and thus she became a terrible example for them. Yhwh next accuses her of indirectly justifying their deeds (v. 51) at the same time that she was judging them for their abominations (v. 53).

By having Yhwh draw particular attention to Jerusalem's family situation, the authorial voice behind vv. 43bβ-58 accentuates Jerusalem's heinous crimes which, for Ezekiel's audience and (re)readers, intensifies the message of divine anger against the people of Jerusalem. But the fact that Jerusalem's and her sisters' corrupt state is attributed to their mother—°thus, the assumption that the seeds of corruption are rooted in and flow from the female gender—presents for the (re)readers a very troublesome view of women and admits of a certain ideological bias that the text betrays.

Finally, in vv. 59-63, Yhwh assumes the role of a forgiving husband who will deal with his wife in a manner that fits her offenses. Then and only then, will he take her back. Yes, Yhwh promises to take back his idolatrous, adulterous whore of a wife, and he will establish a new covenant with her. The silent voice of Jerusalem throughout the story is deafening.

It is this story of Ezekiel 16, with its gender-specific metaphors, that has tremendous implications and serious ramifications for Ezekiel's audience and (re)readers, especially when woman Jerusalem's crimes are viewed in relationship to biblical law and divine judgment.

Ezekiel 16.3-14: First Abhorred, Then Adorned

Ezekiel's address to Jerusalem is in the form of an allegory (vv. 3-43bα); its first part is a judgment speech (vv. 3-14) comprised of three subunits: vv. 3-5, 6-7 and 8-14. In all three subunits, and throughout the entire allegory, Yhwh speaks through the prophet Ezekiel. The address begins with a messenger formula: *kōh-'āmar ''ădōnāy* Yhwh *lîrûšālaim*, 'Thus says the Lord Yhwh to Jerusalem' (v. 3). Here Yhwh is portrayed as quoting his own words addressed to Jerusalem.

In vv. 3-5, Yhwh vividly describes to Jerusalem her origins (v. 3) and painful first days of life (vv. 4-5). From Yhwh through Ezekiel, Jerusalem learns about her roots and early days of life, namely, that she: (1) came from the land of the Canaanites; (2) had an Amorite father and a Hittite mother; (3) did not have her navel cord cut at birth; (4) was not cleansed and rubbed with salt; (5) was not pitied by anyone; and

(6) was thrown out in the open field because she was abhorred on the day she was born. With these verses, Ezekiel's audience and (re)readers are being asked not only to recall how Jerusalem started out as a foundling child,[10] a 'foreigner' of female gender but also to remember Jerusalem's frail, helpless, and unloved condition in her early years. The vivid description in vv. 3-5 aims at jarring the memories of Ezekiel's listeners and (re)readers, while attempting to conjure up feelings of remorse and guilt on the part of some and rage on the part of others.

The metaphorical language of vv. 3-5 raises serious issues and questions for the (re)readers of the text. First, the image of Jerusalem as a female brings to the fore the reality of how children, particularly female children, were treated in some ancient societies.[11]

Second, the mention of the child being from the land of the Canaanites, whose mother was a Hittite and whose father was an Amorite, establishes Jerusalem as a child of mixed ethnic background, who, as an adult, is guilty of abominations (v. 2) that warrant divine rebuke (see vv. 15-58). The focus on Jerusalem's ethnic background and the mention that she is responsible for abominations (see v. 2), emphasizes Jerusalem's pagan roots and plants in the minds of the (re)readers the idea that some people are 'bad seeds' from the beginning because of their ethnic background.[12] A. Cody notes that 'the pejorative reminder that the Israelites were originally indistinguishable from their Canaanite neighbors prepares the accusation of typically Canaanite religious abominations hurled in vv. 15-22. The hearers of the oracle can grasp the insinuation: once a Canaanite always a Canaanite'.[13] The idea of

10. Ezek. 16.3-5 makes clear that no one cared for Jerusalem, thus, neither her parents nor passers-by. So then, Jerusalem was abandoned not only by her mother but by her *father* as well.

11. J. Blenkinsopp (*Ezekiel* [Interpretation; Louisville, KY: John Knox Press, 1990], p.77) comments that 'exposure of unwanted children, especially female children, was the alternative to birth control or abortion in several ancient societies...' For further discussion, see K.W. Carley, *Ezekiel* (Cambridge: Cambridge University Press, 1974), p. 96; Cooper, *Ezekiel*, p. 169.

12. For Ezekiel's audience, the focus on Jerusalem as a foundling child from a mixed ethnic background also functions as a religious polemic against idols and those who believe in them and live their lives accordingly. Yhwh, Israel's God, who is the living God of life, is the one who takes notice of and cares for people, especially when everyone, including the gods and goddesses of other religions, has abandoned them.

13. Cody, *Ezekiel*, pp. 77-78. For further discussion on Jerusalem's ethnic past,

Jerusalem's abominations as something that is related to 'her' ethnic background recurs in vv. 43bβ-52.

Third, the fact that the child was not cared for at the time of birth, which, in the ancient world was the mother's and/or the midwife's responsibility, presents a negative picture of women. And, the fact that the child is a female makes the lack of care and eventual abandonment even harder to swallow—a mother has rejected her own child, her own daughter. The throwing out of the infant female child into the open field suggests metaphorically that Jerusalem was destined for destruction. The use of this gender-specific metaphor admits of a particular attitude that was prevalent in the ancient Israelite social and patriarchal world. This attitude is, to some extent, still prevalent today in certain contemporary social and religious spheres. What connections are the (re)readers of the text being asked to make because of the text's gender-specific metaphors?

Fourth, the fact that no eye pitied the abandoned child to care for it out of compassion can be viewed as a serious indictment against the human community, and by extension, an indictment against the child's father as well. Yet, the focus on the absence of care at birth keeps the image of the woman in the forefront and puts the blame primarily on her. The fact that Yhwh is the speaker in vv. 3-5 creates an underlying tone of judgment. Thus, Ezekiel's audience and (re)readers are being presented with quite a picture. While this picture can stir up feelings of sadness and guilt on the one hand, it can, on the other hand, enrage others because of (1) its overtly ethnic reference with an implied religious statement, and (2) its gender-specific imagery that is used to shape a story filled with demeaning statements and overtones that create both social and theological problems with respect to how women are viewed in society and how certain group(s) of people or individuals are viewed by God.

Finally, the fact that Jerusalem was a 'foundling child' has legal ramifications. In the ancient world, whenever a person or object was cast out, the one doing the casting relinquished all rights and obligations to the object cast out.[14] Hence, Yhwh's description of Jerusalem

see W. Eichrodt, *Ezekiel* (Philadelphia: Westminster Press, 1970), p. 204; Carley, *Ezekiel*, p. 96; and W.H. Brownlee, *Ezekiel 1–19* (WBC, 28; Waco, TX: Word Books, 1986), p. 223.

14. M. Malul ('Adoption of Foundlings in the Bible and Mesopotamian Documents: A Study of Some Legal Metaphors in Ezekiel 16.1-7', *JSOT* [46] 1990,

that he rehearses reminds Jerusalem of her previous orphaned and vulnerable state. The (re)readers of the text are confronted with the sad fact that the law safeguarded the one who casts out and not the one being cast out. The metaphor of Jerusalem as a cast out infant makes one realize how vulnerable children were in the ancient world and still are today. Voiceless infant Jerusalem is unprotected by the law after being rejected by her parents in vv. 3-5. This metaphor with its legal ramifications begs the question, 'Is not Jerusalem's early life situation still happening today in all respects in some circumstances and cultures, particularly, in some cases, when female children are involved'?

In vv. 6-7 Yhwh describes for Jerusalem his first encounter with her. Jerusalem hears that (1) the first time Yhwh passed by her, Yhwh took notice of her;[15] (2) that her life is the result of Yhwh's word, *ḥ*^{a}*yî* 'Live!'; (3) that Yhwh watched her grow physically into womanhood; and (4) that Yhwh seemed to mind that she was 'naked and bare' (v. 7). Hence, Jerusalem is reminded of Yhwh's care for her.

The (re)readers of the text are given a mixed picture of Yhwh as conveyed by the text's metaphorical language. First, Yhwh is someone who takes notice of small, insignificant outcasts in their struggles. In the case of Ezekiel 16, Yhwh cares for Jerusalem, a foundling child.

Second, one sees someone who is rejected, abhorred, abandoned being given the chance for survival and not the kiss of death (see v. 7).

Third, Yhwh is someone who watches attentively the growth process. However, the phrase, *w*^{e}*'at 'ērōm w*^{e}*'eryâ* 'yet, you were naked and bare' (v. 7), has a ring of disdain to it on the part of Yhwh. To be noted is that the word *'ērōm*, 'naked', is used only in Gen. 3.7, 10, 11; Deut. 28.48; and Ezek. 16.22, 39; 18.7, 16; 23.29. In Gen. 3.7 nakedness is associated with transgression and shame; in Deut. 28.48, it is part of a warning of chastisement that Yhwh will inflict on the Israelites if they do not serve him joyfully; Ezek. 16.22, 'nakedness' is part of Jerusalem's foundling condition; in 16.39 and 23.29, it is associated

pp. 97-126 [101]) explains that 'an object or person cast outside the city, in the field or the desert, into a pit, or even in the street, is thereby removed to the outside domain, and no longer has any ties with the person who cast it. The person responsible for casting renounces any right or obligation toward the object cast.'

15. Blenkinsopp (*Ezekiel*, pp. 78-79) notes that 'Yahweh's first "passing by" and his decision to save the child wriggling in its birth blood by the roadside (vv. 6-14) corresponds to the time of the ancestors. A remote parallel might be the story of the endangered ancestress (Gen. 12.10-12 and parallels) or the Aramean ancestor doomed to perish memorialized in Israelite worship (Deut. 26.5).'

with divine judgment and violent actions. Lastly, in Ezek. 18.7, one who covers the 'naked with a garment' is considered 'righteous' (cf. Ezek. 18.16). Is the authorial voice that shaped the text of Ezekiel 16 making some sort of statement here in v. 7, especially with Yhwh as the speaker? And what are Ezekiel's listeners and (re)readers to suppose, especially since it is in reference to, metaphorically, a female as was the case in part in Gen. 3.7, 10, 11 with 'nakedness' being connected to transgression and shame with the assumption that the woman was responsible for leading the man astray?

Fourth, Yhwh's word is seen as efficacious. The command to live goes forth, and the foundling child lives and grows!

With respect to vv. 6-7, T. Craven notes that 'the child lay beside the road, unloved and unattended, when God came by and performed the duties of a midwife'.[16] But Craven's suggestion that Yhwh acted as a midwife is questionable insofar as none of the afterbirth care, that is, cutting the navel cord, washing and cleansing the child of the blood from birth, rubbing it with salt, and swaddling it (see v. 4) were done by Yhwh. Nor is there any evidence that Yhwh acted maternally or paternally as in Hos. 11.1-4. Why did Yhwh not pick up baby Jerusalem who was flailing around in her birth blood? Why did Yhwh not bathe her, salt her, swaddle her, and hold her close to his cheek? What are the (re)readers of the text to suppose? Are they to suppose that Yhwh did not do these things because Jerusalem is, metaphorically, a little girl and not a little boy as is the metaphorical image in Hos. 11.1-4? So far, in Ezekiel 16, Jerusalem has yet to be cared for physically by Yhwh. Such care on the part of Yhwh does occur in vv. 8-14 when Jerusalem is at the age of love. What kind of picture of Yhwh and Yhwh's relationship with Jerusalem is being portrayed by the authorial voice that shaped the text? And, what is Ezekiel's audience and (re)readers to assume about Yhwh with regard to Yhwh's supposedly genuine, wholehearted care of Jerusalem?

In vv. 8-14, Yhwh reminds Jerusalem of how he took notice of her a second time, realized that she was at the age of love, and so spread the edge of his cloak over her, covered her nakedness, pledged himself to her, and entered into covenant with her, which made her 'his' (v. 8). Then, he bathed her, anointed her (v. 9), clothed her (vv. 10-13a); fed her (vv. 13b); complimented her (v. 13c), and informed her that her

16. Craven, 'Ezekiel', p. 545.

beauty was perfect because of his splendor that he bestowed on her (v. 14).

From Yhwh's comments, Jerusalem is made to realize that she was chosen by Yhwh, that she belonged to Yhwh because of Yhwh's pledge of himself to her and because of their covenant, and that all that she is and all that she has, both materially and physically, is on account of Yhwh.

The (re)readers of the text now see Yhwh as a God of tender love who is generous, caring, benevolent, and committed to Jerusalem. But Yhwh's espousal to Jerusalem presents a dilemma. On the one hand, Yhwh's deeds and compliments could be seen and heard as gestures of kindness. On the other hand they could be seen as patronizing since there is no response, verbal or otherwise, by Jerusalem to Yhwh and Yhwh's deeds. The relationship is not portrayed as a mutual one. And the woman is seen to be someone without an identity independent of what Yhwh has turned her into—the resemblance of a queen who would be fit for him, 'the king'.

Through the metaphorical language and imagery used in vv. 8-14, the text's (re)readers are also given a picture of what an ideal relationship between a man and a woman is, supposedly, to look like: when a woman is at the age for love, an age that is within the sphere of a man to notice, it is the place of a man to make the necessary advances that will eventually lead to a commitment and a covenant whereby a woman then becomes a man's possession (v. 8). Then, a man's responsibility is to care for the woman (vv. 9-13) which, against the backdrop of vv. 3-7 is seen more like 'taking care of' the woman whose beauty is the result of his care (v. 13). The woman's fame becomes equated with her beauty (v. 14a), a beauty that is 'perfect' only because of the 'splendor' the man has bestowed on her (v. 14b). Beauty, then, in a man's eyes, is equated with the outward appearance of a woman, and she is valued not for her own independent self but for what she has become through the man's care. In essence, the woman becomes a reflection of her husband's care.

The description of the relationship that exists in vv. 9-13 portrays an image of Yhwh as a husband who is in control of the relationship between his wife and him and essentially, a husband in control of his wife! This covenant–marital model is troublesome insofar as the intrinsic dignity and beauty of a woman are not respected, acknowledged, or affirmed. Her natural beauty is something that needs to be covered over by clothes and jewels that her husband picks out without any comment from her.

Furthermore, the reference to Yhwh washing the blood off of Jerusalem, his wife, is suggestive that the woman was a virgin and the blood was caused by a first coitus.[17]

Finally, the imagery of the regal adornment of Jerusalem and the reference to her as a 'queen' is suggestive of royalty. It is monarchical language. The question emerges, 'Does Jerusalem have to become "regal" in order to remain loved by Yhwh?' What does the text's imagery suggest to its (re)readers of the text about God's relationship with and to people? Or might such regal imagery be the result of a particular cultural and social situation that perhaps influenced the writers and rewriters of the text?

Ezekiel 16.15-34: Affirmation Turns to Accusation

Ezekiel continues his oracle in vv. 15-34. Here, as in vv. 3-14, Yhwh is the speaker and Jerusalem, personified as Yhwh's wife, remains the focus of attention. Yhwh continues to rehearse Jerusalem's past for her, but this time he brings to the fore her abominations (vv. 15-26, 28-35) and recalls for her how he chastised her on account of such deeds (v. 27). He begins his tirade against Jerusalem with the phrase *wattibṭᵉḥî bᵉyopyēk wattiznî ʿal-šᵉmēk*, 'but you trusted in your beauty, and played the harlot because of your fame...' (v. 15). The waw adversative signals a shift in tone.

In vv. 15-22, Yhwh accuses his wife Jerusalem of having trusted in her beauty, having played the harlot because of her fame, having lavished her harlotries on any passer-by. She has misused the clothing, jewels, and food he gave to her (vv. 16-19), and grossly of all, she has having sacrificed their children to her idols as an offering (vv. 20-21). Furthermore, she has forgotten that it was her husband Yhwh who rescued her from death in the days of her youth (v. 22). Thus, Jerusalem is guilty of harlotry, idolatry, murder, and forgetfulness. And, one sees

17. For further discussion, see Brownlee, *Ezekiel 1–19*, p. 225. A woman's virginity and evidence of it was an important issue in the ancient Israelite world (see, e.g., Deut. 22.13-21) because the presence of or loss of it had certain legal ramifications for a man and a woman. Thus, a woman's virginity, an expression of female sexuality, is connected to the law. But whether or not a man is a virgin does not seem to enter into the conversation.

that Yhwh's regal bride is now an unfaithful, idolatrous, murderous, absent-minded wife!

Yhwh's invective against Jerusalem continues in vv. 23-29. Here Yhwh again accuses his wife of having played the whore, and now he specifically names her 'lovers': the Egyptians (v. 26), the Assyrians (v. 28), and the Babylonians (v. 29) and points out that even with all these she was still not satisfied (v. 29).[18] Now, Yhwh has indirectly accused her of being a woman of insatiable lust!

In the midst of these accusations, Yhwh recalls for Jerusalem how he had previously 'chastised' her (v. 27). Here, Jerusalem's enemies are also, metaphorically, females—the daughters of the Philistines—whom Yhwh says were ashamed of her lewd conduct.[19]

Finally, in vv. 30-34, Yhwh ends his list of accusations against Jerusalem with a series of denigrating statements. First, Yhwh exclaims to her how sick her heart is that she did so many abominations (vv. 30-31). Second, he states that she was not like a whore because she refused payment (v. 31). Instead she bribed her lovers to come to her.[20] Yhwh makes clear to her that none of her lovers solicited her (v. 34) and hence, Jerusalem was different from other whores because, according to Yhwh, she sought the men for prostitution instead of vice versa, the more usual way. Third, and worst of all, Yhwh launches a personal and direct attack against his wife: 'Adulterous wife'! She takes strangers instead of her husband (v. 32)! Yhwh is a bitter husband with righteous anger because his wife has broken their covenant (see v. 9), betrayed his faith in her (vv. 16-19), and murdered her sons and daughters—'his' children (vv. 20-21).

Within vv. 15-34, several points need further comment. First, the root *znh*, 'to commit fornication', 'to play the harlot', occurs 18 times throughout this unit[21] and helps to create the unit's overall theme. Second, the image and motif of the unfaithful wife, here in Ezekiel 16 metaphorically applied to Jerusalem, is a common Old Testament

18. The mention of the various names is a historical allusion to Jerusalem's foreign alliances. For further discussion, see Blenkinsopp, *Ezekiel*, p. 78 and Carley, *Ezekiel*, p. 101.

19. Carley (*Ezekiel*, p. 101) notes that 'the metaphor of Jerusalem as a young maiden is sustained by the reference to the Philistine cities as women'.

20. The reference to payment could be an allusion to the tribute paid to foreign powers. For further discussion, see Carley, *Ezekiel*, p. 101.

21. See vv. 15 (twice), 16, 17, 20, 22, 25, 26 (twice), 28 (twice), 29, 30, 31, 33 (twice), 34 (twice).

motif.[22] Third, four abominations that Jerusalem is guilty of, all of which have legal ramifications, are adultery, idolatry, child sacrifice, and forgetfulness of Yhwh.

According to the Law, a man and a woman who commit adultery are both sentenced to death by stoning or the sword (Lev. 20.10; Deut. 22.21-24; Ezek. 23.47; cf. Exod. 20.14). Punishment for idolatry is death by the sword (Deut. 13.12-16; cf. Exod. 20.2-6). Child-sacrifice was also strictly forbidden by the Law (Lev. 18.21; 20.1-5; Deut. 12.30-32; 18.10-12, and is punishable by death.[23] With respect to forgetfulness of Yhwh, especially in times of prosperity, a strong word of caution is put forth in Deut. 6.10-12; 8.11-20.

From these verses, Ezekiel's audience and the (re)readers of the text are presented with a disturbing picture of God and, because of the husband–wife metaphor that is operative throughout much of Ezekiel 16, a distressing portrayal of a husband–wife relationship, along with a horrendous profile of a woman. The authorial voice that shaped the text portrays Yhwh as someone who is controlling, possessive, angry, and abusive. Yhwh is a raving husband, justly angry at his wife, but is verbally abusive in his accusations and has been physically abusive in his punishment (v. 27). Jerusalem, Yhwh's wife, is described as a bride turned harlot. In vv. 1-14, she is a silent, passive woman—a foundling child who grows up to resemble a queen. In vv. 15-34, she becomes an initiator of harlotry, a 'hussy' incapable of being satisfied by lover after lover, and by indirect implication, not even Yhwh can satisfy her! Ethically, she is guilty of breaking four laws, three of which require her to be punished by death. In the case of adultery, both guilty parties are to be put to death. Interestingly enough, though, no rebuke or punishment is mentioned for Jerusalem's 'lovers'.

The authorial voice that has shaped the story has set Jerusalem up for the divine judgment and chastisement that is to follow (see vv. 35-43bα). Thus, the story progresses, but at whose expense? Are the

22. See, e.g., Isa. 1.21; 57.8; Jer. 2.20; 3.2, 6, 20; Ezek. 23.3, 8, 11, 12; Hos. 1.2.

23. For further comment on child sacrifice, see Cooper, *Ezekiel*, p. 172, and Swanepoel, 'Ezekiel 16: Abandoned Child, Bride Adorned, or Unfaithful Wife', p. 97. In the ancient Near East, children were sacrificed to pagan gods such as Molech. By the time of King Josiah, the practice was widespread (2 Kgs. 23.10). Brownlee (*Ezekiel*, p. 231) notes that 'the special place of this evil cult [child sacrifice] was not in the temple, but on a special altar in the valley of Hinnom (2 Kgs. 23.10; 2 Chron. 28.3; 33.6; Jer. 7.31-32; 19.5-6; 32.35)'.

(re)readers being asked to sympathize with Yhwh the 'victim' in a disastrous marriage? Are the woman's deeds being portrayed so horribly so as to accent the strength and power of God's judgments and chastisements? But what about the woman who will suffer death? Are the (re)readers being asked to assume that the woman is going to get 'what she deserves'? (See vv. 35-43.) It is to be noted that the woman is silent throughout every one of the accusations hurled at her. Is this to be understood by the audience and (re)readers as her proper stance before Yhwh? Is this to be seen as 'appropriate behavior' in her relationship to her husband? With the male metaphor for God and the female one for Jerusalem, the image of the woman, as seen in Ezekiel 16, will always be tainted. She will generally be seen as one who is in need of divine redemption not only because of what she has been set up to do, but also by virtue of who she is—a woman! Thus, the (re)readers of the text are presented with a metaphor that not only shaped a story in the past but one that also continues to shape theological imaginations today in a way that is offensive and unacceptable.

Ezekiel 16.35-43bα: 'Therefore, O Whore, Hear the Word of Yhwh'

Following Yhwh's list of accusations that Ezekiel announces is a proclamation of intended divine chastisement. Yhwh, the speaker of vv. 35-43bα, now tells his adulterous and murderous wife what he intends to do to her. The phrases *lākēn zônâ šim'î d^{e}bar-Yhwh*, 'Therefore, O whore, hear the word of Yhwh' (v. 35) and *kōh-'āmar '^{a}dōnāy Yhwh*, 'Thus says the Lord God' (v. 36), introduce Yhwh's speech. The phrase *lākēn*, 'therefore', signals a new unit and prepares Ezekiel's audience and (re)readers for a description of the consequences that Jerusalem will have to endure on account of her abominations. In v. 32, Yhwh has called his wife an 'adulterous wife'; now in v. 35 she is a 'whore'. The vocative, followed by an imperative and an emphasis on Yhwh's word that in turn leads into a prophetic messenger formula, adds a derogatory and authoritative tone to Yhwh's message (vv. 36b-43bα). The unit ends with the phrase *n^e'um '^{a}dōnāy Yhwh*, 'says the Lord Yhwh' (v. 43bα, which harks back to v. 36, the beginning of Yhwh's list of chastisements.

In v. 36b, Yhwh summarizes Jerusalem's abominations and then declares what he plans to do to her on account of them (vv. 37-41). The list of punishments opens with the word *lākēn*, 'therefore' (cf. v. 35).

Because of her wicked deeds Yhwh will: expose her to all her lovers (v. 37), judge her *mišpᵉṭê nōʼᵃpôt wᵉšōpᵉkōt dām*, 'according to judgments of adulteresses and murderers' (v. 38), and then deliver her into the hands of her executioners who will execute judgments on her *lᵉʻênê nāšîm rabbôt*, 'before the eyes of many women' (v. 41a). According to the Law, the legal penalty for harlotry and adultery was stoning (Deut. 22.20-24). The same was true for those who sacrificed their children (Lev. 20.2). Thus, Yhwh was sentencing and handing over his wife to the death penalty.

After the list of consequences, Yhwh continues his speech with a series of personal, self-reflective statements. First, he admits to Jerusalem that his aim in punishing her is to stop her from playing the harlot and from making payments. Next, he admits that the deeds that are about to happen to her will satisfy his fury and his jealousy and so return him to a calm, non-angry state (v. 42). Finally, Yhwh explains to Jerusalem that he will give back to her what she deserves!

The (re)readers of vv. 35-43bα are given a picture of God that is violent and repulsive Ywhw, in vv. 35-41, advocates destruction and death instead of life (cf. v. 6). On the one hand, such rage is understandable when marital love has been betrayed. On the other hand, such rage represents an anger that is out of control and leads to intended action that is in direct contradiction to God's own law in the Decalogue (see Exod. 20.13). Jerusalem has, metaphorically, murdered her children and is now sentenced to death by a law that is contrary to another law. It seems, then, that one is being told that someone cannot take another's life. Yet, a person's life can be taken by another; one can be 'put to death' when certain crimes have been committed. Thus, some of God's laws seem to have an inherent contradiction within them. The spirit of what God says in one law is not carried out in another. What God says in some cases does not apply in other cases, and certainly not to God who wants Jerusalem dead!

Hence, God in vv. 35-43bα is portrayed as a vengeful, angry God who wants his own feelings appeased at the expense of another's life. Furthermore, metaphorically, the fate of a woman is in the hands of her husband. The authorial voice that shaped the text makes clear that God is someone capable of devising wicked deeds against those who act wickedly. The verses serve as a warning to Ezekiel's audience, many of whom are supposedly guilty of wicked deeds. The verses also attest to the fact that God is a God of justice and a jealous God. The punishment advocated by the Law appears to be in conflict with other laws, a situation that raises this question: Can violence to a perpetrator make right the harm done to the perpetrator's victim?

The (re)readers are again confronted with an offensive depiction of women, with the Law on the side of the men. According to the Law, the punishment for adultery is death for both parties. But here, the text makes no mention of Jerusalem's 'lovers' being put to death. Instead, they will publicly humiliate her. The metaphorical language of the text admits of a strong bias against women. In v. 38, judgment is upon Jerusalem as it is upon other adulteresses and murderers. Again, there is no mention of the man being judged or stoned for his part in the act of adultery.

Finally, the idea of the woman's nakedness recurs three times in this unit (vv. 36, 37, 40) and harks back to vv. 7 and 22. In vv. 36, 37, 40, nakedness and bareness are associated with transgression (v. 36), shame (v. 37), and humiliation (v. 40). All three instances, inclusive of vv. 7 and 22, draw attention to the female body and communicate an air of disdain for it. Therefore, one can see from vv. 35-43bα that imagery and metaphors relating to women are used to communicate to Ezekiel's audience and to the text's (re)readers an ethical message: God will not tolerate injustice. Yet, at whose expense is credence being given to the allegorical message?[24] And does the text communicate a truly ethical message?

Ezekiel 16.43bβ-58: 'Like Mother, Like Daughter'

Verses 43bβ-52, a comparison, and vv. 53-58, a promise of restoration, form a continuation of Yhwh's judgment against Jerusalem. This

24. On the issue of female imagery used in relation to divine judgment, Cooper (*Ezekiel*, p. 174) comments that 'through judgment Israel the harlot was to return to the same despised condition of shame, helplessness, and exile she was in before God found and rescued her ("naked and bare" in v. 39, also in vv. 7, 22). The nation would be an example of the justice and judgment of God. The phrase "in the sight of many women" (v. 41) was a reminder that women were made to watch the judgment of an adulteress so that her judgment might be an example and deterrent.' While Cooper tries to explain the metaphorical language in the text here and elsewhere, he does not address the gender-specific metaphors in Ezekiel 16, and so he indirectly accepts the underlying assumptions that the text is making, along with certain attitudes and mindsets that shaped the text at a particular time in a particular culture.

judgment is couched in a harsh, gender-specific simile and related metaphors that accent Jerusalem's corruption while making a statement about a source of wickedness in general.

In v. 43bβ, Yhwh draws attention to Jerusalem's abominations and then tells her that all who now encounter her will ascribe a particular proverb to her: *k^{e}'immâ bittāh*, 'as (the) mother, (so) her daughter' (v. 44). In v. 45, Yhwh unpacks the simile for Jerusalem while drawing her attention to other members of her family. Yhwh points out to Jerusalem that she is like her Hittite mother, an unnamed woman, who 'loathed her husband and children' (v. 45); she is the sister of her sisters who also 'loathed their husbands and children' (v. 45). Jerusalem's older sister is Samaria; her younger sister is Sodom (v. 46), and the children that both loathed were their 'daughters' (v. 46). Hence, Jerusalem is the 'middle child' in the family; she is surrounded by a mother and two sisters who acted corruptly (v. 47) and in time, as Yhwh points out, she became more corrupt than Samaria and Sodom, a situation that made her sisters look 'righteous' (vv. 48-52).

With the words of these verses, Ezekiel points out to his audience the depth, breadth, and magnitude of Jerusalem's abominations and makes the assertion that she was corrupt from birth onward, that the seeds of her corruption were given to her by her mother who also 'infected' her two sisters as well. And from vv. 1-5, one can deduce that Jerusalem's behavior was not 'learned behavior' because she was abandoned at birth. Thus, the suggestion is that Jerusalem's internal make-up is corrupt (cf. 16.30). In addition to bringing Jerusalem's ethnic background to the fore, might not the authorial voice that shaped the text have the Genesis 3 account in mind? In v. 45, there is mention of Jerusalem's father being an Amorite, but clearly the blame for Jerusalem's corrupt state is being placed on Jerusalem's mother.

Thus, the (re)readers of the text are presented with a metaphorical description of Jerusalem's family that highlights the corruption of its female members while accenting Jerusalem's own corrupt state as well. The fact that the message takes the form of a Yhwh speech gives the distinct impression that God disdains Jerusalem, inclusive of her family members. But with the gender-specific imagery that is both quoted and used by Yhwh, are the (re)readers being asked to come to some understanding about the root of wickedness whereby Jerusalem then becomes both an example and a symbol? If this be the case, then one needs to raise a deeper question: To what extent has the text been shaped by an authorial voice(s) that has itself been shaped by a particular theological perspective that has been influenced by and intertwined with certain cultural, social, and religious biases of the day?

In vv. 53-58, Yhwh continues his speech to Jerusalem. He promises to restore all of Jerusalem's and her sisters' fortunes (vv. 53-54) and to return the sisters, their daughters, and Jerusalem's daughters to their former states (v. 55). But, Yhwh's treatment of Jerusalem does not speak of divine benevolence on the part of Jerusalem. Yhwh's restoration of Jerusalem is so that she might become a consolation for her sisters (v. 54). Jerusalem, the most corrupt of her sisters, and therefore, the most undeserving of divine mercy, will be shown mercy. This gift could make her an object of disdain for Sodom, whom she mocked earlier (vv. 56-57), and surely an object of mockery for her neighbors who already despise her (vv. 27, 57). Thus, Yhwh's restoration of Jerusalem and her daughters is meant to make Jerusalem feel guilty and ashamed.[25]

The (re)readers now see God as someone who sometimes does good things for spite. God's favor is meant here to punish Jerusalem indirectly. With goodness, Yhwh is 'getting back' at Jerusalem. Now, this picture of God is problematic. What kind of a God does such things? And were the original (re)readers of the text being asked to accept this spiteful attribute of God as a fully, absolutely determinative quality of God's characterization in the text? Another question arises from v. 55. Yhwh promises that Jerusalem and her daughters will be returned to their former state. Who, then were the sons and daughters that Jerusalem was accused of sacrificing in v. 20? And why are only the daughters being restored and not their sons (cf. vv. 21-22, 45), if, in fact, they all had sons? Is the authorial voice that shaped the text asserting an assumption here, namely, that it is women who are in need of redemption and restoration and not men?

Ezekiel 16.59-63: From Condemnation to Restoration?

Ezekiel brings Yhwh's speech to a close in vv. 59-63. Here Yhwh, once again, is the only speaker who now talks to Jerusalem in a manner that attests to his sense of both justice and mercy. Beginning with the prophetic messenger formula that puts authority behind Yhwh's word, Yhwh continues to promise Jerusalem that he will make her 'pay' for

25. For further discussion, see Carley, *Ezekiel*, p. 106.

her infidelity (v. 59), but that he will remember his covenant with her when she was younger, and will now establish an 'everlasting one' with her. But again, how Yhwh's intentions are portrayed presents a problematic view of who God is and why God entered or enters into covenant. In this unit, one sees that the re-establishment of covenant is meant to make Jerusalem feel ashamed (v. 61) and to assert Yhwh's power and control over Jerusalem (vv. 62-63), all of which is associated with divine forgiveness (v. 63).[26]

What is the authorial voice behind the text asking the original (re)readers of the text to understand about God and covenant? Are they now being asked to accept the fact that as far as God is concerned, there can be no mercy without first having severe justice (see vv. 35-43bα) and humiliation (see vv. 43bβ-58)?[27] And, when mercy and the restoration of the divine–human relationship is re-established, are the (re)readers of the text being told that the restoration of the covenant is primarily for the purpose of humiliating a human person so that God can establish God's power and control over humankind, which here in Ezekiel 16 (see, specifically, v. 63) takes the form of being silenced? What are the (re)readers being asked to understand about covenant and its restoration? That it was for God's self-serving purposes rooted in sensuality (vv. 8-14) and the need for domination (vv. 62-63)? What happened to *ḥesed*, 'lovingkindness' and *raḥ^{a}mîm*, 'compassion' (see, e.g., Hos. 2.21; Mic. 7.19-20)? It seems that Hebrew Law (see, e.g., Lev. 18.21; 20.1-5,10; Deut. 12.30-32; 13.12-16; 18.10-12; 22.21-24)

26. M.S. Odell ('The Inversion of Shame and Forgiveness in Ezekiel 16.59-63', *JSOT* 56 [1992] pp. 101-12 [102]) makes a striking point with respect to vv. 59-63: 'These verses raise a theological problem, since they reverse the sequence of consciousness of sin and forgiveness. Jerusalem feels shame only after God forgives, and furthermore, is commanded to feel shame because God forgives.' By way of clarification, I would add that Odell asserts that Jerusalem feels shame only after God forgives. While this may be true, neither the text nor Jerusalem admits of this feeling. The text points to a future feeling of shame that Jerusalem will have to experience because of Yhwh's restoration of the covenant. Furthermore, Jerusalem is totally silent throughout Ezekiel 16. So, it is difficult to assess just how Jerusalem feels about anything. But, Odell's main theological point remains clear.

27. In commenting on vv. 37-38, two verses that shed light on v. 59, Allen (*Ezekiel 1–19*, p. 242) points out that 'adultery was a capital crime for both men and women (Lev. 20.10; Deut. 22.22), and so was murder, in this case of Jerusalem's children (v. 36). Yahweh, as both cuckolded husband and sovereign judge, would pass the double sentence, with the jealous fury of a husband scorned (cf. Prov. 6.34)'.

as it specifically related to Jerusalem, and metaphorically referred to it as female, has a direct impact on the restoration of covenant with God who has to relate to Jerusalem as husband and judge.

Furthermore, looking at vv. 15-58 as a whole, one notes that Yhwh in his anger said and did some despicable things to Jerusalem as her husband. Although Yhwh is willing to forgive and restore the covenant with Jerusalem, despite the fact that there is no mention of remorse on Jerusalem's part, it seems a bit presumptuous on Yhwh's part to assume that Jerusalem would take him back. After all, he has been verbally and physically abusive to her (see, e.g., vv. 27, 32, 35). Neither is there any mention of Yhwh's heart recoiling or growing warm and tender (see, e.g., Hos. 11.8-9). Jerusalem will pay for her deeds and then Yhwh will restore the covenant with her. Are the (re)readers being given a model of covenant that bespeaks of a tit-for-tat relationship with God? As a model of covenant and marital love, should not Jerusalem ask Yhwh to apologize for his abusiveness?[28] Jerusalem's silence looms large; there is more that needs to flow from the mouth of the prophet and the pen of the author.

Conclusion

This study of Ezekiel 16 has shown that the text is an intricate piece of writing, one that uses a particular form of literary artistry to communicate a message that is most unsettling and very controversial in many scholarly and public circles today. A general theological statement that

28. With respect to the violence of language, particularly in vv. 35-43, Blenkinsopp (*Ezekiel*, p. 79) states that 'the violence of the language is so deliberately offensive that we can well understand why it would be considered unsuitable for liturgical reading. We shall have to make of it what we may, but it may at least serve as a reminder that the kind of pain and anger from which the language springs is, more often than we care to think, integral to the act of loving.' I agree with Blenkinsopp that the violence of the language is offensive, but I disagree with his point that such language is integral to the act of loving. If it were, then we would have no problem with Ezekiel 16 being used as a liturgical reading. While the language may be an expression of anger that springs from the pain of deep love that has been betrayed, this kind of offensive language is not acceptable. It only heaps violence on top of violence. Some sort of acknowledgment of sorrow needs to be expressed afterwards when all is sorted out between the two parties in conflict. Furthermore, Ezekiel would make a wonderful liturgical reading followed by a homily or sermon on violence in interpersonal relationships and marriage.

can be retrieved from the text is that God is faithful and willing to restore covenant despite the fact that humankind may, at times, violate or break it.

The study has also given consideration to gender-specific metaphors and imagery within the text, particularly the male–husband metaphor that the character Yhwh assumes and the female–wife metaphor that is ascribed to Jerusalem by the prophet Ezekiel, the character Yhwh, and the authorial voice of the text. Issues and questions pertaining to biblical law were considered in relation to Jerusalem's metaphorical actions. As a result of a focus on gender and law, several things became clear about Ezekiel 16 and other biblical stories in general.

First, gender-specific imagery and biblical law have an impact on each other, specially when it comes to divine judgment and its relation to the restoration of covenant.

Second, these issues have an impact on the overall and deeper theological message of Ezekiel 16, whose historical prophet and community and literary author(s) were all living in a time and world that was less than positive in its view of and outlook on women. The text reflects this.

Third, the problems that create controversy for the (re)readers of Ezekiel 16 are problems that stem from the text's central metaphors, the underlying ideologies of the people that created the metaphors, this text, and the laws of the Israelite community that were in existence at the time when the text took shape. Clearly, the ideology that underlies Ezekiel 16 admits of a bias against women, whether the bias be conscious or unconscious. God's committed relationship with the people of Jerusalem begins with a metaphorical description of Jerusalem as a foundling child. The relationship is then described as a marriage that goes sour on account of Jerusalem. In a society characterized by patriarchy and hierarchy, whose divine deity is often expressed in metaphorical and gender-related language that is consistent with the attitudes and perceptions of that patriarchal and hierarchical society, the choice of a husband and wife metaphor to express covenant relationship is one that creates theological problems and legitimizes certain oppressive attitudes and actions that are unacceptable.

Fourth, because of the gender-specific imagery in Ezekiel 16, certain legal issues come into play when wife Jerusalem betrays husband Yhwh who must then play the role of judge.

Lastly, the study has looked at how the metaphorical language worked within the 'conversation' between the speaking characters and their audiences within the world of the text, and the 'conversation' between the implied author of the text and the text's actual readership. From such conversations, one can conclude that the metaphorical language of Ezekiel 16 is not helpful to Ezekiel's audience nor to his (re)readers then and now. Furthermore, many biblical laws need to be reappropriated and reassessed, especially when gender, law, and ideological issues—be they metaphorical or real—are intertwined.

Ezekiel 16 is a passage rich in issues related to gender and law. While it speaks of a forgiving God who is faithful to covenant and its restoration, the text is revelatory insofar as it sheds light on many ancient and often oppressive attitudes and actions, some of which are still with us today, that shape(d) and misshape(d) people's lives as they try(ed) to live life together and in relationship with their God whom they are/were trying to know and understand. The text is also revelatory insofar as it presents a picture of a marriage that, in some people's eyes, is sorely in need of transformation on the part of both parties involved. Thus, Ezekiel's allegory could use some further editing. And, it must be acknowledged that the wonderful vision of human and divine love—with all that the relationship entails—that Ezekiel attempts to present to his audience seems to be clouded over by some of the 'stuff' of the day.

VIRGINITY IN THE BIBLE

Tikva Frymer-Kensky

Among the Deuteronomic laws dealing with sexuality and the family, two laws demonstrate Israel's attitude towards the chastity and virginity of daughters: the case of the slandered bride (Deut. 22.13-21) and intercourse with an unmarried daughter (Deut. 22.28-29). Both laws operate on the premise that unmarried girls are supposed to remain virgins until they are married to a man of their father's choosing. In the intercourse provision, the girl's sexual experience is revealed while she is still under her father's jurisdiction. In the case of the slandered bride, the bridegroom of a newly married girl claims that he is not the first. Both circumstances flaunt the assumption of daughterly chastity and both precipitate a crisis that the laws seek to resolve.

The cultural expectation that young girls should remain virgins is embedded in the Hebrew language. As is now generally well known, the term normally translated 'virgin', *b^{e}tûlâ*, means a girl of marriageable age. A passage such as Joel 1.8, 'like a *b^{e}tûlâ* wearing sackcloth for the husband of her youth', cannot refer to a virgin, and the common pairing of *bāḥûr* and *b^{e}tûlâ* (Deut. 32.25; Isa. 23.4; Isa. 42.5; Jer. 51.22; Ezek. 9.6; Ps. 148.12; Ps. 78.63; Lam. 1.18; Lam. 2.21; 2 Chron. 36.17) makes it clear that the word's reference is to 'young man/men and woman/women', and says nothing about their physical characteristics. When the text wants to emphasize the virginal state of a girl, it adds the phrase 'who has not known a man' (Judg. 19.39; Judg. 21.12; Gen. 24.16[1]). On the other hand, the plural word *b^{e}tûlîm* probably means 'virginity' in Judg. 11.37. The same term *b^{e}tûlîm* is used in Lev. 21.13 in a discussion of the High Priest who cannot leave the sanctuary; he must marry a girl in her virginity. So too in Deut. 22.14, the term indicates 'sign of virginity', namely, 'blood of defloration'.[2] The term

1. Masoretic reading of Gen. 24.16: 'a man has not known her'.
2. This despite Wenham's attempt to interpret the passage as a seeking of

b^e^*tûlâ* can also sometimes mean 'virgin'. Leviticus 21.14 stipulates that the High Priest cannot marry a widow, divorcee, profane woman or prostitute; only a '*b*^e^*tûlâ* from his people'. This verse is one verse after the phrase 'a girl in her *b*^e^*tûlîm*', and almost certainly means 'virgin'. The passage in Ezek. 44.22 is more ambiguous. Speaking about all priests, it declares that they cannot take widows or divorcees as wives, only *b*^e^*tûlôt* from the seed of Israel or widows of priests. Here the essential requirement is that she has not been stamped as a non-priest. She is a daughter of Israel, or has been inducted into the priestly caste by another priest.

The ambiguity and variability of the term arises from the basic cultural assumption that young marriageable women are virgins. This virginity is prized. Lot tells the mob that his daughters are virgins to make them want the girls more. The prize has a price: in Exod. 22.16, the girl's lover pays the *mōhar habb*^e^*tûlôt*[3] even if the father refuses to allow him to marry her. It is sometimes assumed that a girl who has been seduced and raped will no longer be marriageable. Of this there is no hint in the biblical text. In an age when many women died in childbirth, and when polygamy was permitted, if not popular, most girls could find husbands. But they would no longer command the *mōhar habb*^e^*tûlôt*.

The serious expectation that daughters be virgins before marriage is shared by other ancient cultures. Classical Greece also had high expectations and strong demands for the virginity of girls. As with Hebrew, the words for 'young girl' and 'virgin' are the same, *parthenos*. Furthermore, the Greek word *sophrosune* 'right action', which refers to cautious moderation for men, means absolute chastity for girls.[4] Ancient Near Eastern laws also show this concern. If the girl has been spoken for (brideprice paid), then sleeping with her is a capital offense. This is an adultery regulation. But Lipit-Ishtar 33 shows us a similar,

menstrual blood, whose absence would indicate pregnancy. This use of a 'bloody sheet' would be without parallel in a world where bloody sheet inspection is a well-known institution for enforcing the virginity of daughters. See G.J. Wenham, 'B^E^TÛLĀH, "A Girl of Marriageable Age"' *VT* 22 (1972), pp. 326-48.

3. Of course, given the ambiguity of the term *b*^e^*tûlôt*, this brideprice might simply mean the appropriate brideprice for young girls.

4. For Greece see initially Michel Foucault, *The Use of Pleasure: The History of Sexuality*, II (trans. Robert Hurley; New York: Vintage Books, 1986) and Giulia Sissa, *Greek Virginity* (trans. Arthur Goldhammer; Cambridge, MA: Harvard University Press, 1990).

though less weighty concern attached to virgin daughters: 'If a man claims that another man's virgin daughter has had sexual relations but it is proven that she has not had sexual relations, he shall weigh and deliver 10 shekels of silver'.[5]

Western culture after the Bible has put so much emphasis on virginity and has attributed such importance to the biological condition of virginity (the 'intact virgin' with the unruptured hymen) that we take such emphasis for granted and rarely ask 'why'? Why should society place such great stock, or indeed care that its young women be virgins at marriage? Adultery can wreak havoc in society, but premarital chastity? When people have thought about this question, the standard explanation has been that men want their wives to be virgins so that they can be sure that any babies are theirs. But, when carefully examined, this explanation will not hold up. There is no reason that societies could not have a convention that any baby born during the first nine months after the marriage belongs to the bride's family—after all, in an agrarian society, there is economic value in the labor of children. Alternatively, societies could have a rule such as Sparta is reputed to have had, wherein biological fatherhood was immaterial and only sociological fatherhood (who raised the child) counted. Even Rome made a distinction between the *progenitor* and the *pater*, with the *pater* the significant father.

A second common 'explanation', that men want the 'property' that they acquire to be new and unused does not make any sense. When sexual pleasure is a concern, experience might outweigh any titillation from tight fits. Women rarely want their bridegrooms to be virgins and when they do, it is because of the ideological value of 'purity' that is culturally learned. And since one of the main purposes of marriage is the production of children, a society could have a convention that a girl who has already gotten pregnant, indeed has already birthed a living baby, has demonstrated that she is fertile and therefore has increased her worth. Some societies do have such a convention and place no

5. LL 26. Except when indicated, all translations are by Martha Roth, *Law Collections from Mesopotamia and Asia Minor* (Atlanta: Scholars Press, 1995). In this text I read 'another sleeps with her' where Roth reads 'deflowers'; in practice, the expectation is that the two mean the same. However, if the man who paid the brideprice has already slept with her so that the second man is not technically deflowering her, the penalty would be the same. The classic study on the sex laws is by Jacob J. Finkelstein, 'Sex Offenses in Sumerian Laws', *JAOS* 86 (1986), pp. 355-72.

stock in a girl's premarital chastity.[6] The desire of men that their wives be virgins results from the cultural supervaluation of virginity, particularly female virginity; it is not its cause.

There have been several noteworthy attempts by anthropologists to explain the virginity ideal. The first, by Jane Schneider,[7] concentrated on the pan-Mediterranean preoccupation with female chastity. She argues that it arose from political-economic and ecological situations in the absence of effective state control. Kin groups competed over land and other scarce resources, and women were an important resource. Guarding access to this resource could symbolize the family's ability to protect its material boundaries. The necessity to guard access could also reinforce intra-familial cooperation in the face of potentially disruptive external forces. The problem with this explanation, provocative as it is, is that it suffers from both historical and ethnological blindness. By concentrating only on the modern Mediterranean complex, it ignores the fact that the same cultural valuation of virginity is found around the globe and existed long before the collapse of the Roman Empire and long before the Bible. The same problem undermines Carol Delaney's hypothesis that when the ideology of monogenesis, namely, the Aristotelian notion that the entire embryo is contained in the sperm, was combined with monotheism, the combination led to the establishment of total patriarchy with its desire to control women.[8] Patriarchy existed long before Greece, and Aristotle's theory of monogenesis was only one of several biological models of procreation in classical Greece. Far from being the cause of patriarchy, it became the dominant reproductive thesis because it fit patriarchal ideals. Nevertheless, despite their flaws, both theories draw attention to the intimate connection between the ideal of virginity and the control of women.

In contrast to Schneider, who emphasized the absence of a state, Sherry Ortner pointed to the historical emergence of the state, with its increasing stratification in kinship forms and the emergence of family as an administrative unity with absolute authority vested in the father as

6. For discussion, see Karen Erickson Paige and Jeffrey M Paige, *The Politics of Reproductive Ritual* (Berkeley: University of California Press, 1981) and Lucy Mair, *Marriage* (London: Scholar's Press, 1977), chapter 10.

7. Jane Schneider, 'Of Vigilance and Virgins', *Ethnology* 10 (1971), pp. 1-24.

8. Carol Delaney, 'Seeds of Honor, Fields of Shame', in D. Gilmore (ed.), *Honor and Shame and the Unity of the Mediterranean* (American Anthropological Association Publications, 22; Washington, DC: American Anthropological Association, 1987), pp. 35-48.

senior male. Thus, in a patriarchy, women are legal minors subject to male control. The state and its legal and religious institutions have formally legitimated, enforced and symbolically justified the codes by differential laws and punishments for female and male adultery; by the 'crimes of honor' that condone by minimal sentencing any homicides committed to avenge the sexual transgression of a female relative; and by religious images like the Madonna which glorify female chastity.[9] In a later work, Ortner herself realized the historical myopia of this study. From her studies in Polynesia she realized that hierarchical social organization historically preceded state formation and economic intensification, and was at least as much cause as effect of these. She suggests that it is hierarchy itself that creates the demand for virginity. In a hierarchical society, the status of a person is based first on his or her position in the hierarchy and secondarily on gender within that rank. At the highest rank, the social organization unites males and females with common interests and tends towards (though it does not reach) gender equality. Women also get their share of the family property: in patrilineal exogamous systems women are dowered, in cognatic endogamous systems they inherit. However, the unexpected fact is that even though marriage is less important in the latter system, nevertheless, both systems place great importance on guarding girls' virginity. Ortner therefore concludes that the stratification itself, by elevating women's position within each strata, creates the high cultural value of virginity. Noting that 'Virginity in its cultural contexts [is] an expression and cultivation of the overall higher "value" of women in such systems', Ortner suggests that this is because 'virginity downplays the uniquely feminine capacity to be penetrated and to give birth to children'.[10]

The most recent study of virginity, by Alice Schlegel, relies on the techniques of cross-cultural analysis. Using the index of cultures, Schlegel notes that the only societies that do not value virginity are those with subsistence technologies, small communities, absence of stratification, matrilineal descent, matrilocal marriage, absence of belief

9. Sherry Ortner, 'The Virgin and the State', *Feminist Studies* 4 (1978), pp. 19-33.

10. Sherry Ortner, 'Gender and Sexuality in Hierarchical Societies', in Sherry Ortner and Harriet Whitehead (eds.), *Sexual Meanings: The Cultural Construction of Gender and Sexuality* (Cambridge: Cambridge University Press, 1981), pp 351-409; quotations are from p. 401.

in high gods, no bridewealth, little or no property exchange at marriage and ascribed rather than achieved status. She therefore suggests that those societies where young men seek to ally with powerful families value virginity because by ensuring the virginity of families, the bride's family prevents young men from claiming girls by making them pregnant. When abortion is freely available, she adds, virginity is less valued.[11]

Schlegel's argument is seriously flawed. As historians, we know of societies—most notably biblical society—in which bridewealth is clearly combined with the valuation of virginity. Schlegel's flaw lies in the very methodology of cross-cultural techniques. She recognizes that there are six gradations of attitudes towards premarital sexuality: expected, tolerated, mildly disapproved but not punished, mildly disapproved and lightly punished, disallowed except with groom and strongly disapproved. However, in order to code her computer search, she takes the first three as 'virginity not valued' and the last three as 'virginity valued'. This simplifies far too much. Moreover, there are societies (like contemporary Saudi Arabia) that do more than strongly disapprove, that kill the girl and/or her lover. There are also societies (early and medieval Christianity) whose valuation of virginity is so high that it becomes the bedrock demonstration of faith. In addition, it is simply not true that virginity is not valued where abortion is available: laws from the ancient and classical world clearly assume the option of abortion or exposure.

Whatever the ultimate causes of the virginity ideal, the anthropologists are right in pointing out the strong connection between such chastity codes and the guarding of girls. The male members of the family have the prerogative and the duty to maintain the chastity of the young women of the family. The chastity of the girl thereby becomes an indicator of the social worth of the family and the men in it. The honor of the family is at stake, for real men have the strength and cunning to protect and control their women.[12] The defilement of the

11. Alice Schlegel, 'Status, Property and the Value on Virginity', *American Ethnologist* 18 (1991), pp. 719-34.

12. This phenomenon has been studied particularly in the societies around the Mediterranean, because chastity codes are universal through that area. But the same patterns have been discerned in very widespread areas. The classic study is by J.G. Peristiany, *Honor and Shame: The Values of Mediterranean Society* (London: Weidenfeld & Nicolson, 1965). More recently, see David Gilmore, 'Introduction', in David Gilmore (ed.), *Honor and Shame and the Unity of the Mediterranean*

females unmans the men: they lose their honor by the demonstration that they lack the qualities of real men. To protect their honor, men of a family may join together to safeguard their women. They view other men with suspicion, and Paige and Paige point out that the period beginning at menarche is a time of great vulnerability for a family, for some men may find it beneficial to seduce or rape a girl rather than negotiate a brideprice.[13] By eloping with a girl, a man both eliminates competing suitors, and demonstrates her father's inability to control his own daughter. The effect is to shame him into lowering the amount of compensation he demands. Gossip can also weaken the father's position in marriage bargains. Even if the girl has not run away, rumors that she has not been chaste reduce the family's status in the same way. The solution is strict surveillance, which protects the 'daughter' against both seduction and accusations of promiscuity.

There is another explanation that could be offered for the importance that maidenly chastity assumes in so many cultures. If Freud is right about the incestuous feelings that fathers and daughters have for each other, and if the 'primal law' against incest is truly universal, then a father's desire for his daughter may be transmuted into his insistence that she belong to no one but him until he marries her off. The primal law has often been considered the origin of both law and morality and of the construction of gender. But the universality of the primal law is itself a theoretical construction[14] and any assumptions derived from it stay speculative.

Another possibility is that the surveillance of girls may itself be part of the reason that virginity is so prized. Virginity becomes a tangible reason for the family's right to control their women. It offers a specific purpose towards which the patriarchal urge to dominate can be directed, and a way in which it can be measured. In this way the control of girls may be a cause of the chastity codes, not their necessary corollary. In any event, control and chastity are intimately related.

(AAA Publications, 22; Washington, DC: American Anthropological Association, 1987), pp. 2-21, and Maureen Giovannini, 'Female Chastity Codes in the Circum-Mediterranean: Comparative Perspectives', in Gilmore (ed.), *Honor and Shame*, pp. 61-74.

13. Paige and Paige, 'Politics'.

14. For discussion of gender and Foucault's theory of the Primal law, see Judith Butler, *Gender Trouble: Feminism and the Subversion of Identity* (London: Routledge, 1990).

Dinah

The biblical story that most dramatically reflects these concerns is Genesis 34, one of the most misunderstood stories in the Bible. A tale of love, betrayal, and war, it is commonly known as 'the rape of Dinah' and has been read and interpreted as a story of rape and revenge.

The first sentence of Genesis 34, 'Out went Dinah, the daughter of Leah whom she bore to Jacob, to visit the girls of the land', is fraught with implications for biblical Israel. The very first word, 'out went', can strike terror in the mind of any patriarch. 'Out' means leaving the family domain, leaving both the protection and the control of the head of household. We often talk about the vulnerability of women who go out without protection. But rarely is it mentioned that when a woman goes out, she leaves her family vulnerable to any disgrace her actions might bring upon them. As a result of this vulnerability, many societies have strongly discouraged girls and women from going out. In Near Eastern society women had responsibilities, such as going to the well, that would take them out into the public sphere. But the woman who went out without a specific chore was viewed with suspicion and condemnation. The Laws of Hammurabi 142 consider the case of a woman who wants a divorce. The local court investigates: if she has been a paragon of a wife and her husband a profligate, she gets her divorce and takes back her dowry; if, on the other hand, her husband has been a proper husband, but she has been a gadabout, (*wāṣiat*) then they throw her into the river (LH 142). An Old Babylonian word list identifies this same word 'gadabout', *wāṣitum* (literally 'goer-out') with *harimtu*, 'prostitute'. The goddess Inanna/Ishtar and female demons and streetwalkers roam the streets; 'proper' women do not. Jewish and Christian commentaries also exhibit this attitude towards women who go out. Rashi calls Dinah a *yōṣ'ānît*, the Hebrew equivalent of *wāṣitum*, with the same connotation. In the Christian tradition, the Renaissance commentator Tyndale declares 'Dinah goeth but forth alone, and how great myscheve and troble followed', and Calvin makes the lesson explicit: 'fathers are taught to keep their daughters under narrow watch'.[15] The control of girls is only slowly disappearing in our own culture, and our

15. Quoted from Ilona N. Rashkow, *Upon the Dark Places: Antisemitism and Sexism in English Renaissance Biblical Translation* (Sheffield: Sheffield Academic Press, 1990), p.97.

languages still encode the same message: the Aramaic word *napqa'*, literally, 'she who goes out', becomes the Yiddish word for prostitute; the English word 'streetwalker' means the same.

With all this cultural background, 'Dinah went out' is not an innocent statement. She is 'out of control' and something is going to happen. And what happens is a father's nightmare: Dinah, who went out to see the girls, is seen by a boy. The story tells us, 'Shechem... the prince of the land, took her and laid her, and degraded her'. Usually, the story is considered a rape story: girl goes out alone and gets attacked. But the key word, *'innâ,* does not mean rape. *'innâ* is one of the key words of relationships in the Bible. It characterizes how Sarah treated Hagar and how the Egyptians treated their Israelite slaves. The basic meaning is to treat someone improperly in a way that degrades or disgraces them by disregarding the proper treatment due people in each status. In the story of Tamar and Amnon, where Amnon raped Tamar, the narrator says specifically 'he overpowered her, abused her and lay with her' (2 Sam. 13.14). Both the use of the verb 'overpower' and the word order are significant. In Amnon's case, where the text tells us specifically that the rape was by force, *'innâ* comes before the verb 'he lay with'. By contrast, in the Dinah story, the verb 'overpower' is not used and *'innâ* comes after the word 'lay with'.[16] Later in the story, the text says that Shechem did an outrage by 'sleeping with the daughter of Jacob'. Nothing is said about forcible rape: any sexual intercourse with a daughter is a moral outrage that may not be done.

There is a reason that the word order counts. In rape, abuse begins before intercourse, from the moment the rapist begins to use force, and so the word *'innâ* comes before the word 'lay with'. In other forms of illicit intercourse, the act of intercourse may not have been abusive. The sex may be sweet and romantic. But the *fact* that the man has intercourse with her degrades her, and the word *'innâ* comes after the word 'lay with'. Shechem did not rape Dinah, but he did wrong. From the Bible's point of view, an unmarried girl's consent does not make the sex a permissible act. She has, after all, no right of consent.

Shechem may not have forced her, but the very fact that he has slept with her means that he has ignored the fact that she is a proper young woman who must be treated within certain protocols. Laws from Sumer and Assyria deal with the possibility that a man might meet a girl in the

16. For the word order, see Lyn Bechtel, 'What if Dinah is not Raped?', *JSOT* 62 (1994), pp. 19-36.

street and sleep with her; the Assyrian law provides that the man must give triple the virgin's price.[17] The proper protocol demands that the man (or his father) approach the girl's parents, and possibly first her mother. A love poem from ancient Sumer that tells of the meeting of the god Dumuzi and the young goddess Inanna demonstrates the way things should happen. As Inanna tells the story, Dumuzi approached her, putting his arm around her shoulders. She, however, tells him 'let me go that I may go home. What stories would I tell my mother?' Dumuzi suggested that she tell her mother that she spent the time in the square with a girlfriend, listening to music: 'with this story confront your mother; as for us—let us be dallying in the moonlight'. She, however, convinced him that he must court her properly by coming to see her mother Ningal.[18]

The meeting of the two gods Enlil and Ninlil is told in two Sumerian myths. In one, 'the marriage of Sud', Enlil negotiates with Sud's (Ninlil's) mother for her hand. But in the myth of 'Enlil and Ninlil', the mating of these two gods is more like that of Dinah and Shechem. Ninlil goes to the banks of the holy canal and Enlil accosts her, 'let me make love with you...let me kiss you!' But she would not agree: 'If my mother learned about it, she would be slapping my hand; if my father learned about it, he would be grabbing hold of me'. But Enlil pursues the matter, sleeps with her and inseminates her with the moon god Su'en. When he comes through the courtyard of the town, he is set upon by the court of the fifty great gods and the seven deciding gods, who decree, 'the sex offender Enlil will leave the town'. Enlil is banished. Ninlil loves him, and indeed follows him, but he is banished nonetheless. His act is too dangerous to the social order to allow him to continue to live in Nippur.[19]

Inanna insists that her suitor come to her mother; Ninlil and Dinah do not. But regardless of the willingness of the maidens, the suitors had no right to sleep with them. Young girls cannot consent legally, for they do not have the right of consent. Even if Dinah was willing, even if

17. Sumerian Laws Exercise tablet 7-8; MAL 55 (Roth, *Law Collections*, pp. 44, 174-75).

18. Dumuzi-Inanna H: critical edition by Yitschak Sefati, 'Love Songs in Sumerian Literature: Critical Edition of the Dumuzi-Inanna Songs' (PhD thesis, Bar-Ilan University, 1985), pp. 209-17; ET *The Harps That Once: Sumerian Poetry in Translation* (trans. Thorkild Jacobsen; New Haven: Yale University Press, 1987), pp. 10-12.

19. Jacobsen, *The Harps that Once*, pp. 167-80.

Dinah would have been the aggressor, it would not matter: Shechem is a ravisher of a young virgin. To use the terminology of Roman law, Shechem's act was not *stumpa per vim*, 'wrongful intercourse by force', but it was certainly *stumpa*, 'wrongful intercourse'. To use contemporary American terminology, sleeping with Dinah was statutory rape. In our society, girls below a certain age (the 'age of consent') are not free to arrange sexual liaisons, and men are not free to sleep with them. Dinah was very young, a *yaldâ* (v. 4). Even today, when a Congressman sleeps with a high school girl, when a cult leader has 'consensual' sex with the young girls of the cult, our society is outraged, and the man can be considered a felon. In ancient society, unmarried girls never acquired the right of consent. Only the prostitute owned her own sexuality. By sleeping with her, Shechem was acting as if she had no family to protect, guard and marry her. As the brothers say, 'should our sister be treated as a whore'? He has disgraced her, and through her, her whole family.

Shechem never intended any harm. As the story says, 'His soul cleaved to Dinah the daughter of Jacob; he loved the girl and spoke to the heart of the girl' (Gen. 34.3). *dbq*, 'cleaving', is the very word that Genesis requires for the love between husband and wife (Gen. 2.24). Solomon cleaved to his wives in love (1 Kgs 11.2), and with this word Israel loves God (Pss. 83.9; 119.25; Deut. 4.4; 13.5 and Josh. 23.8); God loves Israel (Jer. 3.11; 13.11) and Ruth loves Naomi (Ruth 1.14). With the specific subject *nepeš*, 'soul', the psalmist cleaves to God (Ps. 83.9), and the psalmist in depression, is stuck in the mud (Ps. 119.25). In all these contexts, in addition to those in which love is not the subject, the connotation of *dbq* is the permanent nature of the attachment: Shechem is not fickle, and his love is not transitory. The other phrase in the sentence, *wayᵉdabbēr ʻal-lēb* ('spoke to the heart'), employs another special idiom. It only appears eight times in the bible. In all these cases, the one speaking has a superior position: Joseph the Ruler to his brothers after the death of Jacob (Gen. 50.21); the Levite to his concubine (Judg. 19.3); God–husband to Israel–wife (Hos. 2.16); King David to his men (2 Sam. 19:8); King Hezekiah to the Levites and to the people (2 Chron. 30.22; 32.6); Boaz to Ruth the gleaner (Ruth 2.13), and the people to Jerusalem (Isa. 40.2). In all of these instances, the other party may be alienated, as the concubine who has run from the Levite; Israel who has been rejected by God; the destroyed Jerusalem; and David's men who have seen him grieve excessively over Absalom the enemy with whom they have just been at war. Or the other party's position might be insecure, like Joseph's brothers after the death of Jacob, or Ruth as a poor outsider–gleaner in Boaz's fields, or the people of Jerusalem during the siege of Sennacherib. In all of these instances the superior's message 'to the heart' is one of loving assurance that the speaker will rectify the other's insecure or alienated status. In all these passages, the implication is that the speaker not only 'woos', but courts successfully, and the positive response of the other party is not even recorded. The use of these terms in Genesis 34 conveys a picture of Dinah accepting Prince Shechem's loving commitment. She stays with him, we are to understand, not because she has been kidnaped or is a captive. Shechem 'done her wrong' (*'innâ*), but 'he spoke to her heart'.

But even if Dinah has consented, Shechem must make things right with her family. Shechem wants to make amends. He belatedly asks his father to negotiate a marriage. And to restore Jacob's honor, Shechem is willing to pay any brideprice that Jacob wants. Such a high brideprice could restore Jacob's status. But before Hamor can act, Jacob hears about it; people are talking and the affair has become public. Jacob himself keeps quiet until his sons come home from the fields. The matter is a public disgrace, and their future is threatened: they may not be able to get the wives that they want, or they may have to pay exorbitant brideprices.

From Dinah's point of view there is a very big difference if she had been raped. But from the point of view of the family, it may even be worse if the girl has consented rather than if she has been raped. If she has been raped, then Shechem has violated the integrity of the family, breached its boundaries, and left it without honor. But if Dinah has eloped, then Shechem has still transgressed the families boundaries, but, in addition, Dinah has not been faithful to Jacob's right to control her sexuality and, as a result, she too has dishonored him. Shechem has shown its external boundaries to be weak; Dinah has shown its internal order to be chaos. The whole family has been grievously dishonored.

It is in this serious framework that they all meet with Shechem and his father.There are two main ways in which the honor of a family may be restored. One rests with the girl's lover. He can demonstrate that he and his family intend no dishonor to the girl's family by offering a very large brideprice. Shechem and Hamor make it clear that they are willing to offer anything that Jacob's family might ask. The other way to restore honor rests with the girl's kinsmen, who can conduct a reprisal raid. Such a raid demonstrates that the men can protect their boundaries and that outsiders encroach upon their territory, property or personnel at the risk of their own lives. Both methods are represented in the Dinah story: Shechem offers the former, the brothers demand the latter. To restore their virility, they need to react violently. They are willing to sacrifice a very important cultural value—honesty in negotiation—and to demean the prime symbol of Israel—circumcision—to manifest that they are real men who can protect their own. And so, in falsehood, they accept the offer of marriage and then destroy the town.

The story raises the question of honor and self-defence in high drama. Jacob attacks Simeon and Levi, declaring that they have made him stink. First, he has been dishonored by Dinah and Shechem, who showed that he did not guard and control his women, and now he has been totally dishonored by his sons, who show that their word cannot be trusted. Jacob feels that if they lose their reputation as honorable men, the others will attack and destroy them. But Simeon and Levi answer, 'Should our sister be treated as a whore'? They feel that if the others see that they can be taken advantage of, then the others will surely attack and destroy them. Who is right—Jacob, who will negotiate the return of his honor, or Simeon and Levi, who fight for it?

Intercourse with an Unmarried Girl
(Exodus 22.15-16 and Deuteronomy 22.28-29)

In the story of Dinah, Shechem's infraction of the protocols of propriety escalated into a vendetta that entailed a full-scale destruction of his city. Such unregulated reprisals cannot be permitted within society, and the laws of the ancient world seek to normalize the events surrounding illicit sexual encounters by spelling out the consequences in terms of monetary remuneration that the lover has to make. In Exodus, this is spelled out: he must offer the standard brideprice. A man cannot 'love her and leave her': by sleeping with her, he has assumed the obligation to marry her. And he must pay a normal brideprice: he cannot obtain a girl cheaply by first sleeping with her, thus dishonoring her, and lowering her brideprice. But the father is not obligated to give her to him in marriage. He can take the 'virgin's brideprice' from the lover, and then refuse to give her in marriage. Through his demonstrated control over the girl's fate, he repairs the momentary loss of control he had over his daughter and restores his status. The law prevents girls from circumventing their father's authority and finding their own husbands. And it prevents men from grabbing wives without considering the rights of other men.

The laws of Deuteronomy consistently reduce the authority that heads of household have over the members of their household.[20] The wives and children do not thereby become more autonomous or independent, but rather control is taken from the individual head-of-household in favor of the collective power of the local council and the state. As part of this general movement, the rule about intercourse with unwed girls also undergoes a change. In Deuteronomy, the man who grabs a girl and sleeps with her and is discovered must pay 50 shekels to her father, marry her and never divorce her. The word 'grab' is sometimes understood to imply rape, but once again, the text does not really say this. The previous law deals with the case of clear unambiguous rape of a betrothed girl: the man overpowered her in a field where no one could hear her cry out. Once again, as with Tamar and Amnon, the verb 'overpower' is used. In this case, the rapist is killed, but the girl is not touched because, 'for just as when a man rises up against his neighbor and murders him, just so is this matter' (v. 25). But the verb 'grab' in the law of the unwed virgin, seen from the perspective of the girl's family, could simply mean he grabbed what he wanted without showing respect for the family's honor and the protocols of propriety.

In Deuteronomy, the couple has been discovered, so there can be no pretense, and the father has lost his power to decide whether the man who has slept with his daughter can marry her. He is obligated to give her to the man who slept with her. The situation is completely taken out of the realm of personal volition and at the same time out of the realm of honor. In effect, the situation becomes routine: if the man and girl are discovered, the law dictates everyone's actions; the boy must marry, the girl must marry and be given in marriage, and the family's only protection (and the girl's) against frivolous intercourse is that the bridegroom is obligated to pay a high brideprice and marry forever. Theoretically, on the one hand, this law could enable a man who knows that the girl's father would not give her to him in marriage to acquire a girl by 'rape-capture', as the 200 men of Benjamin were invited to do with the girls at Shiloh (Judg. 21.19-21). Such an abduction would force the father's hand. The only deterrent to such abduction is that no matter how miserable an unwilling bride might make his life, he cannot

20. For further discussion, see Tikva Frymer-Kensky, *Victims, Virgins and Victors: A New Reading of the Women of the Bible* (forthcoming).

divorce her. On the other side of the spectrum, the law might enable a Romeo and Juliet to force acceptance of their union by eloping. When faced with a *fait accompli*, the father would have no choice but to accept the 50 shekels and give her in marriage. Elopement has long been a means of circumventing parental decision-making in societies where the father normally decides who the girl should marry. It is the reverse of a shotgun marriage. In a shotgun marriage, the father forces the girl's lover to marry her; in an elopement, the willing bride and groom force the father to accept the marriage. The law in Deuteronomy accomplishes both aims. All the parties have their further actions regulated by the law: the boy must marry, the girl must be given in marriage. The law prevents such an elopement from being embarked upon frivolously by its provision against divorce. If the couple elope, there is no going back.

The Law of the Slandered Bride (Deuteronomy 22.13-21)

A man marries a girl and, disliking her, makes the serious accusation that she was not a virgin. He may be shocked and angry and acting out of a genuine rage. Or he may have base motives and, not finding the girl to his liking, may want to be rid of her without losing his brideprice or her dowry. He thereupon makes the affair a matter of public gossip, thus impugning the girl's father's honor that he cannot control the behavior of his daughter. If the father can prove the girl's virginity, the man must pay 100 shekels, which may be double indemnity for the virgin's brideprice. The parents have a lot at stake. If they prove virginity, they gain 100 shekels; if they do not prove it they will be shamed publicly and will lose status in the community, jeopardizing their chances of marrying the rest of their children off favorably. In the days of Genesis, when Judah thought that Tamar's faithlessness, publicly demonstrated by her pregnancy, had threatened his honor, he had a simple solution. He could restore his control and his reputation for being in control by executing Tamar for unfaithfulness, and so he commands, 'Bring her out and let her be burned!' (Gen. 38.24). But in Deuteronomy, society oversees family affairs and fathers no longer have life and death control over their dependents. The bridegroom's public accusation creates a crisis for the girl's family that profoundly undermines their status in the community. If the accusation is well founded, there can be only two possibilities: either the girl's sexual behavior was never discovered, in which case the affair demonstrates the family's lack of ability to control its members; or the parents knew and conspired with their daughter to pass her off as a virgin, in which case the parents stand revealed as frauds. Either way, their honor is destroyed. There has to be a way to resolve the issue.

Deuteronomy adopts a method of proof used in many chastity-focused cultures: the wedding sheets are to be examined for signs of defloration. The parents bring 'the daughter's virginity' (the bloody sheets) before the elders in the gate, and the father declares that he gave the daughter in marriage, and that her husband, not loving her, has slandered her by his accusation. As a result, the elders beat the man and fine him 100 shekels of silver because 'he has put out a bad name about a virgin of Israel'. They give the money to the father as a kind of double-indemnity. If the bridegroom had tried to back out before marriage, he would have had to pay double the brideprice. He suffers no less a financial loss by his attempt to get out of the marriage after the wedding night. And he can never divorce her.

This provision for no divorce seems odd to our modern sensibility, for remaining married to the man who slandered her seems as much a punishment of the wife as of the husband. But the no divorce provision, here, as in the case of the man who illicitly sleeps with an unmarried girl, is a deterrent to such actions. He will always have to support her financially. Perhaps the law assumes that an angry wife could make his life miserable. Still, the law ignores the girl's wishes or her prospects for a more congenial marriage in its concern to assure that men cannot use this method of ridding themselves of unwanted wives.

The law continues with the case in which the accusation was true and no marks of virginity were found. In that case, she is to be stoned by the men of the city until she dies. The secretly non-virginal bride has seriously disrupted the community's expectations of daughterly obligations and threatened society's control over female sexuality. Convicted by the elders of the community, she is put to death by the entire community. The execution takes place at the entrance to her father's house because 'she did an outrage in Israel by being faithless towards her father's house' (Deut. 22.21). Just as Shechem did an outrage (*nᵉbālâ*) by sleeping with the daughter of Jacob, so the non-virgin daughter did an outrage (*nᵉbālâ*) by not observing her obligation (the sense of *zānâ*) to her father to be chaste. By the execution of the girl, the community of men reinforces the right of fathers to demand that their daughters be chaste.

The law seems very clear, but it contains a strange twist. Even though bloody sheets are a common manifestation of virginity in many cultures, there is a radical and revealing difference between the biblical practice and that found elsewhere. In other cultures, the groom or his parents take possession of the sheets on the wedding night. In Deuteronomy, the parents of the girl take the sheets. They are also entrusted with showing the cloth to the elders, and they do so, not at the consummation of the marriage, but after the public accusation. It is quite easy to imagine a scenario in which the parents, finding a blank cloth and either believing their daughter's protestations of virginity or having a vested interested in 'believing' them, simply falsify the blood on the cloth. If they had known that she was not a virgin and have committed fraud, or if they are more angry at the accusation than at the girl, they can always spread some animal blood on the sheets before they spread them out before the elders. This vindicates their own honor and shames the bridegroom in one fell swoop. The girl will die only if the parents are so enraged at her that they will show the elders clean sheets. In the final analysis, the fate of the girl rests with her parents.

The case of the slandered bride and the case of the rebellious son (Deut. 18–22) both present circumstances in which children endanger their parent's honor and wellbeing, the daughter by lack of chastity and the son by drunkenness and profligacy. The parents do not have the legal authority to execute their children. The authority to sentence them to death resides with the council of elders. But in both cases, the parents have the real power to determine how the council will act. If they become enraged at their son or desperate, they can denounce him to the council of elders, and he will be stoned to death. If they are enraged at their daughter, they in effect denounce her by bringing out an unbloodied sheet. The council will then condemn her, and the public will stone her. Death by stoning is significant. The public acts as executioner because the public community is an injured party. By offending against the hierarchical obligations children owe parents, the son and the daughter have endangered the hierarchical family system upon which society rests. The people must act to 'rid this evil from your midst'. For such an offense against hierarchy, stoning is the most appropriate punishment.[21] By the action of the public, the honor of the parents is restored without unregulated acts damaging the community.

21. See Frymer-Kensky, 'Deuteronomy', in Carol Newsom and Sharon H. Ringe (eds.), *The Women's Bible Commentary* (London: SPCK, 1992), pp. 52-62.

Conclusion

The laws of Deuteronomy and the Dinah story illustrate the complex role of gender in the honor of the family and its limitations. In the biblical family, generation superseded gender. Wives were subordinate to husbands, and girls might be under the control of their brothers, but both daughters and sons were subordinate to both mother and father. Abandonment of these obligations endangered the family's position in the community. In Genesis, in the days before the state, families acted to ensure their own honor: when Dinah dishonored Jacob, the brothers took over to recoup their honor and in the process, Jacob claims, further dishonored him by their behavior. In the more established days of Deuteronomy, the public had an interest in preserving the rights of parents over children and (upon cue from the parents) acted as a unity to restore the honor of the family by executing the offending children. In all these instances, gender does not influence the relationship between the parents, the children and the community. But gender defines the very nature of the obligation of the children. Boys were obligated to be disciplined, act properly, and not squander the family wealth. Girls were certainly not allowed to be drunk or disorderly, but they had the special obligation to stay chaste until marriage as virgins.[22]

22. For the connection between stoning and hierarchy, see J.J. Finkelstein, *The Ox that Gored* (Transactions of the American Philosophical Society NS, 71.2; Philadelphia: American Philosophical Society, 1981).

HONOR AND SHAME IN GENDER-RELATED LEGAL SITUATIONS IN THE HEBREW BIBLE

Victor H. Matthews

When the Book of Deuteronomy (Deut. 12–26) and other legal codes in the Bible refer to women and deal with women's issues, they are seldom interested simply in regulating physical relationships between men and women. Rather, these codes are concerned with more sweeping issues of social justice and the equitable distribution of goods and services through the maintenance of a strong subsistence economy.[1] In addition, the legal vocabulary used when dealing with women and with sexuality is concerned far more with property than with gender and sexual contact. For traditional societies, such as the one that is portrayed in the Bible, social justice and sexual conduct are the basis of morality. Consequently, teachings dealing with virginity, marriage, divorce, infidelity, adultery, promiscuity, and rape are not only concerned with the sexual relationships of individuals or couples, but also with the social and economic relationships between the households in the village as a whole.[2]

When a marriage occurred, this event ratified an important political and economic covenant between the bride's household and the household of her husband.[3] The precise economic significance of a particular

1. D.C. Benjamin, *Deuteronomy and City Life* (Lanham, MD: University Press of America, 1983), pp. 12-18.

2. R. Gordis, 'Love, Marriage, and Business in the Book of Ruth: A Chapter in Hebrew Customary Law', in H.N. Bream, *et al.* (eds.), *A Light unto My Path: Old Testament Studies in Honor of Jacob M. Myers* (Gettysburg Theological Studies, 4; Philadelphia: Temple University Press, 1974), pp. 241-64, and C.L. Meyers, *Discovering Eve: Ancient Israelite Women in Context* (New York: Oxford University Press, 1988), pp.123-24.

3. C.R. Fontaine, 'The Sage in Family and Tribe', in J. Gammie and L. Perdue (eds.), *The Sage in Israel and the Ancient Near East* (Winona Lake, IN:

sexual relationship was indicated by the various titles that households bestowed on women (harlot, concubine, wife, virgin, queen). The rendering of these titles in English today carries almost no economic connotations, but, they may carry unnecessarily negative moral overtones. Each title is not so much an indication of the ethical behavior of a particular woman but rather of the economic and social relationship between her household and the household of her husband.

Shaming as a Means of Social Control

The biblical text is a product of a 'tradition-oriented' society, which places a great deal of value on honorable behavior. Codes of correct behavior are the measure of honor or dishonor. Thus shame, guilt and embarrassment, which are the personal reflections of improper behavior, are based on social experience. They are reinforced by rituals and shared attitudes, and are a product of group processes endowed with the power of coercion.[4] Shame and shaming is less likely to be concealed in traditional societies than in modern ones.[5] They also function as a means of social modification through the imposition of legal measures and procedures. When the shaming mechanism fails to suffice, harsher measures are then prescribed by law to ensure social order.

Every member of a household, which was the primary social unit in ancient Israelite society, had an obligatory social role to uphold the honor of the household through his or her speech and actions. If a member of the household performs or is about to perform some action that would reflect badly on the household, it is the responsibility of every other member to attempt to prevent a repetition of the dishonorable action or to convince the deviant to reconsider his or her action(s) and come back into compliance with honorable behavior. In addition,

Eisenbrauns, 1990), p. 162, and G. Lerner, *The Creation of Patriarchy* (New York: Oxford University Press, 1986), pp. 67-68.

4. S.E. Cahill, 'Embarrassability and Public Civility: Another view of a Much Maligned Emotion', unpublished paper presented to the 1992 Annual Meeting of the Midwest Sociological Society, pp. 3-5, and E. Goffman, *Relations in Public: Microstudies of the Public Order* (New York: Basic Books, 1971).

5. T.J. Scheff and S.M. Retzinger, *Emotions and Violence: Shame and Rage in Destructive Conflicts* (Lexington, MA: D.C. Heath, 1991), pp. 4-6, argues that 'shame cultures' and 'guilt cultures' are not part of an evolutionary process from traditional to modern societies. Rather, 'in modern societies, references to shame still appear frequently but in a disguised form'.

each member must also protect the household's honor against insults by outsiders—both physical and verbal.

Aside from physical retorts in defense of the household, one of the principal methods used, short of legal remedies, is shaming speech. Unlike insults and taunts, which are components of aggressive behavior and may or may not be rationally based,[6] shaming speech is a social control mechanism It is designed, through reasoning or by employing a sort of 'vocabulary of embarrassment',[7] to make the prodigal or the enemy rethink their plans or suppress their unacceptable speech. Shaming speech calls on each person to behave honorably, with carefully thought out actions, not in the manner of fools who act in the height of passion, without thinking.[8] Generally, shaming speech will take the form of a wisdom argument, calling on traditional practice, social codes, and covenantal allegiance.[9]

Embarrassment or shaming can thus be conceived as a positive process, designed to maintain social order and personal civility.[10] Its purpose, when used with a positive intent, is to elicit a reevaluation of actions, feelings, or behavior, and a conclusion of having done something wrong.[11] Thus Tamar's argument against Amnon's sexually

6. R.J. Felson, 'Shame, Anger, and Aggression', *Social Psychology Quarterly* 56 (1993), pp. 305-309, esp. p. 307.

7. E. Goffman, 'Embarrassment and Social Organization,' in *Interaction Rituals* (Garden City, NY: Anchor Books, 1967), pp. 99-112 describes 'incidents' of embarrassment that can cause flustering, loss of composure, hostility, or flight by persons who have committed a social error in their speech or behavior. Similar reactions can also occur among witnesses of this behavior if it is sufficiently embarrassing to them. Thus, much of our social behavior is geared either to avoiding socially unacceptable situations and actions or to suppressing our public reaction to them.

8. There are numerous examples in wisdom literature admonishing the wise to consider the implications of their words before they speak. For instance, the Assyrian sage Ahiqar says, 'Above all else, control your mouth. Do not repeat what you have heard. A human word is a bird. Once released, it can never be recaptured' (V.H. Matthews and D.C. Benjamin, *Old Testament Parallels: Laws and Stories from the Ancient Near East* [Mahwah, NJ: Paulist Press, 1991], p. 180). See also Prov. 26.2 and Sir. 27.4.

9. See my treatment of the story of David and Abigail in V.H. Matthews, 'Female Voices: Upholding the Honor of the Household', *BTB* 24 (1994), pp. 8-15, esp. p. 10.

10. Cahill, 'Embarrassability', p. 1.

11. M. Lewis, *Shame: the Exposed Self* (New York: The Free Press, 1992), p. 2.

aggressive proposal attempts to sketch out both 'proper' or 'wise' action and shameful or foolish behavior (2 Sam. 13.11-13).[12] Of course, shaming speech can also be used to harass and dominate someone else, but in those cases it is not based on upholding honorable behavior, and is better termed malicious speech or slander.[13]

On those occasions when it is necessary to embarrass a person publicly by using shaming speech, the argument must be publicly staged in order to draw on the energies and backing of a desired audience.[14] The aim is the same as in the private setting, to sustain public order, and may be employed by either male or female characters. It should be noted that embarrassment, guilt, and shame all elicit similar behavior reactions and thus will not be greatly distinguished here.[15] Shame can elicit the strongest reactions and is based on the most serious charges, but it, like the others, is intended as a form of behavioral modification.

One particularly good example of this type of public confrontation is found in the law in Deut. 25.5-10. Based on the necessity to ensure a consistent inheritance pattern from one generation to the next, the law of levirate obligation also placed a heavy burden on the levir. It was his responsibility to impregnate his deceased, male kin's wife so that she would produce an heir to the dead man's lands and property. However, this also produced a conflict of personal interest since the levir was therefore, intentionally, lessening his own opportunity to inherit this property.[16]

12. V.H. Matthews and D.C. Benjamin, 'Amnon and Tamar: a Matter of Honor (2 Sam. 13.1-38)', in G.D. Young *et al.* (eds.), *Interconnections: A Festschrift in Honor of Michael Astour* (Baltimore: CDL Press, 1997), pp. 339-66 and V.H. Matthews and D.C. Benjamin, *Social World of Ancient Israel, 1250–587 BCE* (Peabody, MA: Hendrickson, 1993), pp. 182-86.

13. This is not to be confused with the taunt, which is used in political and military situations to an enemy to force them to make a mistake. For examples of taunting, see Marduk's taunting of Tiamat (*Enuma Elish* 4.70-90; *ANET*, pp. 66-67) and the Jebusites' taunting of David as he besieges their city in 2 Sam. 5.6. Perhaps bridging the gap between these two types of speech is the statement by Nabal in 1 Sam. 25.10, which taunts David's messengers and also publicly belittles David as a 'nobody'.

14. H. Kuzmics, 'Embarrassment and Civilization: On Some Similarities and Differences in the Work of Goffman and Elias', *Theory, Culture and Society* 8.2 (1991), p. 3.

15. E. Bedford, 'Emotions and Statements About Them', in R. Harre (ed.), *The Social Construction of Emotions* (Oxford: Basil Blackwell, 1986), p. 21.

16. See Onan's resistance to his levirate obligation in Gen. 38.8-9.

Faced with the reality of this conflict of interest, the Deuteronomic loophole was created which allowed the levir to renounce his obligation publicly.[17] To do so, however, required participation in a ritual in which the widow was allowed to shame him publicly, through speech and gesture.

This legal instruction, like the instructions on siege warfare in Deut. 20.10-20, is concerned with forms of recourse when 'the response is negative'.[18] It is also one of the few instances in which a woman can label a man effectively and permanently stigmatize his 'name' as one who does not uphold his legal and family obligations to perpetuate the 'name' of her dead husband.[19]

What is particularly interesting, however, about the law of levirate obligation in Deuteronomy is that it does contain this loophole. Apparently, no such remedy was available to Tamar in Genesis 38 since she had to resort to subterfuge to obtain the desired result, a pregnancy.[20] This suggests a change in the binding nature of the levirate obligation by the time of the Deuteronomist. However, since the dating of these materials is uncertain, there may actually be other cultural factors at work in the Genesis narrative that require a different solution to Tamar's problem. In any case, the Deuteronomic legislation requires that no further penalty be imposed upon the levir for refusing to uphold his duties to the widow other than facing a prescribed form of ritualized public humiliation.[21]

While not all the ritual aspects of this ceremony are fully understood,[22] it is clear that what has occurred transforms the status and

17. See the slightly altered use of this judicial procedure in the narrative in Ruth 4.1-11. In this case, the woman does not speak publicly, but is represented before the elders by Boaz. The exact chronology for the development of the levirate obligation is uncertain. The variations may be based on cultural–legal evolution or simply the difference between narrative form and legal pronouncement.

18. Benjamin, *Deuteronomy and City Life*, p. 244.

19. D. Daube, 'The Culture of Deuteronomy', *Orita* 3 (1969), p. 35.

20. G.W. Coats, 'Widow's Rights: A Crux in the Structure of Genesis 38', *CBQ* 34 (1972), pp. 461-66, esp. p. 464.

21. E.W. Davies, 'Inheritance Rights and the Hebrew Levirate Marriage, Part 2', *VT* 31.3 (1981), pp. 257-68, esp. p. 261.

22. See Davies, 'Inheritance Rights', pp. 262-63; E. Neufeld, *Ancient Hebrew Marriage Laws* (London: Longmans, Green & Co., 1944), pp. 42-43; and Benjamin, *Deuteronomy and City Life*, p. 254 for the symbolism of removing the sandal. Å. Viberg, *Symbols of Law: A Contextual Analysis of Legal Symbolic Acts in*

applies a new label to the levir. This may have actually been the lesser of two evils for the levir, if the law, as E.W. Davies suggests,[23] is designed to give him the opportunity to refuse the widow while retaining inheritance rights to the land of the deceased kinsman. To bear public humiliation and a pejorative title, while undesirable, may thus be balanced by the desire to keep one's inheritance rights intact.

Endangerment of the Household's Honor

In other cases in which individuals fail to uphold the honor of their household, shaming speech may be employed in addition to symbolic gestures and ritualized procedures. The instances involving women, which are clearly written from the male viewpoint, often center on the fact that the required bonding that should have taken place between a woman and her husband and his household is inadequate. Failure to demonstrate this loyalty results in a dysfunctional relationship, which is manifested by anger and alienation,[24] and in some cases in the imposition of barrenness as a punishment.[25]

Numbers 5.11-31

In this legal situation, the wife is assumed by her husband to be unfaithful and to have had illicit intercourse, even though there are no witnesses. His right to punish her and bring her to trial is based on the marriage contract and the obligations that this document lays on her to remain loyal to his household.[26] Defilement, which serves as the

the Old Testament (ConBOT, 34; Stockholm: Almqvist & Wiksell, 1992), pp. 146-51 stresses that this is not a reciprocal act, nor is it an act of transference of the sandal (or of the widow) in either the Deuteronomic passage or in Ruth 4.8. He points, rightly, to the use of formal and informal language as the keys to legally binding the kinsman–redeemer.

23. Davies, 'Inheritance Rights', p. 263. A. Phillips, 'Another Example of Family Law', *VT* 30 (1980), p. 243, notes that the village elders had no power to impose their will on the levir since this was strictly a family matter. This most likely explains the eventual elimination of the practice of levirate marriage (Lev. 18.16; 20.21).

24. J. Bowlby, *Attachment and Loss*. II. *Separation: Anxiety and Anger* (New York: Basic Books, 1973).

25. See my discussion of enforced barrenness as a punishment in 'Female Voices: Upholding the Honor of the Household', *BTB* 24 (1994), pp. 13-14.

26. R. Westbrook, 'Adultery in Ancient Near Eastern Law', *RB* 97 (1990),

introduction to this chapter (dealing with lepers, and other unclean persons), is considered a breach of faith with God.[27] A protocol is established for restitution and decontamination which requires: (1) confession of sin, (2) full restitution, plus one-fifth more to the person wronged, or to God and the priests if the person wronged has no next of kin.

M. Fishbane has convincingly demonstrated the relationship between the legal situations in vv. 12-13 and v. 14.[28] Although both instances will result in the trial by ordeal,[29] they represent public 'knowledge' and private suspicion of adultery respectively. The actions taken by the husband are based on his unsubstantiated suspicions, described here as a 'spirit of jealousy' (v. 14).[30] It seems unlikely that these suspicions are simply another ploy, as in Deut. 22.13-14, for a man to set aside a wife who does not please him. More likely, there have been accusations made to him privately and rumor (represented by the statement in vv. 12-13) is beginning to bring public shame on his household.[31] If a

pp. 542-80, esp. p. 557. See also A. Phillips, 'Another Look at Adultery', *JSOT* 20 (1981), p. 7.

27. See T. Frymer-Kensky's discussion of defilement as the key issue here in 'The Strange Case of the Suspected *SOTAH* (Numbers V 11-31)', *VT* 34 (1984), pp. 17-18.

28. M. Fishbane, 'Accusations of Adultery: A Study of Law and Scribal Practice in Numbers 5:11-31', *HUCA* 45 (1974), pp. 25-45, esp. pp. 35-39.

29. H.C. Brichto, 'The Case of the Sotah and a Reconsideration of Biblical Law', *HUCA* 46 (1975), pp. 55-70, esp. pp. 64-65, argues that this is not a trial by ordeal. He insists that it is merely 'an invocation of Deity to grant a sign of His verdict'. T. Frymer-Kensky, 'The Suspected *SOTAH*', p. 24, calls this a 'religio-legal procedure' rather than a trial by ordeal on the basis of the delay involved in determining the guilt or innocence and the fact that God has taken over the role of sentencing judge from the courts. I can agree that a sign is expected, but it is the result of a physical test, utilizing ritual procedures, and an execration. As such it is best defined as an ordeal. Even though the potion may not be poison and the danger may be more psychological than real, the expectations of the participants is a transformation of the liquid into a potent force that will evidence the truth of the matter.

30. W. McKane, 'Poison, Trial by Ordeal and the Cup of Wrath', *VT* 30 (1980), pp. 474-92, posits that the woman is already pregnant and her husband's suspicions center around the child's actual paternity. Thus the potion is designed to affect the fetus. If it survives, then innocence and paternity are established. While the woman may in fact be pregnant, the lack of any mention of a fetus in the curse formula and the clearer implication of future sterility for the woman do not support this suggestion.

31. See LU 14 and LH 127. Roth, *Law Collections*, pp. 18, 105.

household could not protect its women, then it was declared insolvent or shamed and unable to fulfill its responsibilities to the community as a whole.[32] Thus any hint of infidelity, however unsubstantiated, could have dangerous consequences for the entire household.

Promiscuity in the world of the Bible is not simply a lack of sexual discretion, but a symptom of the risks that a household is taking with its land and children. Husbands and fathers are responsible for the honor of their women, which is associated with sexual purity. Their own honor derives in large measure from the way they discharge this responsibility.[33] If fathers and husbands protect the women of their household, then they are known to have the ability to protect all its members.

The legal remedy in this case, necessitated by the lack of eye-witnesses,[34] is to resort to the use of a third-party mediator, the priest, and what appears to be a trial by ordeal. The ordeal is a judicial institution designed to resolve conflicts between households which could not be resolved by the elders in a village assembly, and to re-establish harmony within the village. Crimes that carried the death penalty, such as adultery, required that the plaintiff's charge be supported by the testimony of two eye-witnesses. Without two eye-witnesses, the plaintiff has no case to present to the village assembly and the potential threat to the entire community cannot be resolved (Num. 35.30; Deut. 19.15). The village assembly simply cannot function when there are no witnesses.[35] Since harmony in the village is essential for its economy to prosper, the intention of the ordeal is to help break a stalemate and allow God to make a decision between the households involved.

In the protocol for an ordeal, the defendant is exposed to a strenuous, potentially life-threatening experience.[36] If she survives, then the

32. M.J. Giovannini, 'Female Chastity Codes in the Circum-Mediterranean: Comparative Perspectives', in D.D. Gilmore (ed.), *Honor and Shame and the Unity of the Mediterranean* (Washington, DC: American Anthropological Association, 1987), p. 68.

33. J. Pitt-Rivers, 'Honour and Social Status', in J.G. Peristiany (ed.), *Honor and Shame: The Values of Mediterranean Society* (London: Weidenfeld & Nicolson, 1965), p. 78.

34. J. Milgrom, 'The Case of the Suspected Adulteress: Redaction and Meaning', in R.E. Friedman (ed.), *The Creation of Sacred Literature* (Near Eastern Studies, 22; Berkeley, CA: University of California Press, 1981), p. 74, notes the reiteration of this element four times in the indictment against the wife.

35. Benjamin, *Deuteronomy and City Life*, pp. 198-210, 297-98.

36. See the use of the ordeal as a judicial procedure in LH 2 (sorcery) and as a

Divine Assembly has cleared her of the charges made against her and the honor of her household is reaffirmed. If she does not, then her household is shamed. An ordeal was thus a legally constructed 'day of judgment' (Deut. 32.34-36; Pss. 18.7; 32.6; Job 21.30).

The somewhat peculiar procedure in Num. 5.16-28 hinges on a potion that invokes God's judgment on the woman.[37] It is not a poison and most likely does not contain any drug that would induce an abortion.[38] It functions almost as a prop to empower the ritual of execration[39] and is coupled with an oath first spoken by the priest and then repeated by the woman. Certainly, there is an element of shaming involved in having to participate in this ritual and in speaking these words. However, such a public ritual, like a purgative oath,[40] has a positive function as well, to remove all doubt of guilt or suspicion.

The fact that it involves elements of the ordeal rather than just a formal oath 'before God'[41] suggests a blending of judicial procedures to satisfy a case that otherwise could not be proven and would continue to damage a household's reputation. This is why Karel van der Toorn describes the procedure as a 'drinking trial' and compares it to the drink concocted by Moses using the dust from the destroyed Golden Calf

form of oath taking 'before the god' in LH 9, 20, 23, 103, 106, 107, 120, 126, and Exod. 22.10-11. For a discussion of the various forms of the ordeal, see T.S. Frymer-Kensky, *The Judicial Ordeal in the Ancient Near East* (Ann Arbor, MI: University Microfilms, 1977), pp. 11-16.

37. See J. Milgrom, 'On the Suspected Adulteress (Numbers V 11-31)', *VT* 35 (1985), pp. 368-69 for an analysis of the potion and ritual procedures.

38. See D. Pardee's discussion of a Ugaritic text in '*MARIM* in Numbers V', *VT* 35 (1985), pp. 112-13, which clarifies the term *marim* in this passage. It is apparently a term that means both 'bitterness' and 'illness'. Thus the result of drinking this bitter potion would be the fomenting of an illness in the guilty party. Milgrom, 'The Case of the Suspected Adulteress', pp. 73-75, and 'On the Suspected Adulteress', p. 368, suggests that the potential threat of sterility, coupled with the assumption of God's certainly to act in the face of the ritual and curse, is sufficient cause for her to confess her guilt, if there is any. For the opinion that the potion does contain a poison, see McKane, 'Poison', pp. 477-87.

39. See Jeremiah's use of a pot in his execration ritual in Jer. 19.1-13. This sense of purpose for the potion is also found in Num. 5.23-24 in the combination of writing and drinking that enacts the curse.

40. Frymer-Kensky, 'The Suspected *SOTAH*', p. 24. See Job's 'oath of clearance', in Job 31.

41. As is the case in LH 131 (Roth, *Law Collections*, p. 106).

(Exod.32.20). In both cases, their guilt would be revealed by what was otherwise a non-lethal potion.[42]

The closest cuneiform parallel to the Biblical example in Numbers 5 is found in Code of Hammurabi (LH) 131 and 132 (Roth, *Law Collections*, p. 106). In these legal statements, the wife has either been 'accused' (LH 131) or 'charged' (LH 132) with adultery, although there are no witnesses. In the first case, which involves an accusation by the husband, the woman simply has to swear an oath 'in the name of the god' and can then return home. She endangers herself by using the name of the god[43] and pledges in public ceremony that she has upheld her loyalty to her husband's household. However, no more immediately life threatening act is required because, as in Num. 5.14, the issue is one between husband and wife and does not require the participation of the community or the courts.

The more serious nature of the legal procedure described in LH 132, like that in Num. 5.12-13, suggests that the woman has been denounced publicly by others and more stringent measures are required to lift the veil of shame that has been drawn across her household. She must submit to the river ordeal 'to exonerate her husband'.[44] Should she survive and be proven guiltless by the Divine Assembly, she may return to her former status (as in LH 131) and, based on Middle Assyrian Laws

42. K. van der Toorn, 'Ordeal', in ABD, V, p. 40. See other examples of drinking trials in T.S. Frymer-Kensky, 'Suprarational Procedures in Elam and Nuzi', in D.I. Owen and M.A. Morrison (eds.), *Studies on the Civilization and Culture of Nuzi and the Hurrians* (Winona Lake, IN: Eisenbrauns, 1981), pp. 115-31, and J.M. Sasson, 'Numbers 5 and the "Waters of Judgment"', *BZ* 16 (1972), pp. 249-51.

43. See the curse formulas found in such treaties as that between Rameses II and Hattusilis III (*ANET*, pp. 199-201), and in the seriousness with which Jepthath and his daughter took the fulfilment of his oath in Judg. 11.30-40. T.R. Ashley, *The Book of Numbers* (Grand Rapids, MI: Eerdmans, 1993), pp. 124-25, rightly emphasizes the implicit danger to the woman due to the use of the oath and the potion.

44. Fishbane, 'Accusations of Adultery', pp. 38-39, suggests that an oath may have originally proceeded the river ordeal, but has since been dropped from the legal statement in the Code of Hammurabi. He points to a Middle Assyrian text (VAT 9962), which includes a threefold procedure (drink, swear, be pure/innocent) which corresponds to the events of Num. 5.11-31. Frymer-Kensky, 'The Suspected *SOTAH*', p. 17 n. 11, disputes the possible parallel with LH 132, seeing the biblical procedures initiated only by the 'husband's jealousy'.

17-18, any accusers will be dealt with either through fines or physical punishment.[45]

This post-ordeal fine in the Middle Assyrian laws suggests that even the charge against her requires restitution. The false accuser must, as in the case in Num. 5.5-10, make restitution to the wronged party, the woman's husband. The doubt placed against his honor is satisfied by the ordeal, but full payment must also be made by the false accuser in order to prevent rampant use of slander or malicious speech as a means of injuring a household's reputation.[46]

The sense of guilt and the need to clear away a blot on her husband's reputation may also be the basis for the actions in Num. 5.15. Although the required offering that the husband brings to the priest is said to be for the wife, it appears that it also serves to help relieve the husband's anxiety by bringing the shame ('iniquity') forward, rather than letting it mentally consume him and undermine the honor and effectiveness of his household.

The statement at the end of the legal passage (Num. 5.31), which exonerates the husband from any 'iniquity' for having brought his wife to trial, speaks again to the issue of the husband's marital rights. Certainly, it would have been better if he had not had to participate in a public demonstration. H.C. Brichto suggests this may have even been an element of protection for the wife in this drama since it required the husband to 'put up or shut up'.[47] However, the balancing act between upholding the honor of the household and the public embarrassment occasioned by the trial may have forced the issue in much the same way that it does in the case of the 'rebellious son' in Deut. 21.18-21.[48] It also provides some measure of protection for the woman from mob violence or some unsanctioned 'kangaroo court'.[49] The community is

45. See MAL A.17-18 (Roth, *Law Collections*, p. 159) for use of the River Ordeal by the accuser and the imposition of corporal punishment and a huge fine (3,600 shekels of lead) on the false accuser.

46. See LU 10-11 (Roth, *Law Collections*, p. 18) for another example of heavy fines imposed after a river ordeal proved the accused innocent. Deut. 19.16-19 also provides strict punishment against 'a malicious witness'.

47. Brichto 'The Case of the *SOTA*', p. 67.

48. See V.H. Matthews and D.C. Benjamin, 'The Stubborn and the Fool', *TBT* 29.4 (1991), pp. 222-26, and *The Social World of Ancient Israel*, pp. 149-50.

49. Milgrom, 'The Case of the Suspected Adulteress', pp. 74-75.

thus restrained from direct action since the woman's punishment will come directly from God.[50]

The Case of the Suspect Virgin

Female virginity is the legal guarantee of land and children for a household in the world of the Bible.[51] Consequently, households guard their female virgins until they can be married so that their economic status will remain intact.[52] A lack of virginity due to rape or promiscuity threatens a household's social status and precludes future transactions.[53]

The virginity of a bride is an indication that the household of her father is stable. Her fertility represents the mutually beneficial character of their covenant. The assumption is that the marriage will produce land and children for both households. Plus, the certification that she has been protected from violation is an assurance for her husband that his semen will not be mixed with that of any other man. This is the mark of a proper marriage.[54]

Thus a good example demonstrating the role that maintaining honor plays in the village setting is found in the case of the suspect virgin in Deut. 22.13-21. The charge made against the bride in this passage is that she has not proven herself to be a virgin because during initial intercourse the bleeding associated with the breaking of the hymen has not occurred. The husband has stated publicly that she is not what he contracted for when he arranged the marriage with her father. He subsequently 'brings an evil name upon her' (v. 14), which both labels her as one who 'plays the harlot' (v. 21) and charges her family with breach of contract and outright fraud.

In making this accusation, the husband proves that, for whatever reason, he has become disenchanted with his bride after the marriage has

50. J. Milgrom, *The JPS Torah Commentary: Numbers* (Philadelphia: Jewish Publication Society, 1990), p. 43.

51. Giovannini, 'Female Chastity Codes', pp. 67-68.

52. J. Goody, *Production and Reproduction* (Cambridge: Cambridge University Press, 1976), p. 14, and J. Schneider, 'Of Vigilance and Virgins: Honor and Shame and Access to Resources in Mediterranean Societies', *Ethnology* 10 (1971), pp. 20-21.

53. A. Schlegel, 'Status, Property, and the Value of Virginity', *American Ethnologist* 18.4 (1991), p. 724.

54. C. Delaney, 'Seeds of Honor, Fields of Shame', in Gilmore (ed.), *Honor and Shame and the Unity of the Mediterranean*, pp. 41-42.

been consummated. Such a public posture by the husband may have been designed to pressure the parents to settle with him privately.[55] However, since the charge is one that could eventually result in the death penalty, the law may have been designed to prevent such slanderous talk.[56]

Once it has become a public matter, however, it is then the responsibility of her parents to produce the 'tokens of her virginity' (namely, the blood-stained sheets)[57] and show them to the elders at the city gate. The very existence of these tokens suggests that there existed a 'ritual of examination' on the wedding night that required the bridegroom or perhaps an objective witness such as a midwife to present the physical evidence to the in-laws.[58]

As can be seen in this instance, one of the principal uses of labeling is simply to call someone a name. In cases of malicious speech, its intent is either to slander or to cause an injury. Malicious speech is designed to evoke a reaction of public condemnation from a defined audience that will transform the targeted individual into what they have been called and thus change their status downward.[59] Once the name

55. A. Phillips, 'Some Aspects of Family Law in Pre-Exilic Israel', *VT* 23 (1973), pp. 349-61, argues that cases of divorce are strictly family matters and are not to be taken to the courts. The husband in this case, however, has made his accusations public rather than confining them to familial chambers. The result is the possible charge of adultery, if she had had relations during the time that the couple were betrothed, or fraud, if the father was attempting to pass his deflowered daughter off as a virgin. On this latter point, see Phillips, 'Another Example of Family Law', p. 242.

56. See the discussion of which party is the plaintiff in this case in C. Pressler, *The View of Women Found in the Deuteronomic Family Laws* (Berlin: W. de Gruyter, 1993), pp. 23-24. Her conclusion that it is the parents of the slandered bride who are pressing the case fits well with an honor-restoring procedure.

57. See G.J. Wenham, '*Betulah* "A Girl of Marriageable Age"', *VT* 22 (1972), pp. 326-48, for a discussion of this legal episode as an example of adultery in which the 'first night' evidence is lacking because she is not menstruating and thus has had relations and is pregnant prior to marriage. Phillips, 'Another Look at Adultery', p. 8, also points to the possibility of the wife's pre-nuptial pregnancy.

58. Benjamin, *Deuteronomy and City Life*, p. 227, and Giovannini, 'Female Chastity Codes', p. 61. Phillips, 'Another Look at Adultery', p. 22 n. 27, rightly compares this ritual of examination with the waiting period prescribed in Talmudic law (*b. Yeb.* 35a) before a second marriage can be consummated or before an unmarried woman who has had intercourse can marry.

59. E. Goode, 'On Behalf of Labeling Theory', *Social Problems* 22 (1975),

has been applied, it is even possible to lower the labeled person's status legally by employing a 'public status-degradation ceremony'.[60] This drama is performed for the benefit of the audience as much as it is for the individual involved.[61] A modern example would be a criminal trial with all the protocol of the courtroom to identify for the public the defendant, the charges being made, and the sentence for crimes committed.[62]

The husband's slanderous talk has degraded his wife before a select audience. Now it becomes the turn of the parents to answer this slander and, if possible, reverse the procedure by presenting evidence that will either clear or condemn their household of fraud. In this way they attempt to deflect his labeling of their daughter and the potential legal ramifications of a charge of misrepresentation. Thus in addition to the physical evidence, a statement is made by the father of the suspect virgin (Deut. 22.16-17) that could be identified as a form of shaming speech since it (1) repeats the scandalous charges made against the daughter, and (2) provides an opportunity for the husband to repent his statement.

If they do in fact have the garments as proof, then the husband is whipped and fined a hundred shekels of silver 'because he has brought an evil name upon a virgin of Israel', and he is restricted from ever divorcing her (v. 19). Such a punishment provides an equitable restitution since it requires public shaming of the husband[63] and a secure economic future for the bride. Simple dissatisfaction with one's bride is

pp. 570-83, esp. p. 577. One example of this practice would be Jezebel's designation of Jehu as a 'Zimri' (i.e. a 'traitor' who has betrayed his master the king) in 2 Kgs 9.31.

60. H. Garfinkel, 'Conditions of Successful Degradation Ceremonies', *American Journal of Sociology* 61 (1950), pp. 420-24. See Matthews and Benjamin, 'The Stubborn and the Fool', pp. 222-26 on the case of the rebellious son in Deut. 21.18-21.

61. E. Goode, *Deviant Behavior* (Englewood Cliffs, NJ: Prentice-Hall, 3rd edn, 1990), p. 61, and K.T. Erikson, 'Notes on the Sociology of Deviance', *Social Problems* 9 (1962), pp. 307-14.

62. E.M. Schur, *Labeling Deviant Behavior: Its Sociological Implications* (New York: Harper & Row, 1971), p. 52.

63. Note the parallel with the name given the unfaithful levir in Deut. 25.10. In both cases the man involved will take away from the public ceremony a reputation of false dealing.

therefore, by statute, not a grounds for divorce in Israelite law.[64] Furthermore, the honor and legal rights of inheritance of the woman and her children are protected against slanderous or unjustified statements.[65]

It should be noted that in this procedure the woman is never questioned and the physical evidence is the sole determinant of guilt or innocence. The elders are not judges. They are merely the administrators of the public trust and of the social contract that binds them together. The 'instruction' embodied in this text is designed to maintain social standards of conduct and prevent fraud on the part of either the husband or the father of the bride. Furthermore, the instruction here would mandate that material evidence be kept in order to prevent such accusations.

For the charge to be made and the parents to be unable to produce evidence of their daughter's virginity must have been an unusual situation considering the potential for harm involved here to the husband and the 'ritual of examination' mentioned above. Under this stricture, the woman, without the physical evidence to prove otherwise, is automatically assumed to be guilty and the social purging mechanism

64. The statute found in Deut. 24.1-4, which forms the legal basis for divorce, stipulates that the man has found 'something indecent' in his wife. While this is certainly open to interpretation (see the conflict between the schools of Hillel and Shimei in *Giṭ. 9.10* and *b. Giṭ. 90a*, and the quoting of this verse in Mt. 5.31 and Mk 10.4), it seems likely that a matter of ritual impurity or evidence of infertility is the basis for the dissolution of the marriage (see P.C. Craigie, *The Book of Deuteronomy* [Grand Rapids, MI: Eerdmans, 1976], pp. 304-305). Compare the various grounds for divorce found in cuneiform law: LH 138 (Roth, *Law Collections*, p. 107)—wife has not borne children, but she is to receive the equivalent of her marriage price and her dowry; LH 141 (Roth, *Law Collections*, pp. 107-108)—woman leaves her husband to start a business and neglects her duties as a wife, may be divorced without payment of a settlement; MAL 24—woman divorced for deserting her husband and staying with another household; MAL 37—no grounds specified for divorce other than husband's decision and it is his option to pay her a settlement.

65. Note that the law of false accusation (Deut. 19.16-19) does not come into play in this situation. Pressler, *The View of Women*, pp. 24-25 n. 9 and p. 29, has convincingly argued that the husband is only guilty of slanderous statements, not formal accusation in a court of law. See on this issue, A. Phillips, *Ancient Israel's Criminal Law: A New Approach to the Decalogue* (Oxford: Basil Blackwell, 1970), p. 115 n. 28.

comes into play.[66] There is no alternative sentencing, no plea bargaining, no speech by a lawyer. She is simply taken to the door of her father's house and stoned to death.[67] She had dishonored her father and the community as a whole 'by playing the harlot in her father's house' (v. 21). In addition, her family has dishonored itself by contracting a marriage without acknowledging the fact that the young woman involved was not a virgin. Her execution at the door of her father's house marks this spot and this household as frauds, open to sanction by the community due to a breach of contract.

Conclusions

In those legal situations in which the honor of the household comes into question, primarily due to the uncertainty of chastity on the part of the wife, public demonstrations seem to be the best way to resolve the issue. Slander, rumor, and false labels can irreparably injure a household's reputation. Swift action is necessary to prevent a complete loss of credibility and ultimately the extinction of the household when no other family will contract marriages or do business with it. The cases described above provide a brief look at the way in which Israelite society attempted to deal with potential shaming of a household. While they may only represent hypothetical cases, the value of honorable association and the potential danger of shameful behavior are clearly delineated.

66. Phillips, *Ancient Israel's Criminal Law*, p. 116, and H. Reviv, *The Elders in Ancient Israel* (Jerusalem: Magnes Press, 1989), p. 63.

67. Thus the significance attached to her place of execution is fully commensurate with the crime. See V.H. Matthews, 'Entrance Ways and Threshing Floors: Legally Significant Sites in the Ancient Near East', *Fides et Historia* 19 (1987), 32. LH 227 (Roth, *Law Collections*, p. 124) also ties the place of execution to the site of fraud. In this case, a man who attempts to free a slave who does not belong to him by having his 'slave hairlock' shaved is to be hung 'in his own doorway'.

A Riposte Form in The Song of Deborah

Geoffrey P. Miller

The Song of Deborah in the Book of Judges records a stunning victory won by a coalition of Israelite tribes under Deborah and Barak over a powerful army led by the Canaanite Sisera (Judg. 5.1-31). The Song is widely viewed as among the most ancient of all the biblical material;[1] by its own terms, it describes a period early in the history of the Israelite occupation of the Promised Land, a time when, there being 'no king...in Israel' (Judg. 19.1), the common life of the tribes was organized under a loose confederacy under the guidance of 'judges'—inspired leaders who would rise up to rescue the Israelites when they faced aggression from other peoples. Deborah was one of these judges—and, unusually, a woman.

This paper analyzes the Song of Deborah as a riposte form in a literature influenced by norms of honor. A riposte was a form of retaliation against an insult circulated in the culture by a rival group. Characteristic of the riposte is the fact that the insult could not simply be denied or ignored, because its substance had achieved widespread credibility in the broader culture. The riposte deals with this problem by accepting part of a stereotype as true, but reversing the honor-value of the attribution and returning the insult, with interest, to the group from which it originated. Riposte forms can be found at several points in the early biblical texts, and thus may represent a rhetorical form that has not been fully recognized by critical analysis.[2]

This paper proposes that the Song of Deborah responds to a negative stereotype about the people of the hill country of Canaan (i.e. the Israelites) that may have enjoyed popularity among their city-dwelling

1. See, e.g., J. Alberto Soggin, *Judges: A Commentary* (Philadelphia: Westminster Press, 1981), p. 80.

2. For analysis of another biblical riposte, see G.P. Miller, 'Verbal Feud in the Hebrew Bible: Judg. 3:12-30 and 19-21', *JNES* 55 (1995), pp. 105-17.

neighbors (i.e. the Canaanites). The stereotype was to the effect that the hill people lacked social graces and refinement, and that their women behaved like men. This appears to be a common cultural stereotype that people of the towns and the plains have used against the uncouth hill people in other times and places.

The Song of Deborah accepts the essential attributes of the stereotype, but reverses their honor value by demonstrating that it is good to have nature on your side, that cultural refinement is an empty promise when stacked up against wily resourcefulness, and that any group should be glad to be led by women when the result is a victory as spectacular as the one secured by Deborah and her general.[3] The Song then returns the insult to sender: the sophisticated war machine of the Canaanite forces is swept away by the forces of nature that are allied with the Israelites, and the Canaanite commander is feminized, raped, and vanquished by a woman allied with the Israelite forces.

This paper is structured as follows. Part I discusses some of the prior literature on Judges 5, and argues that the characterization of the story as a riposte is new in the literature. Part II outlines a theory of verbal feud and places the riposte form within a broader typology of honor stories. Part III illustrates the nature of the riposte in the Song of Deborah. I end with a brief conclusion.

Prior Scholarship

For a number of reasons—the remarkable reversal of sexual roles, the extraordinary poetry, the apparent antiquity of the text—the story of Deborah and Barak in Judges 5 has generated a substantial body of modern commentary.

Several scholars have analyzed the text as history, and reached varying conclusions about the historical veracity of the text and the

3. It is appropriate to consider norms of honor in a volume devoted to the topic of gender and law in the Hebrew Bible and the ancient Near East, because these norms exercised a form of social control in settings where formal legal control, through the medium of an established state, was weak or lacking. Honor-based codes tend to assume importance where state-imposed law is weak; their function, however, is similar, in that they may induce people to act in socially responsible ways and discourage socially irresponsible behavior. Norms of honor may also cement social coherence within a group by providing a self-identity to which pride is attached and offering a means to look down on rival groups.

probable geopolitical background.[4] A.D.H. Mayes sees the text as a fairly accurate account of a battle sometime in the course of the second half of the eleventh century BCE, and as representing a 'stage in the course of transition by which the Israelite tribes progressed from acting as independent units to employing their combined strength in time of battle'.[5]

L.E. Stager provides interesting insight into why some tribes answered the call to battle and some did not.[6] Stager argues that four of the ten tribes mentioned in the Song did not participate because their economic interests were tied up with the Canaanites: Dan and Asher served as maritime client workers, while Reuben and Gilead–Gad were pastoralists who depended on the Canaanites for trade. David Schloen supplements Stager's account by arguing that the stimulus for the conflict was the exorbitant tolls that were being charged by Sisera and his Canaanite allies, which was stifling caravan traffic vital to the economic interests of the Israelites and their Midianite (Kenite and Amalekite) allies.[7]

Norman Gottwald argues, in contrast to Stager and Schloen, that it was the Israelites who were exercising control over caravans through plunder and brigandage, and that the Canaanites were the organizers of the caravan routes.[8] Gottwald views the poem as recording the victory

4. For a discussion of Judges 4 as representing a later historian's attempt to interpret the earlier poetic text, see Baruch Halpern, 'The Resourceful Israelite Historian: The Song of Deborah and Israelite Historiography', *HTR* 76 (1983), pp. 379-401. In an earlier article on the Song of Deborah, I analyze the text as reflecting the difficulties of organizing an alliance for mutual protection given the dangers of free-riding and defection, and the difficulties of reliably recording in oral form a group's history of cooperating or defecting. Geoffrey Miller, 'The Song of Deborah: A Legal-Economic Analysis', *University of Pennsylvania Law Review* 144 (1996), pp. 2293-320.

5. A.D.H. Mayes, 'The Historical Context of the Battle Against Sisera', *VT* 19 (1969), pp. 353-60.

6. L.E. Stager, 'Archaeology, Ecology and Social History: Background Themes to the Song of Deborah', in J.A. Emerton (ed.), *Congress Volume: Jerusalem, 1986* (VTSup, 40; Leiden: E.J. Brill, 1988), p. 221.

7. J. David Schloen, 'Caravans, Kenites, and *Casus Belli*: Enmity and Alliance in the Song of Deborah', *CBQ* 55 (1993), pp. 18-38.

8. Norman Gottwald, *The Tribes of Yahweh: A Sociology of the Religion of Liberated Israel, 1250–1050 B.C.E.* (Maryknoll, New York: Orbis Books 1979), pp. 503-507. See also Norman Gottwald, *The Hebrew Bible in its Social World and in Ours* (Atlanta, GA: Scholars Press, 1993), p. 63.

of 'Israel's egalitarian peasant army' against the 'imperial ventures' of the Canaanite city states.

G.W. Ahlstrom is more skeptical about the historical value of the text.[9] While not denying that there may have been an underlying local conflict, Ahlstrom concludes that the account of a major battle between competing coalitions is not historically accurate, but rather reflects the efforts by a later author or authors to give the events an 'all-Israelite' cast.

Much of the scholarship on Judges 5 (and its parallel prose account in Judges 4) concerns artistic, cultural or narrative elements of the text rather than its historical veracity or background. D.F. Murray's study of the prose narrative in Judges 4[10] sees it as a complex and skillful narrative by an author who makes liberal use of irony in order to accomplish artistic ends. Murray views the pericope as a unified work that reflects the 'controlling influence of an author'[11] whose interests are primarily literary rather than historical. The overall theme of the story, in Murray's view, is to comment on the relationship between men and women.

Victor Matthews and Don Benjamin offer a social-scientific analysis of the tradition.[12] They argue that Jael is not a femme fatale, nor a host who breaks the covenant of her household with its guest, but a hero or judge who defends her household from Sisera, who is not a guest but an intruder. The basis of their argument is the protocol of hospitality, which they reconstruct and then apply to the tradition.

Robert Alter provides a sensitive analysis of the complex and subtle gender reversals found in the Deborah story.[13] In Alter's account, the 'firmly insistent' Deborah assumes a leadership position throughout in her relations with Barak, the 'very hesitant male field commander'.[14] Alter recognizes some of the sexual imagery in the story. Thus, he

9. G.W. Ahlstrom, *The History of Ancient Palestine* (Minneapolis: Fortress Press, 1993), pp. 40-41, 379-81.

10. D.F. Murray, 'Narrative Structure and Technique in the Deborah–Barak Story (Judges IV 4-22)', in J.A. Emerton (ed.), *Studies in the Historical Books of the Old Testament* (VTSup, 30; Leiden: E.J. Brill, 1979), pp. 155-89.

11. Murray, 'Narrative Structure', p. 184.

12. Victor Matthews and Don Benjamin, *The Social World Of Ancient Israel, 1250–587 BCE* (Peabody, MA: Hendrickson 1993), pp. 82-95.

13. Robert Alter, *The World of Biblical Literature* (New York: Basic Books, 1992), pp. 41-46; Robert Alter, *The Art of Biblical Poetry* (New York: Basic Books, 1985), pp. 43-49.

14. Alter, *World of Biblical Literature*, p. 42.

describes the fallen Sisera as 'lying shattered between [Jael's] legs in a hideous parody of a soldierly assault on the woman of a defeated foe'.[15] Jael's position in standing over Sisera, in Alter's view, 'may be perhaps, an ironic glance at the time-honored martial custom of rape'.[16]

Susan Niditch's analysis of the role of Jael extends Alter's work by emphasizing the linkage of sexuality and violence in the story's[17] imagery. In Niditch's view,

> Double meanings of violent death and sexuality emerge in every line. He [Sisera] is at her feet in a pose of defeat and humiliation; he kneels between her legs in a sexual pose. He falls and lies, a dead warrior assassinated by a warrior better than he; he is a supplicant and a would-be lover. This one verse [Judg. 5.27] holds an entire story. The final twist and nuance of the tale awaits the last line, which nevertheless retains the doubleness of meaning. He is despoiled/destroyed. The woman Jael becomes not the object of sexual advances... and not the complacent responder to requests for mercy, but herself is the aggressor, the despoiler.[18]

Niditch carries the analysis forward with her thoroughgoing insistence on exploring the sexualized double entendres running throughout the text.

The gender-based implications of the Song of Deborah are explored at length in Mieke Bal's work. In her book, *Murder and Difference*,[19] she offers a complex analysis of Judges 4 and 5 from the standpoint of a number of separate disciplinary and interdisciplinary 'codes'. Bal, like Niditch, identifies a sexualized meaning in the killing of Sisera. She also identifies the contrast between honor and shame as central to the narrative structure.[20]

None of the prior literature appears to have analyzed the Song of Deborah as part of a literature of verbal feud, or to have identified the

15. Robert Alter, 'From Line to Story in Biblical Verse', *Poetics Today* 4 (1983), pp. 615-37, esp. p. 633.

16. Alter, 'From Line to Story', p. 635.

17. Susan Niditch, 'Eroticism and Death in the Tale of Jael', in Peggy L. Day (ed.), *Gender and Difference in Ancient Israel* (Minneapolis: Fortress Press 1989), pp. 43-74. See also Susan Niditch, *War in the Hebrew Bible* (New York: Oxford University Press, 1993), pp. 113-16.

18. Niditch, 'Eroticism and Death', p. 50.

19. Mieke Bal, *Murder and Difference: Gender, Genre, and Scholarship on Sisera's Death* (Bloomington: Indiana University Press, 1988).

20. Bal, *Murder and Difference*, pp. 116-20.

existence of the literary forms of the boast, the taunt, and the riposte in the text. Thus, the discussion that follows may represent a contribution to the understanding of the social background of Judges 5.

A Theory of Verbal Feud

In an earlier paper,[21] I set out a general theory of verbal feud in the Hebrew Bible, and applied that theory to certain other texts in the book of Judges. The theory draws on the premise that the Hebrew Bible is deeply concerned with norms of honor.

Honor appears to be an important element in many societies, especially societies that function outside the organizing power of an established state.[22] The existence of shame and honor as elements of social control in the Hebrew Bible is indisputable, although prior scholarship has not always recognized the importance of these institutions within the society of ancient Israel.

As I argue in the previous article, ancient Israelite society was deeply concerned about honor—not only the honor of the individual, but also that of the family, clan, and tribe. To be honorable was to be generous, brave, and productive, the father of respectful sons and chaste daughters. One's honor was a valuable asset: it 'elevated a man in the eyes of his peers, enhanced his children's marriage prospects, reassured allies and vassals, awed enemies, and aided in commercial dealings'.[23] People seek the high status that comes with a reputation for acting honorably, and eschew behaviors that could be judged dishonorable. Honor can also come to be an end in itself, so that people may seek to act in honorable ways, and avoid dishonorable ones, even though their behavior is not observable by others. Norms of honor can be internalized, and thus become part of a person's structure of self-esteem; a person who has thoroughly internalized the norm feels diminished if he or she acts dishonorably.

Norms of honor are likely to assume heightened importance in settings where the state, with its dispute-resolving and norm-creating apparatus of police, courts, and the like, is weak or absent. Thus, we

21. Miller, 'Verbal Feud'.

22. For norms of honor among contemporary Bedouin, see Lila Abu-Lughod, *Veiled Sentiments: Honor and Poetry in a Bedouin Society* (Berkeley: University of California Press, 1986).

23. Miller, 'Verbal Feud', pp. 105-106.

find honor norms in frontier lands (the tradition of the western gunfight appears to have evolved out of the European duel); in ghettoes where the police are ineffective (the slang word 'dis' means 'disrespect'); in territories dominated by clan authority (traditional Mediterranean villages or Bedouin culture); or in elite cultural segments whose members claim dispensation from ordinary civil authority (in many cultures, including the early United States, dueling was an accepted means for resolving 'affairs of honor' among the aristocracy, but was considered inappropriate for the lower classes).

The process of losing honor was that of being shamed. As described by Lyn Bechtel in a recent, valuable article,[24] one important function of shame was status manipulation:

> In group-oriented societies status was largely (but not entirely) dependent on the evaluation and opinions of others. The more recognition, respect, or honor nations or people had in the eyes of others, the more influence, superiority, dominance, and status they had. These qualities were not conferred 'once for all time'; tenuous, shifting entities which shaming threatened. One way of maintaining or raising an individual's or group's status was by lowering the status of other people or groups.[25]

As Bechtel analyzes the institution, shaming was a potent form of social control in ancient Israel because the social structure of Israelite society was heavily group-oriented: 'Part of the socialization process of the Israelite society involved developing a sensitivity to shaming. The reaction people had to being shamed was to take revenge or save face. This need for revenge suggested that their pride had been violated by their shaming. Revenge would restore pride by reversing the positions of those involved.'

The book of Judges presents the social setting of the tribal confederacy as one strongly influenced by norms of honor. Indeed, one can detect in this book, as in some of the other early biblical books, the vestiges of what must have been a richly nuanced literature of honor and dishonor.[26] Groups would attempt to establish honor for themselves with stories or attributes that reflected on them in a good light, while at

24. Lyn M. Bechtel, 'Shame as a Sanction of Social Control in Biblical Israel: Judicial, Political, and Social Shaming', *JSOT* 49 (1991), pp. 47-76.

25. Bechtel, 'Shame as a Sanction', p. 64.

26. For a valuable account, see Niditch, *War in the Hebrew Bible*. For an interesting recent article discussing the institution of 'flyting' (verbal dueling), see M.R. Eaton, 'Some Instances of Flyting in the Hebrew Bible', *JSOT* 61 (1994), pp. 3-14.

the same time attempting to diminish the honor of competing groups with shaming stories or attributes.

These honor-based texts fall into certain distinctive patterns. The Bible instances at least four different types of honor stories: boasts (including vaunts), in which a group claimed exceedingly honorable attributes for itself; insults, in which a group attributed grossly dishonorable attributes to a rival; parries (including parodies and taunts) which responded to another group's boasts in situations where the boast had achieved acceptance in the broader culture; and ripostes, which responded to insults from another group in situations where those insults had achieved acceptance in the broader culture.[27] The most complex form is the riposte, which (a) accepts as true part of an insult (because rejecting the insult wholesale would not be effective); (b) reverses the honor-value of the insult by claiming that to the extent that the insult is true, the supposedly bad qualities that have been attributed to the insulted party are, in fact, good; and (c) returns the insult to the sender, with interest, by asserting that the bad attributes involved in the insult are in fact attributes of the group within which the insult originated. In the next section, I argue that the Song of Deborah is fundamentally structured according to these norms of honor, and, in particular, that it contains within it a distinctive riposte—a response to a shaming story that circulated in the broader culture about Israelite society or a portion of that society.

The Song of Deborah Riposte

The Song is, in form, a vaunt uttered by a member of the victorious group after a military victory. The vaunt is a form of boast: it records the vaunting group's superior skill in battle and the favor it enjoys in the eyes of a mighty god. Thus, the vaunt is a direct claim of honor for the vaunting party.[28]

27. When an insult has achieved acceptance in the broader culture, simple denials may do no more than heighten the credibility of the initial accusation. Consider the following widely disbelieved denials from American politics: 'I am not a crook' (Nixon); 'I am not a liberal' (Dukakis); 'I am not a wimp' (Bush).

28. Vaunts were a well-developed literary form; the Song of Deborah bears a remarkable resemblance to the other great biblical vaunt, the song of Moses and Miriam after the miracle of the Red Sea, Exod. 15.1-21. Both texts celebrate a victory over superior military force; in both the overwhelming power of the chariots is defeated by a flood of water; and both are sung, in part, by a woman.

Contained within the Song is also a parry formation. The Song not only boasts of the military skill and divine favor enjoyed by the Israelite forces; it also directly responds to the honor-claims made by the Canaanites about themselves. The Canaanites evidently appear in battle with a vastly superior chariot force, of which we may infer they are enormously proud. The mother of Sisera anxiously awaits the clatter of the chariots' wheels as they return, victorious, to the city. The Canaanites, moreover, appear to take pride in their organized, sophisticated, and segmented society: we hear that it is the 'kings' of Canaan who come to do battle. They are supremely confident, when they go out to battle, that they will return with rich spoils: and even when they are late returning, the Canaanite princess concludes that the delay is due to the richness of the spoils the chariot force is taking, rather than to defeat in battle. All this pride is turned back on the Canaanites in the form of a taunt, harshly contrasting the Canaanites' boastful claims to power and valor with their humiliating defeat at the hands of a hastily organized coalition of amateur Israelite warriors.

The most complex structure in the Song of Deborah, however, involves a riposte. The Song follows the riposte pattern in that it (a) deals with an insult about the Israelites widely credited in the overall culture; (b) accepts a part of the insult as true but reverses the honor-value of the attribution by claiming that to the extent there is truth in the insult, it reflects honor on the Israelites, not shame; and (c) returns the insult with interest to the hostile group.

The first element of the riposte form is the presence of an insulting negative stereotype of the affected group. In the case of the Song of Deborah, the stereotype is roughly this: the Israelites are backward hill people who lack culture, refinement and sophistication; who adhere to absurd norms of hospitality; and whose men are dominated by masculine women. Such a stereotype would have had considerable substance in the social conditions of Iron Age I culture. The Israelites were people of the hills, who lived in a rural setting of small hamlets and farms; the Canaanites were people of the plains whose social life was organized around cities.[29] The people of the hills were not wealthy, and there is no

29. For the archeology of the settlement of the highlands during the Iron Age I period, see I. Finkelstein and N. Na'aman, *From Nomadism to Monarchy: Archaeological and Historical Aspects of Early Israel* (Jerusalem: Israel Exploration Society; Washington: Biblical Archaeology Society, 1994); I. Finkelstein, 'The Great Transformation: The "Conquest" of the Highlands Frontiers

evidence of an urban elite. Conditions of life were difficult, and it is probable that women as well as men had to engage in arduous physical labor. Country women could not have had much luxury to beautify themselves with costumes, cosmetics, or coiffures.

The contrast between city and country appears to be nearly a human universal: country folk, especially people of the hills, are often seen from the urban standpoint as lacking in education, refinement, and social graces, and as economically, politically, and socially inferior compared with the high society of the cities. Country folk tend to display different norms of hospitality, taking in strangers passing through without questioning their origin or credentials—something that would have been impossible in an urban setting. Country women are often stereotyped as plain and vigorous, but lacking in the beauty and refinement of city women. Urbanites of the Canaanite cities may have looked down on and mocked the Israelites for their strange and rude ways.

This stereotype had enough credibility that simply denying it would not have been effective. Consistently with the riposte form, the Song of Deborah does not deny that some elements of the stereotype are, indeed, true. The text explicitly portrays the Israelites as country folk, lacking in kings, chariots, shields, lances and the other accoutrements of organized urban life. The Song itself is to be performed in the open air, at the 'places where the women draw water' (Judg. 5.11). As depicted in the Song, the Israelites have no professional army, no chariots, no shields or lances (Judg. 5.8). The only weapon attributed to the Israelite coalition is the rude tent-peg wielded by Jael. The Israelite ally Jael lives exposed to the elements in a tent pitched in the open air. The Canaanites, on the other hand, are creatures of urban culture. They rely on kings, chariots, and an organized army to win their battles—the products of urban culture. Their women live in a city, sequestered behind walls and peering through the lattice of a window (5.28), listening for the 'clatter of chariots' in the streets (5.28).

The Song of Deborah admits the truth of certain elements of the stereotype of the country culture. Thus, country folk are indeed hospitable to strangers. When Sisera appears at Jael's tent, she does not turn him away even though he is a complete stranger and she is a

and the Rise of the Territorial State', in T.E. Levy (ed.), *The Archaeology of Society in the Holy Land* (London: Leicester University Press, 1995), pp. 349-65; I. Finkelstein, *The Archaeology of the Israelite Settlement* (Jerusalem: Israel Exploration Society, 1988).

woman, apparently alone without the protection of her husband. He asks for water and she gives him milk. She offers him curds in a bowl fit for a chieftain (5.25). During the first part of their interaction, Jael appears hospitable to a fault.

The Song concedes that Israelite women have man-like qualities.[30] For starters, Deborah herself, a woman, has become judge over Israel. It would appear unusual for a woman to exercise authority in her own capacity and not as stand-in or regent for some male figure. Deborah's role becomes even more unusual when we consider that the judges were not selected by dynastic succession. The most common ways in which women rose to power in the ancient world—default of male heirs or relationship with a male authority figure—were not present. Deborah rose on merit: 'champions there were none, none left in Israel, until I, Deborah, arose, arose, a mother in Israel' (Judg. 5.7). Deborah is clearly the leader of the military coalition; the people call on her to rouse herself and 'lead out the host' (5.12). Deborah indeed displays masculine traits: bold, courageous and determined, she assumes a man's position, and exercises personal authority that does not depend on men. Jael also has qualities that do not fit an ideal of protected femininity. She is alone in a tent in open country when Sisera appears. She is not afraid to entertain a strange man, probably in battle dress and disheveled from his flight. And she has no difficulty in taking matters into her own hand—quite literally—when she drives the tent-peg into Sisera's skull. Canaanite women, in contrast, are depicted as timid and retiring, closeted behind walls and dreaming of the house servants and the booty of dyed cloth their menfolk will bring home from the battle (5.30).

Thus, the Song accepts, as valid, certain essential elements of the negative stereotype of the Israelite hill people: they lack urban culture, they live by strong norms of hospitality, and their women play an important role that can even involve leadership positions.

The second element of the riposte form is that the elements of the negative stereotype that are admitted to be true are shown to be honorable and desirable: the honor-value of the stereotype is reversed.

The Song of Deborah tells us quite clearly that, to the extent that the

30. For an interesting account from a feminist perspective, that highlights the contrast between Deborah and the mother of Sisera, see Mieke Bal, *Death and Dissymmetry: The Politics of Coherence in the Book of Judges* (Chicago: University of Chicago Press, 1988), pp. 206-11.

stereotype of Israelite culture is true, the qualities involved are honorable and good, not shameful and bad. Thus, it is true that the Israelites lack chariots, organized armies, and kings, but they have something better. In place of these urban amenities, the Israelites of the countryside possess the protection of a powerful god who descends from the mountains with earthquakes and tempests (Judg. 5.4-5). This god enlists the forces of nature as allies of the Israelites: the stars and the rivers fight on their behalf (5.20-21). Even the hills become an asset: it is the topography of the battle site that causes the Kishon to flood and carry away the Canaanite chariots. On the other hand, the vaunted superiority of the Canaanite forces turns out to be a deficit. Their chariots might be effective on the plains, but in the hill country they can be washed away by a sudden flood from the heights (5.21). Their horses might offer an overwhelming tactical advantage under normal conditions, but in the chaos of a thunderstorm and flood, they are likely to panic and gallop away (5.22). Organized military forces may work well when confronting a similar force on level ground, but they may become trapped and disorganized when attacked from the heights by a fierce rebel force (5.13-15). The message of the text is that the rudeness of Israelite country life is far to be preferred in a time of crisis.

The text also tells us that to the degree that the Israelites are hospitable, this is a good thing and not a bad. We learn here that the hospitality of the country folk is not the same as foolishness. Quite to the contrary, country folk can be much wilier than their city rivals. Sisera implicitly invokes the country norm of hospitality when he appears at Jael's tent and asks for water. The exhausted Sisera, apparently lulled by Jael's ministrations, is no match for the fate that awaits him at her hands. We may infer that Sisera's confidence in Jael is due, at least in part, to the false stereotype to which he and other city folk subscribe as to the excesses of country hospitality. In fact, as Victor Matthews and Don Benjamin argue, Sisera's invasion of Jael's tent is itself a gross breach of the norms of hospitality as applied to a guest, justifying Jael's violent response.[31] The message of the text here appears to be something like the following: Yes, we country folk are hospitable to strangers who deserve our hospitality. But our hospitality is not a mark of weakness but of strength. If someone comes under false pretenses to

31. Matthews and Benjamin, *Social World Of Ancient Israel*, p. 94.

seek our shelter, they are likely to be fooled into making a serious mistake.[32]

The text also reverses the honor-value of the stereotype of Israelite women, demonstrating that a fierce Israelite woman is to be valued, not mocked. It is only because of Deborah's willingness to assume a male role that the Israelites free themselves from oppression. Her activity, courage, and authority contrast with the passivity, timidity, and subordination displayed by the royal women of the Canaanite city, just as her milieu in open country contrasts with the housebound environment of Sisera's mother. Sisera's mother lusts after 'dyed stuff' (Judg. 5.30); Deborah seeks honor and victory. The contrast between Deborah and Sisera's mother is reinforced through the subsidiary female characters, the Canaanite princess and the Kenite Jael. The princess lives in a palace and Jael in a tent, but Jael's familiarity with tents and tent-pegs turns out to be more useful than feminine arts. Jael acts; the princess prattles. The princess's 'wisdom' is nothing but fantasy and foolishness; her cleverness has no object and no effect. Jael is truly clever: she soothes Sisera by giving him milk when he asks for water, causing him to lower his guard and allowing her to administer the coup de grâce. The text tells us that Israelite women may indeed have manly qualities, but these are attributes much to be appreciated in a crisis.

The third distinguishing feature of a riposte story is that the insult is returned, with interest, to the insulting party. The Song of Deborah administers its riposte with exquisite skill and accuracy. Consider the norm of hospitality. It is the very hospitality, displayed in excess measure by Jael, that fools the credulous Sisera into allowing her to administer the fatal blow. If she were not so hospitable as to give him milk when he asks for water and to offer him curds in a fine bowl, he would probably have been more on guard. Moreover, the tent-peg with which Jael administers the fatal blow is itself a symbol of the house. The pegs are what hold the tent up, and thus are fundamental to its stability. Sisera, in a sense, is destroyed by the house, and by the hospitality, on which he has imposed himself.

The Song also administers a riposte against the Canaanites on the issue of country versus city. The Canaanite forces are destroyed by the very forces of nature that rally on the Israelites' behalf, summoned by Israel's powerful mountain god: 'Oh Lord, at thy setting forth from

32. For an argument that Jael does not in fact violate traditional norms of hospitality, see Matthews and Benjamin, *Social World of Ancient Israel*, pp. 82-95.

Seir, when thou camest marching out of the plains of Edom, earth trembled; heaven quaked; the clouds streamed down in torrents. Mountains shook in fear before the Lord, the lord of Sinai' (Judg. 5.4-5).

Finally, the insult that the Israelites are led by women—and, implicitly, that Israelite men are emasculated and feminine—is returned back to the Canaanites with a vengeance. Jael drives a tent-peg into Sisera's skull, a violent parody of the sexual act in which the woman wields the phallic object and the man is feminized and raped.[33] Moreover, the power relation of man and woman is reversed. The text describes precisely how Sisera died: 'at her feet he sank down and fell, at her feet he sank down and fell. Where he sank down, there he fell, done to death' (Judg. 5.26). With this image of Jael standing over Sisera, holding in her hand an object now to be visualized as a staff or rod, the author evokes traditional images of power in the ancient Near East, in which the king stood holding a rod or scepter in his hand as his subjects knelt or groveled before him. Sisera has become a vassal, humiliated and prostrate before his ruler. Sisera is condemned to the ultimate warrior's humiliation—to be killed by a woman.[34] Thus the insult is returned, with interest: it is the Canaanites who are feminized and the Israelites and Kenites who emerge as the victorious warriors.[35]

33. The sexual connotation has been noted by previous commentators, for example, Alter, *The Art of Biblical Poetry*, p. 46 ; Bal, *Death and Dissymmetry*, p. 215; Bal, *Murder and Difference*, pp. 130-34; Matthews and Benjamin, *Social World Of Ancient Israel*, p. 94; Niditch, *War in the Hebrew Bible*, pp. 113-17. Compare the story of Eglon and Ehud, in which the Benjaminite Ehud retaliates against an implication of homosexuality by means of a violent parody of the sexual act in which he thrusts his dagger into his enemy's belly. Judges 3.22; see Miller, 'Verbal Feud'.

34. Calum Carmichael observes in private correspondence that the Bible contains other examples of such a fate—for example, the death of Abimelech.

35. In this respect D.F. Murray misses part of the key to the story when he claims that at the deep structure of the narrative (in Judg. 4), Barak and Sisera are 'united in a tragic fate: ignominious subjection to the effective power of a woman'. Murray, 'Narrative Structure', p. 173. The narrative does make the comparison between the two men, but not in order to equate their fates. It would be completely contrary to the overall thrust of the biblical narrative to cast Barak and Sisera in the same role. The comparison is made rather to contrast the two in the form of a riposte: the narrative admits that Barak is under the control of a woman, but observes that this inversion of normal sex roles is good (the Israelites win a great battle and the Canaanites are humiliated), while returning the insult with interest to

Conclusion

This paper analyzes the Song of Deborah as structured, in part, by norms of honor within a rhetorical culture of verbal feud. One function of the Song may have been to support the coherence of Israelite hill country society by laying claim to honor, shaming the rival culture of the cities, and returning, with interest, the insulting stereotypes about the hill people that were likely to have had currency in the urban areas. An important aspect of the Song was its function as a riposte story. The Song admits that the Israelites lack high urban culture, but argues that the Israelites' closeness to nature is a good thing, not a bad thing, since it allows them to call on their powerful god and to enlist the very stars and rivers as allies in their successful battle against the Canaanite chariots. The hospitality displayed by the people of the hills is also shown to be a positive virtue associated with wily resourcefulness rather than naïvety. As to the issue of gender, the Song admits some truth to the stereotype that Israelite women are man-like and un-feminine, and that Israelite men can be led by women; but it reverses the honor value of the stereotype by claiming that to have such powerful women on one's side is greatly to be wished, and then returns the insult, with interest, to the Canaanites by having a lowly woman in the Israelite coalition feminize, rape, and vanquish the leader of the Canaanite forces. To the best of my knowledge, the Song of Deborah has not heretofore been analyzed as a riposte form. Future scholarship may reveal whether similar rhetorical structures can be identified elsewhere in the Hebrew Bible.

the Canaanites by observing that it is Sisera, not Barak, who ends up being vanquished and humiliated sexually by a member of the 'weaker' sex.

FALSE WEIGHTS IN THE SCALES OF BIBLICAL JUSTICE? DIFFERENT VIEWS OF WOMEN FROM PATRIARCHAL HIERARCHY TO RELIGIOUS EQUALITY IN THE BOOK OF DEUTERONOMY

Eckart Otto

Introduction

In 1929 Walter Baumgartner wrote a review article on scholarly publications about the book of Deuteronomy, which he entitled 'Der Kampf um das Deuteronomium' ('The Battle for Deuteronomy').[1] This could also be a present-day headline for our debate about this biblical book, not only with regard to its literary historical problems but also to its legal and ethical substance. In 1991 Carolyn Pressler published her cutting edge dissertation on the status of women in the Deuteronomic family laws[2] and came to the conclusion that they

> serve a two-fold purpose. In the first place, they undergird the traditional structures of the family, the interests of which are, for the most part, identified with the interests of the male head of the household. In the second place, the laws protect the rights of dependent family members. They do so, however, without challenging the subordinate status of women in any fundamental way.[3]

Lately G. Braulik[4], one of the best scholars of the book of Deuteronomy, came to the exactly opposite result:

1. See W. Baumgartner, 'Der Kampf um das Deuteronomium', *TRev* 1 (1929), pp. 1-25.

2. See C. Pressler, *The View of Women Found in the Deuteronomic Family Laws* (BZAW, 216; Berlin: W. de Gruyter, 1991).

3. See Pressler, *The View of Women*, p. 96.

4. See C. Braulik, 'Haben in Israel auch Frauen geopfert? Beobachtungen am Deuteronomium', in S. Kreuzer and K. Lüthi (eds.), *Zur Aktualität des Alten Testaments: Festschrift für Georg Sauer* (Frankfurt/Main: Peter Lang, 1991), pp. 19-28; *idem*, 'Die Ablehnung der Göttin Aschera in Israel: War sie erst deuteronomistisch, diente sie der Unterdrückung der Frauen?', in M.-T. Wacker and

> Das alttestamentliche Recht enthält allerdings einen *Entwurf von 'Welt'*, der sich von den altorientalischen und den übrigen biblischen Gesetzgebungen dadurch unterscheidet, daß er nicht einfach männerorientiert, sondern *geschwisterlich konzipiert* ist: das Deuteronomium.[5] (The Old Testament law contains a draft version of the world one, which differs from ancient Near Eastern and other biblical collections by the fact that it is not simply male, but brother-and-sister orientated: this is the book of Deuteronomy.)

Both scholars were basing their research on a final text of Deuteronomy. So G. Braulik added: 'Das gilt zumindest für die Endgestalt des Buches, die als systematische Gesamtkonstruktion der Gesellschaft "Israel" verstanden werden will' ('this at least is valid for the final shape of the book, which should be understood as a systematical construction of the entire society of Israel').[6] C. Pressler divorces herself from a diachronic analysis of the Deuteronomic texts.[7] Both scholars deal with different parts of Deuteronomic law. Whereas G. Braulik bases his assumption of an equal status for men and women on the cultic law, C. Pressler restricts her analysis to the family law. But could it be without any importance for the interpretation of the family law if the cultic law had as its context an entirely different approach to women and vice versa? And how were these different views of the status of women in Israelite society related to each other? The debate is still open.

When W. Baumgartner characterized the scholarly discussions of the book of Deuteronomy as a conflict, he thought of the divergent alternatives for the literary formation of this biblical book: was it originally a programme for the Josianic reform with some additions, especially in the family laws,[8] a (post-)exilic utopia using some older material,

E. Zenger (eds.), *Der eine Gott und die Göttin: Gottesvorstellungen des biblischen Israel im Horizont feministischer Theologie* (QD, 135; Freiburg: Herder, 1991), pp. 106-36 (pp. 129-36).

5. See Braulik, 'Haben in Israel auch Frauen geopfert?', p. 20.

6. See Braulik, 'Haben in Israel auch Frauen geopfert?', p. 20.

7. See E. Otto, review of *The View of Women Found in the Deuteronomic Family Laws*, in *TLZ* 119 (1994), cols. 983-86. For the methodological problems of a synchronic approach to biblical law see E. Otto, 'Diachronie und Synchronie im Depositenrecht des "Bundesbuches": Zur jüngsten literatur- und rechtshistorischen Diskussion von Ex 22,6-14', *ZAR* 2 (1996), pp. 76-85.

8. See A.F. Puukko, *Das Deuteronomium: Eine literarkritische Untersuchung* (BWANT, 5; Leipzig: J.C. Hinrichs, 1910), esp. p. 237. This position was lately restated by J.C. Gertz, *Die Gerichtsorganisation Israels im deuteronomischen*

especially in the family laws,[9] or a law code, which was formed in pre-Josianic centuries with some later additions, especially in the family laws?[10] More than sixty years later we are still discussing the same alternatives. But there is some hope for progress in the debate. Our precursors did not yet know much of the ancient Near Eastern legal legacy: the Neo-Assyrian loyalty oaths and vassal treaties particularly were unknown to them. They were directly quoted in the pre-exilic Deuteronomy[11] and can gain the function of an Archimedean point for our current debates.[12] And our precursors were not aware of the fundamental meaning of the phenomenon of inner-biblical exegesis for the literary history of biblical law.[13] The pre-Deuteronomistic laws of

Gesetz (FRLANT, 165; Göttingen: Vandenhoeck & Ruprecht, 1994), pp. 173-233 esp. p. 173; for this dissertation see E. Otto, review of *Die Gerichtsorganisation Israels im deuteronomischen Gesetz*, by J.C. Gertz, in *TLZ* 121 (1996), cols. 1130-33.

9. See G. Hölscher, 'Komposition und Ursprung des Deuteronomiums', *ZAW* 40 (1922), pp. 161-255. This position was lately reprised by E. Würthwein, 'Die josianische Reform und das Deuteronomium', *ZTK* 73 (1976), pp. 394-423.

10. See J. Hempel, *Die Schichten des Deuteronomiums: Ein Beitrag zur israelitischen Literatur- und Rechtsgeschichte* (Beiträge zur Kultur- und Universalgeschichte, 33; Leipzig: Voigtländer, 1914); T. Oestreicher, *Das deuteronomische Grundgesetz* (BFCT, 27.4; Gütersloh: C. Bertelsmann, 1923); *idem, Reichstempel und Ortsheiligtümer in Israel* (BFCT, 33.3; Gütersloh: Bertelsmann, 1930). Lately this position was espoused by J.G. McConville, *Law and Theology in Deuteronomy* (JSOTSup, 33; Sheffield: JSOT Press, 1984); J.G. McConville and J.G. Millar, *Time and Place in Deuteronomy* (JSOTSup, 179; Sheffield: Sheffield Academic Press, 1994). For this latter monograph see the review by R. Achenbach in *ZAR* 1 (1995), pp. 149-55.

11. See E. Otto, 'Treueid und Gesetz: Die Ursprünge des Deuteronomiums im Horizont neuassyrischen Vertragsrechts', *ZAR* 2 (1996), pp. 1-52; H.U. Steymans, *Deuteronomium 28 und die* adê *zur Thronfolgeregelung Asarhaddons: Segen und Fluch im Alten Orient und in Israel* (OBO, 145; Freiburg/Göttingen: Universitätsverlag: Vandenhoeck & Ruprecht, 1995).

12. For an overview of the present state of debate see G. Braulik, 'Das Buch Deuteronomium', in E. Zenger *et al.* (eds.), *Einleitung in das Alte Testament* (Kohlhammer Studienbücher Theologie, 1.1; Stuttgart: W. Kohlhammer, 1995), pp. 76-88; for the recent German commentaries on the book of Deuteronomy by E. Nielsen (*Deuteronomium* [HAT, 1.6; Tübingen: J.C.B. Mohr, 1995]) and M. Rose (*5. Mose* [ZBK, 5.12; Zürich: Theologischer Verlag, 1994]) see R. Achenbach, 'Zwei neue Kommentare zum Deuteronomium', *ZAR* 2 (1996), pp. 86-113.

13. See M. Fishbane, *Biblical Interpretation in Ancient Israel* (Oxford: Clarendon Press, 1985), pp. 91-277.

Deuteronomy were in many points a revision of laws of the covenant code. The provisions for the centralization of the cult in Deuteronomy 12 were the hermeneutical key for this revision.[14] All the laws of the Covenant Code on which the cult-centralization had an impact were revised in the Deuteronomic law. In order to stabilize a brotherly ethos in the desacralized country[15] the Deuteronomic author also integrated the social and ethical provisions of the Covenant Code into the Deuteronomic law. In other parts the Deuteronomic law has supplemented the law of the Covenant Code. The Covenant Code deals with legal matters of the family only in Exod. 22.15-16, but extensively with material damages and bodily injuries in Exod. 21.18-22.14. However, the Deuteronomic law is extensively concerned with family matters, but has no provisions for material damages and only one provision for bodily injuries, in Deut. 25.11-12. The best explanation of this striking feature is the assumption that laws indifferent to cult centralization were not incorporated into the Deuteronomic law, because there was no reason to revise them. In their stead the redactor integrated a collection of family laws in Deut. 21.15-21; 22.13-21a, 22a, 23, 24a, 25, 27, 28-29; 24.1-4aα, 5; 25.5-10[16] into the Deuteronomic law in order to sup-

14. See B.M. Levinson, *The Hermeneutics of Innovation: The Impact of Centralization upon the Structure, Sequence, and Reformulation of Legal Material in Deuteronomy* (Ann Arbor: University Microfilms International, 1991); E. Otto, 'Vom Bundesbuch zum Deuteronomium: Die deuteronomische Redaktion in Dtn 12–26', in G. Braulik *et al.*(eds.), *Gesellschaftlicher Wandel und biblische Theologie. Festschrift für Norbert Lohfink SJ* (Freiburg: Herder, 1993), pp. 260-78; *idem*, 'The Pre-exilic Deuteronomy as a Revision of the Covenant Code', in *idem*, *Kontinuum und Proprium: Studien zur Sozial- und Rechtsgeschichte des Alten Orients und des Alten Testaments* (Orientalia Biblica et Christiana, 8; Wiesbaden: Otto Harrassowitz, 1996), pp. 112-22; *idem*, 'Gesetzesfortschreibung und Pentateuchredaktion', *ZAW* 107 (1995), pp. 373-92. For a contrasting view see J. van Seters, 'Cultic Laws of the Covenant Code (Exodus 20,22-23,33), and their Relationship to Deuteronomy and the Holiness Code', in M. Vervenne (ed.), *Studies in the Book of Exodus: Redaction—Reception—Interpretation* (BETL, 136; Leuven: Peeters, 1996), pp. 319-45; *idem*, 'The Law of the Hebrew Slave', *ZAW* 108 (1996), pp. 534-46.

15. See E. Otto, *Theologische Ethik des Alten Testaments* (Theologische Wissenschaft, 3.2; Stuttgart: W. Kohlhammer, 1994), pp. 180-92 (2; ET forthcoming).

16. See E. Otto, 'Soziale Verantwortung und Reinheit des Landes: Zur Redaktion der kasuistischen Rechtssätze in Deuteronomium 19–25', in *idem*, *Kontinuum und Proprium*, pp. 123-38.

plement the Covenant Code.[17] As a consequence of this view of the literary formation of the Deuteronomic law I shall first analyse the status of women in the pre-Deuteronomic collection of family law and secondly their Deuteronomic interpretation and the Deuteronomic and Deuteronomistic views of women in the Deuteronomic cultic law.

The View of Women in Deuteronomic Family Laws

The laws of adultery and rape in Deut. 22.20-29* show a firmly tied redactional structure. They form a core-section of the family law collection, so that it is useful to start the analysis with this legal section.

Deuteronomy 22.20-29: Laws of Adultery and Rape*

The provision in Deut. 22.22a and its counter case in Deut. 22.28-29 form the literary and legal historical core of the section in Deut. 22.22a, 23, 24, 25, 27-29.[18] Deuteronomy 22.22a was originally a *môt yûmat*-law, which was superficially transformed into a casuistic legal sentence.[19] It has its nearest parallels in Lev. 18.20 and Deut. 5.18 // Exod. 20.14. That both, man and woman, were sentenced to death and executed in a case of adultery was not an innovation of the pre-Deuteronomic provision in Deut. 22.22a, but a traditional feature of Judaean law.[20] The prohibition against adultery in Deut. 22.22a is connected

17. The covenant code remained a legal authority in legal matters even after the formation of the Deuteronomic law. This explains best why the Covenant Code was inserted into the Sinai pericope even after the formation of the Deuteronomic law was finished; see E. Otto, 'Die nachpriesterschriftliche Pentateuchredaktion im Buch Exodus', in M. Vervenne (ed.), *Studies in the Book of Exodus*, pp. 61-111 (70-78). For a divergent view see N. Lohfink, 'Gibt es eine deuteronomistische Bearbeitung im Bundesbuch?' in *idem*, *Studien zum Deuteronomium und zur deuteronomistischen Literatur III* (SBAB, 20; Stuttgart: Katholisches Bibelwerk, 1995), pp. 39-64.

18. The *bi'artā*-formulas in Deut. 22.22b, 24b and the verse Deut. 22.26, which connected the family law with the blood law in Deut. 19.11 (see Fishbane, *Biblical Interpretation*, pp. 217-20), were added by the Deuteronomic redactor; see below.

19. See G. Seitz, *Redaktionsgeschichtliche Studien zum Deuteronomium* (BWANT, 93; Stuttgart: W. Kohlhammer, 1971), p. 120; H.D. Preuss, *Deuteronomium* (EdF, 164; Darmstadt: Wissenschaftliche Buchgesellschaft, 1982), pp.125-26.

20. See also Pressler, *The View of Women*, pp. 33-34, who rejects the thesis of D. Daube ('Biblical Landmarks in the Struggle for Women's Rights', *Juridical Review* 23.3 [1978], pp. 177-97 [177-80]) and A. Phillips (*Ancient Israel's Crimi-*

with its counter-case, the provision on sexual intercourse with an unmarried girl in Deut. 22.28-29. Doubtless these two laws have been shaped by their supposition of a patrilineal family structure. Deut. 22.22a protects the privileges of a married man and Deut. 22.28-29 those of the father of an unmarried girl.[21] But compared with its parallel in Exod. 22.15-16 there is a decisive progress towards protecting the rights and titles of young women rather than those of their fathers. In Exod. 22.15-16 the father was entitled to deny the marriage of his daughter in order to prevent the automatism of a *Raubehe* (marriage by prey). In Deut. 22.28-29 the culprit is forced to marry the girl and renounce his right to divorce her. This is a fundamental improvement of the status of women, especially if this change reflects an increased frequency of divorces during the period of the Judaean monarchy.[22] Whereas Exod. 22.15-16 deals with seduction, Deut. 22.28-29 stresses the aspects of violence and rape, which connect Deut. 22.28-29 with the scholarly extension of Deut. 22.22a, 28–29 in Deut. 22.23-27*. These concentrically arranged provisions differentiate, in contrast to Deut. 22.22a, between the facts of rape and adultery. The redactor has framed Deut. 22.23-27* with the provisions in Deut. 22.22a, 28–29, by which Deut. 22.22a has obtained the function of a principle provision.[23] The scholarly character of the extension in Deut. 22.23-27* is underlined by the fact that MAL (A) §§12-16 (*ANET*, p. 181) has the next parallel to the redactional structure of Deut. 22.22–29*,[24] so that the

nal Law: A New Approach to the Decalogue [Oxford: Basil Blackwell, 1970], pp. 110-12) that the liability of women to the law of adultery was a Deuteronomic innovation. It was evidently not even a pre-Deuteronomic innovation.

21. For the origin and function of these laws within a patrilineally structured society see E. Otto, 'Zur Stellung der Frau in den ältesten Rechtstexten des Alten Testaments (Ex 20,14; 22,15f.)—wieder die hermeneutische Naivität im Umgang mit dem Alten Testament', in *idem, Kontinuum und Proprium,* pp. 30-48.

22. See Pressler, *The View of Women*, pp. 40-41. I cannot see that the redactional intention to protect the girl contradicts a reaction to an increased frequency of divorces. On the contrary, if there was such an increase, the provision in Deut. 22.28-29 was all the more useful as a protective measure.

23. For principle provisions in cuneiform law see R. Haase, 'Über allgemeine Rechtsregeln in den keilschriftlichen Rechtscorpora', *ZAR* 2 (1996), pp. 135-39.

24. See E. Otto, 'Das Eherecht im Mittelassyrischen Kodex und im Deuteronomium. Tradition und Redaktion in den §§12-16 der Tafel A des Mittelassyrischen Kodex und in Dtn 22,22-29', in *idem, Kontinuum und Proprium*, pp. 172-91; *idem*, 'Rechtsreformen in Deuteronomium XII-XXVI und im Mittelassyrischen Kodex der Tafel A (KAV 1)', in J.A. Emerton (ed.), *Congress Volume*

redactor of Deut. 22–29* has depended on redactional techniques in cuneiform law.[25] Deuteronomy 22.23-27* expands the adultery law, incorporating the inchoate marriage and differentiating between adultery and rape. In Deut. 22.22a extra-marital sexual intercourse is at any rate a capital offence, if it is detected *in flagranti delicto*, irrespective of whether the woman has been forced to engage in intercourse or not—it is simply a matter of *Erfolgshaftung* (responsibility for results), irrespective of subjective aspects of intention. The original *môt yûmat* law in Deut. 22.22a reflected a patrilineal family structure. Intercourse between a married woman and another man violated her husband's rights and titles and was at any rate a capital offence. The scholarly author of Deut. 22.23-27* overcomes the simple *Erfolgshaftung* of objective evidence in favour of a *Verschuldenshaftung* (responsibility for guilt) of subjective evidence. For him the woman is a legal subject on her own, irrespective of and independent from her husband and his legal status. Her own will and intention becomes legally decisive.

The provisions in Deut. 22.22a and Deut. 22.23-27* cover only a very small range of cases of adultery, that is, those that have been detected *in flagranti delicto* (*Kî yimmaṣēʾ ʾîš šokeb ʿim ʾiššâ*). The factual differentiation between rape and adultery could only function in these very special cases. The original law in Deut. 22.22a already provided a clear cut proceeding of probative evidence *in flagranti delicto* in order to protect the woman. The same interest in probative evidence can be found in Deut. 22.13-21*.

Deuteronomy 22.13-21: The Slandered Bride*

The law of the slandered bride in Deut. 22.13-21* has its core passage in Deut. 22.13-19, which is extended by Deut. 22.20–21a.[26] The original provision in Deut. 22.13-19 was derived from a court record or a corresponding court narrative.[27] The heading sentence formed by *lqḥ*

Paris 1992 (VTSup, 61; Leiden: E.J. Brill, 1995), pp. 239-73 (243-47, 257-61).

25. See E. Otto, 'Town and Rural Countryside in Ancient Israelite Law: Reception and Redaction in Cuneiform and Israelite Law', *JSOT* 57 (1993), pp. 3-22; reprinted in J.W. Rogerson (ed.), *The Pentateuch: A Sheffield Reader* (The Biblical Seminar, 39; Sheffield: Sheffield Academic Press, 1996), pp. 203-21.

26. See e.g. Pressler, *The View of Women*, pp. 22-23.

27. See C. Locher, 'Deuteronomium 22,13-21: Vom Prozessprotokoll zum kasuistischen Gesetz', in N. Lohfink (ed.), *Das Deuteronomium: Entstehung, Gestalt und Botschaft* (BETL, 68; Leuven: Peeters, 1985), pp. 298-303.

'iš 'iššâ[28] indicates from the very beginning that the provision deals with a problem of marriage, the continuation with *śn'* that it is a matter of divorce.[29] As Deut. 22.14 unfolds, the man intends to divorce his wife by spreading malicious rumours about her, in order to save dowry and divorce-money.[30] A woman charged with premarital unchastity had to leave her house without any financial compensation.[31] The provision is concerned to prevent any abuse of this practice. If the charge can be refuted, the man loses the title to divorce his wife all his days and he has to pay the *duplum* of the dowry. The provision is definitely intended to protect women from unfair divorce.[32]

The extension of Deut. 22.13-19 in Deut. 22.20-21 interprets Deut. 22.13-19 as a case of adultery during an inchoate marriage, and this

28. For the Akkadian equivalent *aḫāzu(m)* see R. Westbrook, *Old Babylonian Marriage Law* (AfO.B, 23; Horn/Österreich: Ferdinand Berger, 1988), pp. 10-16.

29. For *śn'/zêru(m)* as divorce-terminology see Judg. 15.2; Sir. 7.26; cf. R. Yaron, 'On Divorce in Old Testament Times', *RIDA* 3.4 (1957), pp. 117-28; A.J. Skaist, 'Studies in Ancient Mesopotamian Family Law Pertaining to Marriage and Divorce' (PhD dissertation, University of Pennsylvania, 1963), pp. 54-56, 112, 129; S. Greengus, 'The Old Babylonian Marriage Contract', *JAOS* 89 (1969), pp. 505-32 (518 n. 61); Westbrook, *Marriage Law*, pp. 22-23, 80-81. For *śn'* in the Elephantine papyri see P. Koschaker, 'Eheschließung und Kauf nach alten Rechten, mit besonderer Berücksichtigung der älteren Keilschriftrechte', *ArOr* 18 (1950), pp. 210-96 (200 n. 2); R. Yaron, *Introduction to the Law of the Aramaic Papyri* (Oxford: Clarendon Press, 1961), pp. 54-55.

30. For financial compensation of an innocently divorced woman see LU 6; 7; LH 138-40 and *m. Ket.* 2, *b. B. Qam.* 82b. For a divorce without financial compensation, which was caused by the woman, see LH 141; MAL(A) 29 and *m. Ket.* 7.6.

31. The Neo-Sumerian record ITT 3/2, 5286: 18-26 underlines that a man was entitled to divorce his wife because of premarital unchastity; see C. Locher, *Die Ehre einer Frau in Israel: Exegetische und rechtsvergleichende Studien zu Deuteronomium 22,13-21* (OBO, 70; Freiburg/Göttingen: Universitätsverlag/Vandenhoeck & Ruprecht, 1986), pp. 203-208.

32. See Otto, *Theologische Ethik*, pp. 42-43. Pressler (*The View of Women*, pp. 28-29) is of the opinion that not the woman but her father and his household were the injured party, because he received compensation. But to whom else but to him should the culprit pay the fine? His own wife would have been the wrong addressee of the *duplum* of the dowry as long as there was no separation of property between a married couple as in present times. The dowry in the hand of the bride's father functioned as a kind of insurance for his daughter in case of divorce or widowhood. The *duplum* had the same function. It was the slandered bride who indirectly got the money. The penalty for the man corresponded to his offense. He lost the title to divorce his wife and had to pay the *duplum* of the dowry.

means: as a capital offence. The execution at the father's door indicates that this is the case of a woman who has been married but lives in her father's house.[33]

The death penalty was not the usual reaction to adultery of women. Deuteronomy 22.21, 23-27* restricts it to the clear-cut cases detected *in flagranti delicto*, which even required, in a Deuteronomic perspective, two witnesses (Deut. 19.15). This was certainly a rather rare case. The normal reaction to the suspicion of adultery was divorce (Hos. 2.4-5).[34] It was the usual legal practice that a man who suspected his wife to be adulterous had a *Dispositionsverfügung*, that is, was entitled to decide, whether to divorce and humilate her in public[35] or not.[36] The family law in Deut. 22.13-27* restricted the *Dispositionsverfügung* of private penalty of divorce and humiliation to cases of suspected adultery. Definitely proved cases of adultery were a matter of public trial and penalty.[37] This was a decisive improvement for women because they

33. For the standard inchoate marriage see Westbrook, *Marriage Law*, pp. 34-36. There is insufficient evidence for the assumption of an institution of betrothal beside that of inchoate marriage, as Westbrook (*Marriage Law*, pp. 29-34) supposed; see the review of his dissertation by Otto in *ZA* 81 (1991), pp. 308-314. The progressive character of Deut. 22.13-19 remains undetected, if Deut. 21.13-21 is taken as a literary unit. This is the case with C. Locher (*Die Ehre einer Frau*, esp. p. 385) who admits that premarital intercourse as a capital offense has no parallel in ancient Near Eastern law. A diachronic analysis of Deut. 22.13-21 avoids this difficult assumption; see my review of his dissertation in *WO* 20-21 (1989–90), pp. 308-11. Pressler (*The View of women*, pp. 22-31) arrives at the same result as Locher, although she differentiates from a literary critical perspective, between Deut. 22.13-19 and Deut. 22.20-21. Since she interprets Deut. 22.13-19 as related to a conflict between two men, she does not realize the progressive character of this provision.

34. See R. Westbrook, 'Adultery in Ancient Near Eastern Law', *RB* 97 (1990), pp. 542-80 (561-62, 577-80).

35. For the institution of the public humiliation of adulterous women, see for example, the marriage record BRM IV 52 : 11-15 from Hana; see C. Kuhl, 'Neue Dokumente zum Verständnis von Hos 2,4-15', *ZAW* 52 (1934), pp. 102-109 (105) and *CAD* E, p. 320.

36. If he intended to confirm his suspicion he could subject his wife to an ordeal, which had the effect of a self-effective curse in case the suspicion was true (Num. 5.11-31); see Otto, *Theologische Ethik*, pp. 43-44. The object of this cultic procedure was certainty rather than truth. In this respect cultic procedures differed from court procedures.

37. A parallel restriction of private *Dispositionsverfügung* and penalty in favour of public legal procedures characterizes the redaction of the Middle Assyrian Law

became legal subjects of their own not dependent on the legal decision of a husband. Referring to this legally progressive evolution, Deut. 22.20.21a was added to Deut. 22.13-19. Also, in the case of suspected adultery during an inchoate marriage, the man had to prove the alleged offence in court. The redactor used Deut. 22.13-19 for this reform of family law, restricting the male disposal, although Deut. 22.13-19 did not fit this purpose exactly. The evidence of the garment does not really prove adultery during an inchoate marriage. Also, the man's punishment for a wrong charge of adultery does not fit the fatal consequences for the woman if his charge was proved. But the redactor put up with these inconsistencies in order to restrict the legal right of disposal by men and install women as legal subjects of their own.

Since we are already in the midst of the discussion of the rather complicated problems of legal theory and practice of divorce I now turn to the very controversial interpretation of Deut. 24.1-4*.

Deuteronomy 24.1-4aα: The Prohibition Against the Restoration of Marriage

It was to Reuven Yaron's merit that he freed Deut. 24.1-4 from moral and theological speculations in favor of a consistently legal interpretation.[38] He interpreted Deut. 24.1-4 analogously to the prohibitions against incest. Deuteronomy 24.1-4 was meant to protect the second marriage from any attempt to restore the first marriage. But this explanation failed to give reasons why the first marriage should not be restored if the second husband died. So R. Westbrook has assumed that the first divorce, caused by the woman, was executed without compensation, whereas the second was caused by the man, so that he had to compensate his wife. The provision in Deut. 24.1-4 was to prevent the first husband from profiting by the second divorce.[39] Not only Jer. 3.1

(A); see E. Otto, 'Die Einschränkung des Privatstrafrechts durch öffentliches Strafrecht in der Redaktion der Paragraphen 1-24; 50-59 des Mittelassyrischen Kodex der Tafel A (KAV 1)', in W. Zwickel (ed.), *Biblische Welten: Festschrift für Martin Metzger* (OBO, 123; Freiburg: Universitätsverlag; Göttingen: Vandenhoeck & Ruprecht, 1993), pp. 131-66.

38. See R. Yaron, 'The Restoration of Marriage', *JSS* 17 (1966), pp. 1-11. For a summary of the discussion see E. Otto, 'Das Verbot der Wiederherstellung einer geschiedenen Ehe: Deuteronomium 24,1-4 im Kontext des israelitischen und judäischen Eherechts, *UF* 24 (1992), pp. 301-10 (301-305).

39. See R. Westbrook, 'The Prohibition of Restoration of Marriage in Deuteronomy 24,1-4', in S. Japhet (ed.), *Studies in Bible* (ScrHie, 31; Jerusalem: Magnes

contradicts this assumption, but also the fact that Deut. 24.1-4 does not give any substantial reference to a divorce with or without grounds and compensation.[40] Pressler interprets Deut. 24.1-4 in analogy to the prohibitions against adultery.[41] Sexual relations of a woman with the first man, then a second man and again with the first man were considered polluting. Sexual relations, whether legal or not, which bound a woman to men in an A–B–A pattern 'confused the boundaries which defined the (patrilineal) family'.[42] But Pressler has to admit that the text of Deut. 24.1-4 does not give a hint as to why a legally contracted and legally dissolved relationship should have a polluting character. The prohibition against restoration of a divorced marriage is not only a provision analogous to those against adultery but deals with adultery. If one realizes that Deut. 22.22a, 23-27* only deals with the special case of adultery proved by detection *in flagranti delicto*, whereas other cases of adultery, which are not proved in court, are a matter of divorce, then there is no reason to exclude adultery from the semantic spectrum of *'erwāt dābār* in Deut. 24.1.[43] The first husband, who divorced his wife and declared her unclean (*huṭṭammā'â*), was bound by his decision, even if his wife married another man and was divorced again or was widowed.[44] The provision was formulated as a borderline case: even the fact of a second marriage, which was dissolved, did not annul his decision. The man's title to his wife was restricted not in order to preserve the patriarchal family, but to limit male titles of disposal and to give women the dignity of being legal subjects of their own, independent of titles and the decisions of men.

Deuteronomy 25.5-10: The Law of Levirate Marriage

No other Deuteronomic family law in the book of Deuteronomy reflects the patrilineal structure of the Judaean family so directly as the law of levirate marriage in Deut. 25.5-10. The 'name' of the family, that is, its genealogy, was carried down from father to son. It was doubtless the main concern of this institution to provide the patrilineal family with

Press, 1986), pp. 387-405.

40. See Otto, 'Verbot', pp. 303-305; Pressler, *The View of Women*, pp. 56-59.

41. Pressler, *The View of Women*, pp. 60-62.

42. Pressler, *The View of Women*, p. 61.

43. See A. Toeg, 'Does Deuteronomy 24,1-4 Incorporate a General Law on Divorce?', *Dine Israel* 2 (1970), pp. V-XXIV (VII). It is a pity that A. Toeg separates Deut. 24.1 literary critically from its context in Deut. 24.1-4.

44. Otto, 'Verbot', pp. 305-10; *idem*, *Theologische Ethik*, pp. 54-55.

male progeny in case the wife was widowed without a male heir. But looking more closely at the provision in Deut. 25.5-10, it becomes obvious that this law was not simply a mirror of the legal institution of the levirate and its main concern of stabilizing the patrilineal family, but that its intention was to improve the legal and economic position of a widowed woman in a special case of undivided property of her deceased husband (Deut. 25.5),[45] a circumstance that made her especially vulnerable.[46] Normally the *levir* disposed of the usufruct of the property of his deceased brother when he fulfilled his levirate obligation. This was an economic compensation for his obligation to provide for the living of his sister-in-law and the children she got by the levirate marriage and who counted as offspring of her deceased husband. In the case of undivided property there was no such economic stimulus to fulfil the levirate obligation because the property of the deceased fell automatically to his brother's share. Normally the local courts had nothing to do with the institution of levirate marriage, but in this special case their help was needed. The legal symbolic act of removing the sandal in Deut. 25.9 did not only express the humiliation of the reluctant *levir* living on an undivided property, but also the loss of his title to his brother's property.[47] The local court was not entitled to enforce the fulfilment of a levirate obligation. But as a notary it could attest the

45. See LE 16; LH 165; MAL(A) 25; (B) related to MAL 2; 3; cf. M. de J. Ellis, 'The Division of Property at Tell Harmal', *JCS* 26 (1974), pp. 133-53; R. Westbrook, *Property and Family in Biblical Law* (JSOTSup, 113; Sheffield: JSOT Press, 1991), pp. 118-41.

46. See Otto, *Theologische Ethik*, p. 59; Pressler, *The View of Women*, p. 64.

47. See Å. Viberg, *Symbols of Law: A Contextual Analysis of Legal Symbolic Acts in the Old Testament* (ConBOT, 34; Lund: Almquist & Wiksell, 1992), pp. 145-64. For a discussion of Deut. 25.9 see my review of this book in *TLZ* 118 (1993), cols. 506-509. D.A. Leggett (*The Levirate and Goel Institution of the Old Testament* [Cherry Hill: Mack Publishing Company, 1974], pp. 55-62) correctly claimed that the ceremony of the removal of the sandal was primarily intended to protect the widow, not to humiliate the unwilling *levir*, and that 'this ceremony would then constitute a kind of release' (p. 57). But this does not mean that a kind of divorce was executed, but rather that the widow received the temporary usufruct of her husband's share of the undivided property. So there is no reason to interpret the ceremony of the removal of the sandal as a *rite of passage*, as was lately suggested by P.A. Kruger ('The Removal of the Sandal in Deuteronomy XXXV 9: "A Rite of Passage"?', *VT* 46 [1996], pp. 534-38). The inheritance-right of a widow is now confirmed by an ostracon published by P. Bordreuil *et al.* in *Semitica* 46 (1996), pp. 49-76.

temporary cancellation of the title of the obstinate *levir* to his brother's property. The widow received the usufruct of her husband's share as long as she lived or until she remarried. In case she married her brother-in-law or another man or died, the usufruct of the property remained with or fell back to her brother-in-law. Deuteronomy 25.5-10 was a provision that was concerned with the legal and economic protection of a woman living in an especially vulnerable position. As with the other family laws the woman was installed by this provision as a legal subject in her own right.[48] Accordingly she was the plaintiff in the local court and carried out the symbolic legal acts against the obstinate *levir*. In this case the widow defended her own right and not that of her deceased husband.

The family laws in the book of Deuteronomy had a progressive and protective attitude to the legal status of women. They were deeply concerned with the restriction of male predominance. This did by no means imply that these provisions really overcame the patrilineal and patriarchal pattern of Judean society, but they were intended to install women even in matters of family law as legal subjects vested with rights and titles of their own that were not derived from rights and decisions of men. In modern eyes this may be too little and by no means enough—but in antiquity and for women living at that time it meant very much. We do not even know how many and how much of these biblical laws were really executed in pre-canonical times. Obviously there was, as is indicated especially by the relation between MAL(A) 12-16 and Deut. 22.22-29*, a lot of juridical sophistication and legal theory in these laws.[49] But these provisions of the Deuteronomic family law paved the way for the modern emancipation of women already, in antiquity, and their authors deserve our respect.

What began with the pre-Deuteronomic collection of family laws, which became part of the Deuteronomic law, was continued by their Deuteronomic and Deuteronomistic context in this book.

48. For a different view see C. Pressler, *The View of Women*, p. 74.

49. See E. Otto, *Körperverletzungen in den Keilschriftrechten und im Alten Testament: Studien zum Rechtstransfer im Alten Orient* (AOAT, 226; Kevelaer: Butzon & Bercker; Neukirchen–Vluyn: Neukirchener Verlag, 1991), pp. 165-87; *idem*, 'Vom Rechtsbruch zur Sünde: Priesterliche Interpretationen des Rechts', *JBTh* 9 (1994), pp. 25-52. For the role of intellectuals in Greek society see C. Meier, *Athen: Ein Neubeginn der Weltgeschichte* (Berlin: Wolf Jobst Siedler, 1995), pp. 171-81.

The Status of Women in Deuteronomic and Deuteronomistic Theology

In Deut. 22.1-12*, 23.16-26* and 24.6-25.4* the Deuteronomic redactor joined provisions of social solidarity with other cultic and legal rules in an A–B pattern. The provisions of social solidarity formed the *cantus firmus* in this series of rules and for the whole Deuteronomic law. A great number of provisions of the pre-Deuteronomic family law coincided with concern about brotherly and sisterly solidarity and the protection of the status and rights of women. Those family laws that did not fit this redactional intention were interpreted as relating to the purity of the land and people of Israel by adding a *bi'artā-* or corresponding formula. This was the case with the prohibitions against adultery in Deut. 22.22b, 24b, whereas such a formula was not added to the laws of rape and seduction in Deut. 22.25, 27*, 28, 29, which served as protection for women. In Deut. 22.13-21 the same redactional logic dominated. The prohibition against adultery got a *bi'artā*-formula, but not the law against slandering a bride in Deut. 22.13-19, which protected her against a wrongful charge. The law of the rebellious son in Deut. 21.18-21, which had no concern with the protection of the underprivileged and the vulnerable, was closed by an expanded *bi'artā*-formula, but not the law of the levirate marriage in Deut. 25.5-10, which served the rights of the widowed women.[50] The logic of the Deuteronomic interpretation corresponded nearly completely with that of the pre-Deuteronomic collection of family law. Only the prohibition against the restoration of marriage in Deut. 24.1-4 was interpreted by the Deuteronomic author as a law against the pollution of the country. Only here he did not realize the socially progressive impact. But as for the provisions against slandering a bride, rape, seduction, and impoverishment of a widow he realized their progressive character as elements of his vision of a brotherly and sisterly society. In Deut. 22.26 he explicitly equates rape and murder in favour of women as victims.

With the help of the ethos of brotherly solidarity[51] the Deuteronomic

50. For the Deuteronomic redaction in Deut. 19-25 and its intentions see Otto, 'Soziale Verantwortung', pp. 134-38; *idem, Theologische Ethik*, pp. 186-92.

51. See L. Perlitt, '"Ein einzig Volk von Brüdern": Zur deuteronomischen Herkunft der biblischen Bezeichnung "Bruder"', in *idem, Deuteronomium-Studien* (FAT, 8; Tübingen: J.C.B. Mohr, 1994), pp. 50-73.

author reacted to the political and cultural upheavals of the Neo-Assyrian crisis in Judah during the seventh century BCE.[52] In Deut. 15.12 he defined this ethos as equally pertaining to men and women. The law of release in Deuteronomy 15 applies explicitly to men and women, which is different from Exod. 21.7, where a release of the maidservant is excluded. But this alone does not indicate a progressive attitude of the Deuteronomic author,[53] since Exod. 21.7-11 only deals with women purchased for concubinage.[54] Deut. 15.12 was not to replace the provision in Exod. 21.7-11, but that in Exod. 21.2-6, which had to be revised according to the hermeneutical key of cult centralization.[55] That women were explicitly included in the protection by release regulations was traditional in ancient Near Eastern release law.[56] In Exod. 21.2-6 women who were not bought for marriage were implicitly subject to this provision. Decisive for the attitude of the Deuteronomic author towards women is the fact that in Deut. 15.12 men and women were equally called *'aḥ*,[57] brother and sister, so that both of them were embraced by the concept of a brotherly and sisterly solidarity, which should be interpreted inclusively.

The inclusive character of this concept is supported by the Deuteronomic cultic law. In Deut. 14.26; 15.20 (cf. 26.11), 'you and your

52. See B. Halpern, 'Jerusalem and the Lineages in the Seventh Century BCE: Kinship and the Rise of Individual Moral Liability', in B. Halpern and D.W. Hobson (eds.), *Law and Ideology in Monarchic Israel* (JSOTSup, 124; Sheffield: JSOT Press, 1991), pp. 11-107; cf. also my review of this volume in *TLZ* 117 (1992), cols. 827-30.

53. For a different view see M. Weinfeld, *Deuteronomy and the Deuteronomic School* (Oxford: Clarendon Press, 1972), p. 282.

54. See G. Chirichigno, *Debt-Slavery in Israel and the Ancient Near East* (JSOTSup, 141; Sheffield: JSOT Press, 1993), pp. 280-82.

55. See E. Otto, review of *Debt Slavery in Israel and the Ancient Near East*, by C. Chirichigno, in *Bib* 76 (1995), pp. 254-261 (259-60).

56. See e.g. LH 117 (cf. I. Cardellini, *Die biblischen 'Sklaven'-Gesetze im Lichte des keilschriftlichen Sklavenrechts: Ein Beitrag zur Tradition, Überlieferung und Redaktion der alttestamentlichen Rechtstexte* [BBB, 55; Bonn: Peter Hanstein, 1981], pp. 79-81) and the Edict of Ammi-ṣaduqa §20 (cf. F.R. Kraus, *Königliche Verfügungen in altbabylonischer Zeit* (SDIO, 11; Leiden: E.J. Brill, 1984), pp. 264-78.

57. For the meaning of this term in Deut. 15 see J.M. Hamilton, *Social Justice and Deuteronomy: The Case of Deuteronomy 15* (SBLDS, 136; Atlanta: Scholars Press, 1992), pp. 34-40.

family' were addressed to take part in the sacrifices at the central sanctuary.[58] In Deut. 12.18, a Deuteronomic core provision,[59] these addressees were specified as 'you and your son and your daughter, your manservant, and your maidservant'. We find the same explanation of the house of the addressee in the Sabbath and feast of weeks provisions in Deut. 5.14; 16.11, 14. In Deut. 12.12 this list has been taken over by the Deuteronomistic redactor. The 'you' included also the wives, because it was impossible for them not to be allowed to take part in feasts and sacrifices, if their daughters and maidservants did so.[60] Since for the Deuteronomic author men and women were equally *'aḥîm* they were also equally addressed by 'you'. E. Reuter[61] supposes that the implicit address of women might indicate that they were entitled but not obliged to take part in cultic events at the central sanctuary because typical female reasons like pregnancy and childbirth could prevent them from leaving their homes. The liberation of women from cultic obligations could possibly have been intended by the Deuteronomic author—but one should not overstress such a consideration, because the Deuteronomic concept of an ideal society with equal cultic rights of men and women was of a theoretical more than a practical character. The cult at the central sanctuary was the place to realize symbolically the unity of Israel:

> In jeder der fröhlichen Mahlgemeinschaften im Zentralheiligtum ist Israel gewissermaßen in seinem Wesen dargestellt. Alle Glieder Israels sind beisammen, ohne daß es einen sozialen Unterschied gäbe. Alle sind voller Freude. Genau in diesem Augenblick sind sie 'vor Jahwe deinem Gott'. Nirgendwann und nirgendwo kann Israel dichter es selbst sein. (Each joyful feast-community at the central sanctuary represents to a certain degree Israel's identity. All the members of Israel are together

58. For these Deuteronomic provisions see Otto, *Theologische Ethik*, pp. 181-86.

59. See E. Reuter, *Kultzentralisation und Theologie von Dtn 12* (BBB, 87; Frankfurt/Main: Anton Hain Verlag, 1993), pp. 76-77; cf. the review of this book by N. Lohfink: 'Kultzentralisation und Deuteronomium: Zu einem Buch von Eleonore Reuter', *ZAR* 1 (1995), pp. 117-48.

60. See Braulik, 'Haben in Israel auch Frauen geopfert?', pp. 23-24; cf. *idem*, 'Die Ablehnung der Göttin Aschera', pp. 132-33; *idem*, 'Die Freude des Festes: Das Kultverständnis des Deuteronomiums—die älteste biblische Festtheorie', in *idem*, *Studien zur Theologie des Deuteronomiums* (SBAB, 2; Stuttgart: Katholisches Bibelwerk, 1988), pp. 161-218 (199-200).

61. See Reuter, *Kultzentralisation*, pp. 150-51.

> without any social distinction. All of them are full of joy. Precisely at this moment they are 'before Yahweh your God. Never and nowhere else could Israel be more itself.)[62]

The Deuteronomic author had to answer a basic ethical question: What was, for men, the benefit of an equal treatment of men and women? Men had to renounce their immediate advantage and had to be convinced that their immediate advantage was changed for a future greater advantage. The idea of a cultic community representing the unity of an ideal society without marginalized people was his answer. How progressive this concept was becomes obvious if one considers that not even Aristotle's concept of justice as equality extended beyond people of equal rank; it protected neither women nor slaves from discrimination.

Exilic and postexilic Deuteronomistic authors interpreted the Deuteronomic law as an ideal constitution for the New Israel after the exile.[63] Even more explicitly than in the pre-exilic Deuteronomic concept women received equal cultic rights. In Deut. 29.9-10 men and women took part in the Moab covenant (Deut. 29.9-14)[64] and, according to Deut. 31.12, in the assembly heard the Deuteronomic law every seventh year (Deut. 31.10-13):[65]

62. See N. Lohfink, 'Opferzentralisation, Säkularisierungstheorie und mimetische Theorie', in *idem, Studien III*, pp. 219-60 (243).

63. See E. Otto, 'Von der Programmschrift einer Rechtsreform zum Verfassungsentwurf des Neuen Israel: Die Stellung des Deuteronomiums in der Rechtsgeschichte Israels', in G. Braulik (ed.), *Bundesdokument und Gesetz: Studien zum Deuteronomium* (Herders Biblische Studien, 4; Freiburg: Herder, 1995), pp. 93-104; N. Lohfink, 'Das deuteronomische Gesetz in der Endgestalt: Entwurf einer Gesellschaft ohne marginale Gruppen', in *idem, Studien III*, pp. 205-218.

64. For the late-Deuteronomistic concept of the Moab covenant see D. Knapp, *Deuteronomium 4: Literarische Analyse und theologische Interpretation* (Göttinger Theologische Arbeiten, 35; Göttingen: Vandenhoeck & Ruprecht, 1987), pp. 141-56; E. Otto, 'Deuteronomium 4: Die Pentateuchredaktion im Deuteronomiumsrahmen', in T. Veijola (ed.), *Das Deuteronomium und seine Querbeziehungen* (SESJ, 62; Göttingen: Vandenhoeck & Ruprecht; Helsinki: Finnische Exegetische Gesellschaft, 1996), pp. 196-222 (199-204).

65. For the late-Deuteronomistic context of Deut. 31.10-13 see N. Lohfink, 'Zur Fabel von Dtn 31-32', in R. Bartelmus *et al.* (eds.), *Konsequente Traditionsgeschichte: Festschrift für Klaus Baltzer* (OBO, 126; Freiburg/Göttingen: Universitätsverlag/Vandenhoeck & Ruprecht, 1993), pp. 255-79.

> Assemble the people, men, women, and children and the stranger, and the sojourner within your towns, that they may hear and learn to fear YHWH, your God, and be watchful to do all the words of this law (Deut. 31.12).

In Deut. 21.10-14, the provision for a captive bride, which was part of the Deuteronomistic law of warfare in Deut. 20.1-20; 21.10-14; 23.10-15; 25.17-19,[66] but not of the Deuteronomic family law,[67] the Deuteronomistic redactor exemplified the obligation to legal solidarity with the weak and poor with the case of the foreign woman taken captive in a distant town (Deut. 20.14). Her personal dignity has to be secured and this includes freedom for marriage and protection from sexual exploitation.[68] This provision surely did not present the right opportunity to overthrow the patriarchal features of society, since it was intended to protect the most vulnerable women. But compared with the average and usual treatment of captive women in antiquity this provision in Deut. 21.10-14 was a moral revolution on the long road towards equal dignity and rights of men and women. The Deuteronomic and Deuteronomistic concepts of an ideal society were the cradle for the modern world—not only for its market economy,[69] but also for the modern humanism of human rights, including equal rights of men and women. Also in this respect the book of Deuteronomy was the gospel of the modern world.[70] But it would be ahistorical to expect that in the book of Deuteronomy the allocation of values by status relations was overthrown. Deuteronomy became the 'gospel' of the modern world, but perforce it was not this modern world itself. Only when modern

66. See Otto, *Theologische Ethik*, pp. 198-201.

67. So Pressler, *The View of Women*, pp. 9-15.

68. There are some good reasons for G. Braulik ('Das Deuteronomium und die Menschenrechte', in *idem, Studien*, pp. 301-323 [302]) to rank Deut. 21.10-14 among these Deuteronomic laws, which have an equivalent in modern declarations of human rights.

69. See M. Weber, *Ancient Judaism* (New York: Free Press; London: Collier–Macmillan, 1952). B.N. Nelson, *The Idea of Usury: From Tribal Brotherhood to Universal Otherhood* (Princeton, NJ: Princeton University Press, 1949).

70. See E. Otto, 'Gerechtigkeit und Erbarmen im Recht des Alten Testaments und seiner christlichen Rezeption', in *idem, Kontinuum und Proprium*, pp. 342-57; *idem*, '"Um Gerechtigkeit im Land sichtbar werden zu lassen": Zur Vermittlung von Recht und Gerechtigkeit im Alten Orient, in der Hebräischen Bibel und in der Moderne', in J. Mehlhausen (ed.), *Recht—Moral—Gerechtigkeit* (Gütersloh: Kaiser/Gütersloher Verlagshaus, 1998), forthcoming.

constitutional law took the concept of 'human rights' as its basis did the principle of equality came to dominate the law. But if equality is a tenet of all modern concepts of law, that all humans are to be treated alike, then a decisive step into this direction was made by the Deuteronomistic concept of a society without marginalized people.[71] The idea that individuals could change their social surroundings was not a fruit of the Renaissance but already of the Hebrew Bible. The Deuteronomic and Deuteronomistic authors provide us with a brilliant example of this idea in antiquity.

71. For a valid value judgment of historical phenomena of the Bible one should consider the whole cultural situation and avoid working with modern categories and expectations which tend to be disappointed when dealing with the legal phenomena of antiquity. Modifying Karl Barth, who said 'kritischer müssen sie sein, die Historisch-Kritischen', one could say that perforce exegetes should be more aware of the historical dimension when dealing with such precarious and controversial subjects as the status of women in the book of Deuteronomy. Taking this into account one can notice that the weights in the scale of biblical justice are less false than some suppose.

WIVES AND DAUGHTERS, BOND AND FREE: VIEWS OF WOMEN IN THE SLAVE LAWS OF EXODUS 21.2-11*

Carolyn Pressler

1. *Introduction*

The Book of the Covenant contains two ancient laws designed to protect freeborn persons forced into servitude by debt or poverty (Exod. 21.2-6, 7-11).[1] These laws offer sharply contrasting protections for a Hebrew slave and for a daughter sold into bondage. The Hebrew slave (*'ebed 'ibrî*) is to be released at the end of six years (21.2); the enslaved daughter does not go free (21.7). Instead, four subcases of the law of the enslaved daughter seek to protect her by setting forth the master's obligations toward her if he has purchased her as a concubine for himself (21.8, 10, 11) or his son (21.9). Subcases of the law of the Hebrew slave adjudicate competing claims of the slave and his master to the released slave's wife (21.3, 4), and offer the slave the possibility of choosing to remain in bondage. The contrast between the release of the Hebrew slave and the non-release of the enslaved daughter in the main cases and the delineation of male claims over and obligations

* I am indebted to Jeff Rogers for first calling my attention to the overly general ways in which the role of the slavewoman in Exod. 21.2-11 has been interpreted.

1. The two laws are found at the beginning of the *mišpāṭîm*, a series of case laws (Exod. 21.2–22.16) recognized as the oldest legal collection in the Hebrew Bible. Beyond acknowledging that the *mišpāṭîm* predate the Deuteronomic or priestly collections there is little agreement on when these laws emerged, however. The slave laws of Exod 21.2-11 presuppose a certain amount of social stratification; some freeborn persons are forced by poverty or insolvency to sell themselves or their dependents, while others have enough wealth to acquire slaves through purchase or debt-foreclosure or at least have the capacity to feed and clothe additional dependents. This may suggest that the slave laws stem from the more stratified monarchical period rather than pre-monarchical times. We lack the evidence to date the laws with certainty or precision.

towards females in the subcases invite investigation into the assumptions and ideals about women implicit in these laws.

Indeed, the contrast between the treatment of the *'ebed 'ibrî* and daughter sold as an *'āmâ* has been the focus of a fair amount of discussion about women's status(es) in pentateuchal law. Section 2 of this essay briefly examines previous discussions of women and the slave laws. Section 3 considers the ancient Near Eastern background of the laws. Section 4 establishes my position on key exegetical issues.

'Women' in the Book of the Covenant is not a homogeneous category. Rather, the texts depict women with differing roles and statuses determined only partly by their gender. Exodus 21.2-11 explicitly refers to women in the roles of wife, daughter, slave wife of a free man and slave wife of a bondsman. Section 5 investigates the views of women in the roles explicitly named.

An assessment of the understanding of gender underlying these laws depends in part on assessing the contrast between the release of the bondsman in v. 2 and the non-release of the enslaved daughter in v. 7. That is, were the laws intended to exclude all Hebrew bondswomen from the release mandated for all Hebrew bondsmen or would the law of the *'ebed 'ibrî* have applied to some female slaves? Section 6 of this paper asks whether the terms 'master', 'father', and 'bondsman' implicitly include some mistresses, mothers, and bondswomen.

The roles and statuses of women explicitly or implicitly found in these laws are diverse, reflecting not only gender but also generation, ethnicity, and class (free, freeborn slave or slave). I conclude with an effort to identify what among these various factors is specifically determined by the woman's gender.

A caveat is in order. This essay focuses on assumptions and ideals about women expressed by the laws, not on legal practice. There is real doubt about whether the law of release was ever enforced; certainly it was not consistently observed (see Jer. 34.14). The relationship of Pentateuchal law to the lived experience of ancient Israelite women is highly problematic.

2. *Previous Discussion of Women and the Slave Laws*

The contrast between the law of release (Exod. 21.2) and the exclusion of the enslaved daughter from that release (Exod. 21.7), and the contrast between the exclusion of the enslaved daughter in Exodus and the pointed inclusion of the *'āmâ* in the Deuteronomic version of the law of release (Deut. 15.12-18) has generated a good deal of discussion about the status of women presupposed by the laws. A number of scholars, especially those of an earlier generation, have used these laws to make claims about ancient Israelite women's legal status that are both overly sweeping and overly negative. Martin Noth, for example, suggests that the distinction between the treatment of the Hebrew slave and that of the enslaved daughter 'may rest on the view that only the man is a person, while the woman on the other hand is a possession'.[2] Gerhard von Rad believes that Exod. 21.2 has to do with enslavement for debts incurred by landowners. He assumes that in the early period of Israel's history women could not own property, and so could not be forced into debt slavery.[3] Anthony Phillips interprets the purpose of the law of release as restoring 'to a member of Israel his rightful place under the law'. Since, in Phillips's view, women were not full members of the covenant community and hence not subject to the law at the time the covenant code came into being, they were not included in the stipulated release.[4]

A majority of more recent scholars rightly believe that the bondswoman of Exod. 21.7 is excepted from release because she has been sold for sexual and reproductive purposes.[5] The most recent discussions of women and the slave laws argue that Exod. 21.7 has to do only with daughters sold as wives for their masters, and thus constitutes a very narrow exception to the law of release. Gregory Chirichigno[6] and Joe M. Sprinkle believe the laws reflect a very positive attitude toward women. According to Sprinkle, Exod. 21.7-11 has to do with only 'one kind of female servitude. Where sexual favors are not involved a bondswoman would go free at the same time as a

2. Martin Noth, *Exodus: A Commentary* (trans. J.S. Bowden; OTL; Philadelphia: Westminster Press, 1962), p. 177. Noth does acknowledge that the protections in vv. 8-11 already contradict the view that women are chattels.

3. Gerhard von Rad, *Deuteronomy: A Commentary* (trans. Dorothea Barton; OTL; Philadelphia: Westminster Press, 1966), p. 107.

4. Anthony Phillips, 'The Law of Slavery: Exodus 21.2-11', *JSOT* 30 (1984), pp. 51-66 (61).

5. See, for example, Dale Patrick, *Old Testament Law* (Atlanta: John Knox Press, 1985), p. 71.

6. Gregory Chirichigno, *Debt-Slavery in Israel and the Ancient Near East* (JSOTSup, 141; Sheffield: JSOT Press, 1993), pp. 244-55.

bondsman...'[7] Chirichigno and Sprinkle each assert that the law of the enslaved daughter was intended to provide the girl with the status of a free wife. Chirichigno writes 'this law should be understood as an attempt to guarantee to a girl who is sold as a wife those rights that were normally afforded to daughters who were married in the customary manner'.[8]

My assessment of the views of women found in the slave law is neither as negative as that of earlier scholars, nor as positive as the more recent studies by Chirichigno and Sprinkle. It is also less generalized. Women in different roles were assumed to have differing statuses only partly determined by their gender. Thus the appropriate question is not 'how do these laws view women'? but 'how do the laws treat women in the roles of "wife", "daughter", "widow", and so forth'?

3. *Background to Exodus 21.2-11*

Biblical texts attest that freeborn persons in Israel could be forced into slavery under varying circumstances. A creditor could seize a defaulting debtor or the debtor's dependents and either exploit their labor or sell them (2 Kgs. 4.1; Amos 8.6; 2.6; Isa.. 50.1; Neh. 5.5).[9] Destitution

7. Joe M. Sprinkle, *The Book of the Covenant: A Literary Approach* (JSOTSup, 174; Sheffield: JSOT Press, 1994), p. 51. Chirichigno and Sprinkle develop more fully a position already taken by U. Cassuto (*A Commentary on the Book of Exodus* [trans. Israel Abrahams; Jerusalem: Magnes Press, 1967], pp. 266-68). Cassuto challenges the common assumption that *'ebed 'ibrî* automatically excludes women, asserting that bondswomen were implicitly included in the law of release (v. 2) and that the exception of v. 7 was 'enacted for the benefit of the girl...who...is a legal wife in the full sense of the term'.

8. Chirichigno, *Debt-Slavery*, p. 251. Timothy John Turnbam ('Male and Female Slaves in the Sabbath Year Laws of Exodus 21.1-11', in Kent Harold Richards (ed.), *SBL Seminar Papers 1987* [Atlanta: Scholars Press, 1987], pp. 545-49) similarly argues that Exod. 21.7-11 is intended to guarantee the daughter the 'high status' of wife or to let her go free. Turnbam's position differs from those of Chirichigno and Sprinkle, in that he does not agree that many daughters would have been sold for general labor and thus would have been included in the release of v. 2.

9. The enslavement of a convicted thief who is unable to make restitution (Exod. 22.2) may be considered a form of debt-slavery. Poverty or insolvency could also force small landowners to give over themselves and their lands as serfs or sharecroppers (Gen. 47.13-19). Because Exod. 21.2-6 does not refer to land, it probably does not pertain to those forced to sharecrop.

could force a person to give himself or herself into slavery in order to survive (Deut. 28.68). Exodus 21.2-6 represents efforts to prevent such bondage from being permanent; Exod. 21.7-11 attempts to protect the enslaved daughter whose bondage is permanent.[10]

The problem of freeborn persons being forced into servitude by debt or poverty was common throughout the ancient Near East. Two sets of cuneiform texts provide partial parallels to the law of the Hebrew slave; scholars argue over which provides the closest analogy to the Exodus law. In my opinion, the comparative materials suggest attitudes and practices towards bondswomen that may shed light on Exod. 21.2-11, but neither set of cuneiform documents resembles the biblical laws so closely that one may simply read elements from the cuneiform materials into the biblical laws.

Documents from Nuzi record the voluntary self-sale of the *Ḫabiru*, a class of landless refugees, in exchange for the means of survival. Shalom Paul and others have understood Exod. 21.2-6 as 'a later reflex' of the *Ḫabiru* documents.[11]

The centerpiece of the argument of those who relate Exod. 21.2-6 to the Nuzi documents is the connection that they draw between *Ḫabiru* and 'Hebrew'. After a century of debate, the relationship of 'Hebrew' and *Ḫabiru* is still unresolved. Perhaps the most persuasive discussion of the problem is that of Nadav Na'aman. Noting that the Bible depicts bands of marginalized people who were uprooted from their tribes and were later reintegrated into Israelite society, he posits that *Ḫabiru*, originally a sociological term for landless migrants, came to be applied

10. Both laws also seek to protect the master's interests. The law of release affirms the master's property rights over the slavewoman with whom he provided his bondsman as well as over any children they might have had. The law of the enslaved daughter protects the master whose purpose in purchasing her would have been thwarted by her release.

11. Shalom Paul, *Studies in the Book of the Covenant in the Light of Cuneiform and Biblical Law* (Leiden: E.J. Brill, 1970), p. 46. See also Niels Lemche, ' "The Hebrew Slave": Comments on the Slave Law Ex xxi 2-11', *VT* 25 (1975), pp. 129-44. Paul documents parallels between the Nuzi documents and Exod. 21.2-6. Like the Exodus law, the *Ḫabiru* materials indicate that a man's family followed him into bondage and affirm the master's claims to ownership of the woman should he provide his unmarried *Ḫabiru* servant with a wife. In my opinion, however, the parallels do not outweigh the fact that the *Ḫabiru* documents do not include the main stipulation of the Exodus law, that is, a limitation to the period of time that the slave must serve.

to such bands. Na'aman calls the term a 'social ethnonym', that is, a term with both social and ethnic connotations. He rightly notes that the biblical term 'Hebrew' is used to refer to Israelites in exceptional and precarious situations, such as migrants or slaves.[12] Thus, it seems unlikely that one may simply equate *Ḫabiru* and 'Hebrew', or that one may assume that Exod. 21.2-6 is a 'later reflex' of the *Ḫabiru* texts. Moreover, the main thrust of the law of the Hebrew slave is to limit the amount of time that the slave must serve the master. The *Ḫabiru* documents include no such time limits. This fundamental difference outweighs the similarities between the *Ḫabiru* documents and the biblical slave laws.

Old Babylonian texts offer closer parallels to the law of release. Exodus 21.2 stands in the same ancient Near Eastern legal tradition as the Code of Hammurabi (LH) and the Edict of Ammiṣaduqa (*ANET*, p. 528), which attempt to limit the period of bondage of a person enslaved because of debt. LH 117 (Roth, *Law Collections*, p. 103) mandates that the wife, son, or daughter sold into slavery by a defaulting debtor shall be freed after a period of three years. The Edict of Ammiṣaduqa emancipates any person who has sold himself or been sold into slavery because of debt.

The Old Babylonian documents are not so similar to Exod. 21.2-6, however, that one may assume that they concern precisely the same situation. The Exodus law uses the terminology 'slave'; LH 117 and the Edict of Ammiṣaduqa do not. The Old Babylonian materials explicitly state that the case concerns debt slavery; Exod. 21.2 does not. Exodus 21.3, 4 presupposes that a wife automatically follows her husband into slavery; the cuneiform texts do not. Rather, LH 117 envisions the debtor pledging or selling some particular dependent to avoid being seized for debt.

Scholars have used Nuzi or Old Babylonian texts to determine the possible applicability of the law of release to certain bondswomen. For example, the fact that three *Ḫabiru* documents recording the sale of women use prohibitively harsh penalty clauses has led some to conclude that in Nuzi *Ḫabiru* women generally could not gain manumission. Taking the Exodus laws as a 'later reflex' of the *Ḫabiru* documents, they cite the non-release of *Ḫabiru* women as a parallel to the

12. Nadav Na'aman, 'Ḫabiru and Hebrews: The Transfer of a Social Term to the Literary Sphere', *JNES* 45 (1986), pp. 271-88. For bibliography, see, p. 271 n. 1.

non-release of bondswomen in the Exodus law.[13] In contrast, Gregory Chirichigno uses LH 117 (Roth, *Law Collections*, p. 103), which seeks to set a limit on how long a man's wife, son or daughter whose husband or father has sold them must stay in bondage to argue that the release of Exod. 21.2 pertains specifically to daughters and sons. In his view, the exception of Exod. 21.7 applies only to a narrowly defined group of daughters, those destined to become wives of their master or his son.[14]

Neither set of documents is sufficiently similar to the biblical passage to justify limiting the biblical case to the situations in Nuzi or in Babylon. Given the differences between the biblical slave laws and the cuneiform texts, one may not simply equate the statuses of *Ḫabiru* women in Nuzi or pledged dependents in Babylon with the statuses of women in Exod. 21.2-11.

The law of the Hebrew slave is illuminated but not defined by the *Ḫabiru* documents from Nuzi, and by edicts and laws from Old Babylonia. Similarly, the law of the enslaved daughter is illuminated but not defined by 'daughter and daughter-in-law' adoption contracts from Nuzi. These contracts document the transfer of authority over girls in exchange for payment or cancellation of debt; the 'adopting' party gains the right to the girl's bridewealth. The contracts include certain conditions; in some cases the girl may be married to one of the adopter's sons or to any other free man; in some cases she may be married to a slave or (should the first slave die or be manumitted) a series of slaves; in some cases she may be prostituted. The daughter and daughter-in-law tablets amount to the conditional sale of young

13. See, for example, Lemche, 'The Hebrew Slave', p. 139. In fact, it is far from certain that enslaved *Ḫabiru* women in Nuzi could not attain freedom. Prohibitively harsh penalties found in a document involving the self-sale of a male *Ḫabiru* suggests that the possibility of release was not tied to gender. Moshe Greenberg (*The Ḫap/biru* [AOS, 39; New Haven: American Oriental Society, 1955], p. 66) suggests that the harsh penalties in the *Ḫabiru* self-sale documents apply to those of either sex who leave before the death of their master, while the option of providing a substitute and leaving was available only after the master died. Moreover, at least two Nuzi texts refer to bondswomen who have been released from bondage 'because of a liberation'. (Cited by N.P. Lemche, 'ANDURARUM AND MISARUM: Comments on the Problem of the Social Edicts and Their Application in the Ancient Near East', *JNES* 38 [1979], p.19 n. 55.) Whether or not *Ḫabiru* women of Nuzi could attain release, however, their status cannot be directly imputed to Hebrew bondswomen.

14. Chirichigno, *Debt-Slavery*, pp. 244-46.

girls for sexual and reproductive purposes.[15] There are differences between the Nuzi contracts and the biblical law. The Nuzi documents stress the adopter's right to the girl's bridewealth; the subcases of the biblical law focus on situations where the girl is to be kept within the family. The cuneiform tablets speak of giving daughters or sisters into adoption; presumably this legal fiction was necessary because the outright sale of girls was illegal in Nuzi. The biblical law explicitly refers to the exchange as a sale. We cannot simply read elements from these contracts into the biblical law. We can use them to shed light on the biblical case in that they suggest the range of purposes for which daughters might be sold and the range of contractual provisions and protections that might be imposed.

4. *Exegesis*

Exodus 21.2

The main issue in scholarly discussion of Exod. 21.2 has been the identity of the *'ebed 'ibrî*, the Hebrew slave. The debate has focused on whether the term *'ibrî* ought to be identified with the *Ḫabiru* and so taken as a sociological term referring to a class of landless refugees or whether by the time that the *mišpāṭîm* were collected, the term had already come to be used as a gentilic. As noted above, I find the latter position most compelling; with a majority of commentators, I understand *'ibrî* as referring to economically marginalized Israelites.

The identity of the *'ebed 'ibrî* is pertinent to an investigation of the views of women found in Exod. 21.2-11. For the purpose of this discussion, however, the most important question about the identity of the Hebrew slave is not whether the term refers to Israelites, non-Israelites, or a mixture of both, but whether the term refers exclusively to males. That question will be taken up in section 6 of this paper.

Exodus 21.3-6

The four subcases in the law of the Hebrew slave are fairly straightforward. Verses 3-4 adjudicate the competing claims of the released

15. I. Mendelsohn ('The Conditional Sale into Slavery of Free-born Daughters in Nuzi and the Law of Ex. 21.7-11', *JAOS* 55 [1935], pp. 190-95) first demonstrated the parallels between Exod. 21.7-11 and the Nuzi 'daughter and daughter-in-law' contracts. The parallels have been further discussed by Shalom Paul, who notes that a similar Assyrian contract has been found in which a young woman voluntarily gives herself to be adopted (Paul, *Studies*, p. 55).

slave and his master over the slave's wife and children. If the slave was married prior to his enslavement, his dependents are released with him. If his master provided him with a wife, she and the children remain the master's property. Verses 5-6 provide a way for the slave to choose to remain in bondage. The option to remain enslaved may in part reflect the difficulty that a released slave would have making a living apart from the master's house. The law clearly considers the slave's desire to remain with his wife and children a primary motive for choosing perpetual servitude, however. A waw links the subcase permitting the choice of continued slavery to the previous subcase, which recognizes the master's claims over the woman he had provided. Verse 5 explicitly names the bondsman's love of master, wife and children as his reason for remaining enslaved.

Exodus 21.7

Verses 7-11 except a daughter sold as a bondswoman from the release of v. 2. The contrast between v. 2 and v. 7 is explicit: 'She shall not go out as the slaves do'.[16]

The question at hand is who is included in the exception. The meaning of 'daughter' is clear. The daughter is a minor girl who is unbetrothed. If she were betrothed, her father would not have the right to sell her, at least, not without breaching the marriage contract. Exodus 21.7 applies not to all freeborn bondswomen, but to unbetrothed girls sold into bondage.

We may assume that an unbetrothed girl's primary economic value is her sexual and reproductive capacity, and that she typically would be purchased for sexual use and for breeding children, as well as for general labor. A major concern of biblical and cuneiform legal texts having to do with unbetrothed daughters is the economic value of their

16. As Turnbam ('Male and Female Slaves', pp. 545-49), Chirichigno (*Debt-Slavery*, pp. 196-99), and Sprinkle (*The Book of the Covenant*, pp. 51-54) demonstrate, the contrast was carefully crafted. The structure of the laws stresses that they are interrelated; vv. 7-11 are to be read in light of vv. 2-6. Each law consists of a main case and four subcases; the subcases of each law revolve around different marital situations. The language of v. 2 and v. 7 sharply contrasts the slave, who 'shall go out' and the enslaved daughter who 'shall not go out'. Moreover, v. 6 provides the slave with the opportunity to remain with his master, who presumably is obligated to support the slave. The choice is the slave's. Verses 10-11 allow the enslaved daughter to go free if her master withholds provisions from her. The choice is the master's.

sexuality. This is seen in Exod. 22.15, 16 (Heb) and Deut. 22.28, 29, which require a man who seduces or rapes an unbetrothed girl to pay her father, and in Middle Assyrian Law (MAL) 48, which deals with whether a creditor can marry off a girl he holds as a pledge. It is especially obvious in the Nuzi 'daughter and daughter-in-law' contracts that specify the sum the 'adopter' pays in exchange for a claim to the girl's bridewealth, or, in the case of prostitution, her fees.[17]

The meaning of 'daughter' is clear, as are the implications of the term for the purpose of the sale. What is less certain is how generally or specifically to interpret the case. Does the exception to the law of release set out in v. 7 apply to any daughter sold into slavery, or only to a daughter who is sold conditionally as the slave wife of the master or his son? The answer to this question depends upon two further questions. First, is the main case of a law restricted to or defined by its subcases, and second, how is the term *'āmâ* to be understood?

The subcases in Exod. 21.8-11 envision situations where the enslaved girl is assigned either to the master or to his son for concubinage.[18] Several commentators assume that the exception in v. 7 is restricted to the situations delineated in the subcases. Chirichigno, for example, holds that a father could sell his daughter as a general household slave. In that case, however, he argues that the daughter would go free at the end of six years. Only the daughter purchased as a wife for the master or his son is excepted from release.[19] Others assume that the law prohibits the sale of freeborn daughters except for the purpose of marriage to a free man.[20]

The subcases of laws elsewhere in the *mišpāṭîm* and in the cuneiform codes are not comprehensive; they do not exhaust all the possibilities suggested by the main case. The subcases of the law of homicide (Exod. 21.12-14), for example, deal with some but not all of the ramifications of the main case. They treat unintentional but not unpremeditated instances of homicide; they mandate what to do if a deliberate murderer claims sanctuary, but not what to do with the unintentional

17. That young girls were valued primarily for their sexuality is also apparent in biblical references to virgins taken as booty in war (Num. 31.17, 18; Judg. 5.30, etc.)

18. The differences between a slave wife (or, more accurately, an enslaved concubine) and a primary wife are considered below, p. 164 n. 42.

19. Chirichigno, *Debt Slavery*, pp. 253-54.

20. See Turnbam 'Male and Female Slaves'.

killer who legitimately flees to the sanctuary. The law of the seduced virgin for whom the brideprice has not been paid does not address the case of a virgin who is betrothed. It states that in the event that the father does not choose for his daughter to marry her seducer the seducer must still pay the bridewealth, but it does not say what the father should do with the girl.[21]

Chirichigno rightly argues that the selection of the subcases in Exod. 21.2-6 and Exod. 21.7-11 do not exhaust the possible situations covered by the main cases. Rather, the subcases reflect the literary structure of the two laws, which carefully juxtaposes the marital rights and release of the bondsman with that of the enslaved daughter.[22] Situations in which the main cases would apply but which do not relate to the question of marital rights are not discussed by these laws.

The second question related to the scope of the exception in v. 7 is the meaning of the word *'āmâ* as it is used in this context. Several scholars hold that *'āmâ* refers specifically to the slave wife of a free man.[23] Verse 7 would then pertain only to cases where the girl becomes a wife or concubine within the master's family.

A. Jepsen wrote the study that first brought the question of the meaning of *'āmâ* to scholars' attention. In his opinion, *'āmâ* refers to an 'unfree woman as well as the second wife of a free man and also an unfree woman of an unfree man, a slave'.[24] In relationship to the use of the term in legal materials, Jepsen's conclusions are subject to challenge. Elsewhere in the Book of the Covenant, *'āmâ* is used in the general sense of 'bondswoman' (Exod. 21.20-21, 26-27, 32; 23.12). In fact,

21. The adultery laws of Deut. 22.22-29 and of the cuneiform codes provide particularly clear examples of laws in which the subcases do not exhaust the possibilities suggested by the main case. The main case in Deuteronomy (v. 22) rules that the sentence for adultery between a man and a consenting married woman is death for both parties. The Deuteronomic subcases address sex between a man and a consenting betrothed girl, the rape of a betrothed girl, and sex between a man and an unbetrothed virgin. They do not address the rape of a married woman and, unlike comparable laws in the cuneiform codes, they do not consider the case of a man who was unaware that the woman who seduced him was married. The cuneiform codes, on the other hand, omit the case of a betrothed girl who consents to sex with someone besides her betrothed husband.

22. Chirichigno, *Debt-Slavery*, p. 246.

23. See, e.g., Brevard Childs, *Exodus: A Commentary* (OTL; Philadelphia: Westminster Press, 1974), p. 469.

24. A. Jepsen, 'Amah und Schiphchah', *VT* 8 (1958), pp. 293-97.

with one exception (Lev. 19.20), *'āmâ* is the word used for 'bondswoman' in all Pentatuechal laws; in none of the other laws does the term refer to a slave wife. It seems likely that *'āmâ*, used in the context of law, is a general term meaning 'bondswoman'.

An unbetrothed female was likely to have been purchased for sexual use and to get heirs or to increase one's possession of slaves. It seems overly narrow, however, to assume that a master could purchase a daughter only if he were going to marry her himself or were going to give her to his son. The Nuzi materials suggest the range of sexual purposes for which a master might acquire a nubile girl. Nothing in Exod. 21.7-11 rules out the possibility that the master could give the girl to a slave or marry her to another man in order to keep her bridewealth. The exception mandated in v. 7 to the law of release most likely applies to any daughter sold into slavery. It was enacted because unbetrothed girls would usually have been purchased for sexual and reproductive purposes; the purpose of the sale would have been frustrated if the girl were later released. The exception would have applied to girls purchased to be the concubines of slaves, or to be given in marriage or concubinage to someone outside of the household.[25]

Exodus 21.8-11

The subcases of the law of the enslaved daughter provide protections for those girls who are purchased to be the master or son's concubine. Verse 8 prohibits a man who has purchased a freeborn girl to be his slave wife from selling her.[26] If, once she is old enough to be a concubine, he finds he dislikes her, he has violated the terms of the purchase and must allow her kinfolk to buy her back.[27]

25. The possibility that a daughter might have been sold into prostitution cannot be ruled out. The Nuzi adoption contracts attest to parents selling their daughters to be used as prostitutes. The priestly prohibition against prostituting one's daughter (Lev. 19.29) suggests that such practices were found in Israel.

26. The *qere*, *lô y*ᵉ*'ādāh*, 'has appointed her for himself' found in the LXX, Vg., *Targ. Onq.*, and several Hebrew MSS, is to be preferred to the *kethib* of the MT, *lô' y*ᵉ*'ādāh*, 'not appointed her', because the *qere* offers the better parallel to v. 9, 'appoints her for his son', and because the verb *y'd* makes better sense with a dative.

27. With a number of commentators, I interpret the phrase *'am nokrî* to mean anyone outside the enslaved daughter's extended family or clan. Within the context of the law, selling the girl to an *'am nokrî* is contrasted with allowing her to be redeemed, presumably by her father or his kindred (cf. Lev. 25.47-49), and refers to

Verse 9 rules that if the master has purchased the girl as a slave wife for his son, he must accord her the customary rights of a daughter (*k^e^mišpaṭ-habbānôt*). Paul interprets the phrase 'to treat *k^e^mišpaṭ-habbānôt*' as a technical phrase meaning 'to treat as a free(-born) woman'. His widely followed argument is based on three supposedly analogous cuneiform texts. In the two texts where the word 'daughter' clearly means 'citizen', however, it is found in construct with either the word 'city', or the name of a city. These cannot be used to determine the meaning of the absolute form of the noun 'daughters' in Exod. 21.9. Paul's third cuneiform text concerns a man adopting a girl who agrees to 'treat her as his own daughter, an Assyrian'. This text does provide an analogy to the phrase in v. 9. It seems likely, however, that in this latter text the phrase 'his own daughter' is intended literally; the girl must be treated as a member of the family.[28] Actually, the closest parallel to *mišpaṭ-habbānôt* is found in Deut. 21.17, which accords *mišpaṭ-habb^e^kōrâ*, 'the customary rights of the firstborn', to the chronologically oldest son. Both phrases refer to rights that accrue to a specific role within the family. Paul's third text suggests what the rights of a daughter might be. The adopting father promises that 'he will not ill-treat (her) nor prostitute (her); he must treat her as his own daughter'.[29]

Verses 1-11 require the master to continue to provide his slave wife with the provisions that she needs, even if he chooses to take another wife or concubine. If he fails to maintain her provisions, he must allow her to go free.[30] Unfortunately, it is not possible to determine exactly

anyone except those who might redeem her. The term *'am* meaning is found in the phrase 'gathered to his/her kin', Gen. 25.8, 17; 35.29; 49.33. (Nahum Sarna, *Exodus: The JPS Torah Commentary* [Philadelphia: The Jewish Publication Society, 1991], pp. 121 and 252 n. 23 notes that it is also preserved in several theophoric names.) For *nokrî* used to refer specifically to one outside of the family, see Job 19.15; Ps. 69.9; and Gen. 31.15; cf. also Prov. 5.10, 20; 27.2.

28. Paul, *Studies* p. 55. The meaning of *Aš-šu-ra-ia-e*, 'Assyrian', is debated; in the Middle Assyrian Laws it appears to refer to a member of the lower class, rather than to any citizen of Assyria.

29. Paul, *Studies*, p. 55.

30. Some commentators interpret v. 11, 'if he fails to do these three things for her, she shall go out free...' as a reference to the three protections set forth in vv. 8-10, rather than to the three provisions listed in v. 10. This is possible. Verses 10 and 11 are linked by a waw, however, which suggests that the 'three things' in v. 11 refer to v. 10. Moreover, v. 10 very clearly identifies three items that the master must provide the slave wife. Identifying 'three things' in the subcases is less

what the master must continue to provide his slave wife. The first two items are clear; he must continue to give her food and clothing. The third item, *'ōnātāh*, is a *hapax legomenon*. Tradition has interpreted the word to mean 'conjugal rights'. Paul has built an impressive case for translating the word 'oil' or 'ointment', however. Numerous cuneiform texts list three provisions that one party is required to supply another; the list consistently includes food, clothing, and oil. According to Paul, this 'formulaic triad' epitomized 'the necessities of life' in Mesopotamia.[31] Without philological evidence, however, the meaning of the term remains uncertain. One can say that the purpose of vv. 10-11 was to ensure that the slave wife was provided with basic necessities or else set free. As in v. 8, the master is explicitly prohibited from selling a woman whom he has purchased for a marriage-like relationship.

5. *Ideals and Assumptions about Women in Exodus 21.2-11*

Both slave laws are unquestionably written from an androcentric perspective. The presumed audience is male. Verse 2 is addressed to the master. 'when you [2 m.s.] acquire a Hebrew slave...' The laws seek to regulate the master's behavior. Female subjects are found only in v. 3b, which rules that a wife brought into bondage with the Hebrew slave 'shall go out' with him, and v. 11b, which allows a slave wife deprived of the necessities of life to 'go out free'. Women are referred to in these texts as objects of men's claims and obligations (vv. 3-4, 8-10). Indeed, here as elsewhere in Pentateuchal law, the legal status of a woman is understood first of all in terms of male claims and obligations.[32] Her specific status varies, depending in large measure on her role within (or outside) of the male-headed family. In this section, I will look at the assumptions and ideals about women in their various familial roles found in Exodus 21.2-11.

clear. Indeed, the commentators who interpret v. 11 as referring to vv. 8-10 as a whole do not agree on what 'three things' those verses require.

31. Paul, *Studies*, pp. 56-61, especially p. 59.

32. The exception is the mother, whose status is defined largely in terms of her authority over her offspring. For further discussion of the status of mother, wife and daughter implicit in other Pentateuchal laws, see my *The View of Women Found in the Deuteronomic Family Laws* (BZAW, 216; Berlin: W. de Gruyter, 1993), pp. 79-94.

Wife

The law of the Hebrew slave assumes that the wife of a free man has no independent legal status. Verse 3 rules that if a man is married when he is enslaved, his wife is released when he is released. The rule does not explicitly indicate that the wife has been enslaved with him; it assumes that if her freeborn husband is forced into bondage, she is enslaved with him.

The laws assume that a woman did not remain free when her husband was enslaved. Do they allow her to be enslaved if he remains free? The cuneiform codes allow a man to sell his wife in order to avoid being enslaved himself. LH 117 (Roth, *Law Collections*, p. 103) rules that when a defaulting debtor sells his wife she should be freed after a period of three years. MAL A.32 (Roth, *Law Collections*, p. 165) states that a girl is liable for her husband's debts and crimes as soon as he has paid the bridewealth to her father. In contrast, the law of the enslaved daughter implies that an Israelite husband was not to sell his wife into slavery. Two provisions in the law attempt to prevent a master from selling a girl whom he has purchased as a slave–concubine (vv. 8, 11). If a wife with the lowest possible status, that is, a slave–concubine, was not to be sold, then, arguing from lesser to greater, free concubines and primary wives also were not to be sold.[33] The wife, then, goes into slavery and out again with her husband. Her status depends upon his. Neither 21.2 nor 21.7 directly apply to her.

The language used in vv. 3-4 provides some clues about the nature of a free man's claims over his wife. The drafters of this law have used the phrase *ba'al 'iššâ* to distinguish a man who was married before he was enslaved, and thus may claim his wife when he goes free from a man whose master has provided him with a wife. In the latter case, the man cannot lay claim to his wife; she is the master's property. *Ba'al 'iššâ* (usually translated 'husband') thus indicates that the man has authority

33. A much later law, Deut. 21.10-14, clearly assumes that a man could not sell his wife. Deut. 21.14 prohibits the sale of a captive woman whom a man has chosen to marry precisely because she then has the status of a wife. The biblical texts are altogether silent on whether a man could pledge his wife's labor to pay off the interest of a debt. The cuneiform evidence is too mixed to permit deductions to be drawn about early Israelite practice. The pledging of wives is reflected in Old Babylonian and Middle Assyrian materials, but not in the Neo-Babylonian material, according to Muhammad Dandamaev (*Slavery in Babylonia* [trans. Victoria Powell; revd edn; De Kalb: University Northern Illinois Press, rev. edn, 1984], p. 169).

over the woman. The term *ba'al* does not imply ownership, however. The drafters of these laws distinguish the *ba'al*, husband, from the *'adôn*, owner.[34]

Daughter

The law of the enslaved daughter highlights the extensive authority a father has over his daughter. He may sell her into bondage. She is one of his economic assets; her economic worth is, first of all, her sexuality and her reproductive capacity. Because she is purchased for sexual purposes, the daughter, if sold, does not go free at the end of six years.

This appraisal of the daughter's status must be qualified in three ways. First, the father's legal right to sell his daughter is a matter of generation, not gender. Later biblical texts indicate that fathers and mothers may also sell their sons (2 Kgs 4.1; Neh. 5.5). The assumption that both sons and daughters are the property of their parents, and may thus be enslaved to pay for their parents' debts is attested throughout the ancient Near East; we may assume that it was true in early Israel.[35]

The second qualification to the description of the daughter's status as an economic asset is less ambiguous. That is, daughters did have some rights; they were not merely chattels. Verse 9 requires a master who purchases a concubine for his son to grant her the 'customary rights of a daughter'. As was noted above, an Assyrian adoption contract suggests that these rights include the right not to be ill-treated or prostituted.

Thirdly, one should not assume that parents did not care about their daughters. The subcases discussed in vv. 8-11 envision a father's efforts to secure the best possible situation for his daughter, given his poverty. Both biblical and cuneiform evidence indicate that parents sold or surrendered their children into bondage only when they were

34. This distinction has long been noted. See Johannes Pedersen, *Israel: Its Life and Culture* (London: Oxford University Press, 1926), I, p. 63.

35. There is some biblical and cuneiform evidence that in practice, if parents were forced to sell their children they were likely to surrender their daughters into slavery before they would give up their sons. Neh. 5.5 reads, 'we are about to be forced to subject our sons and our daughters to slavery—*some of our daughters are already enslaved*' (italics added). Dandamaev (*Slavery in Babylonia*, pp. 170-71) discusses nine contracts from Nippur in the Neo-Babylonian period that record the sale of children by free persons. One of the children sold was a boy; the rest were girls.

forced by great poverty to do so (2 Kgs 4.1; Neh. 5.5; cf. Deut. 28.32). Neo-Babylonian documents recording the sale of children stress that the parents were forced to sell their offspring to ensure their survival.[36]

Slave Wife of a Free Man

One must begin by noting that the texts assume that a man could purchase a concubine whose status remained that of a slave. Several scholars argue that the law of the enslaved daughter ensures her the status of a free wife. Turnbam, for example, writes. 'This is not concubinage...for she is given the title "wife" '.[37] Chirichigno argues, 'this law should be understood as an attempt to guarantee to a girl who is sold as a wife those rights that were normally afforded to daughters who were married in the customary manner'.[38]

Three factors indicate that the daughter assigned to her master (v. 8) or his son (v. 9) was regarded as a slave rather than a 'full wife' or 'free wife'. First, the drafters of Exod. 21.7-11 carefully use terminology that distinguishes the girl from a free wife. Despite Turnbaum's claim, she is called an *'āmâ*, not an *'iššâ*. She is sold (*mkr*), not given in marriage (*ntn*).[39] The purchaser is referred to as her master or owner (*'adôn*), not her husband (*ba'al*).

Secondly, if her master dislikes her, he causes her to be redeemed; if he deprives her of food, clothing, or oil (?), he must let her go free for no payment. Redemption and letting go free are ways of speaking about the manumission of slaves, not the divorce of a wife. In contrast to legal rhetoric about divorce, the rhetoric of Exod. 21.7-11 suggests that 'going free' is desirable.

Thirdly, the view that the girl is a free wife rather than a slave wife is based largely on v. 9, which accords her the customary rights of a daughter, and v. 11, which requires her master to provide her with clothing, food and oil (?). Neither phrase demonstrates that the *'āmâ*

36. Dandamaev, *Slavery in Babylonia*, pp. 170-71.

37. Turnbam, 'Male and Female Slaves', p. 548.

38. Chirichigno, *Debt-Slavery*, p. 251.

39. Zeev Falk ('Hebrew Legal Terms, II', *JSS* 5 [1954], pp. 114-17) mistakenly asserts that *mkr* is used to refer to the giving of a bride into a free marriage. The only instance in the Hebrew Bible where *mkr* is used in reference to such a marriage is found in the story of Leah and Rachel, as they protest that their father 'has sold us and devoured our purchase price' (Gen. 31.14). The verse is not evidence that the marriage of a free woman was considered a sale, or their bridewealth a purchase price. Leah and Rachel are complaining that their father has acted wrongly.

has the status of a free wife. We have seen that a 'daughter', though not merely a chattel, may be sold. Cuneiform laws require a man to provide clothing, food and oil to a harlot that has borne him children (LL 27 [Roth, *Law Collections*, p. 31]), to his child's wet-nurse (LL 32 [Roth, *Law Collections*, p. 64]) and possibly to a slave.[40]

The slave wife is distinguished from 'daughters who were married in the customary manner'. Indeed, the laws offer her less freedom of choice than the Hebrew slave. The laws seek to give the Hebrew slave the choice of going free at the end of six years, or of remaining with his family. The law of the enslaved daughter denies the slave wife the option of release; it also denies her the power to choose to remain with her master–husband unless he wishes it. In the case of the Hebrew slave, the slave is to decide whether or not the master must maintain him. In the case of the slave wife, the master is to decide whether to continue her provisions or to let her go free.[41]

If the slave wife is not 'highly regarded', she is also not regarded as a mere chattel. The laws are concerned with her welfare. She is not to be resold. The master is obligated to fulfil his contract concerning her. The laws attempt to protect her from ill-treatment and to ensure that she is either given basic necessities of life or allowed to go free.[42] While the value of such 'freedom' may be questioned, the rhetoric of Exod. 21.7-11 and of Exod. 21.26, 27 reflects the assumption that freedom was desirable.

Slave Wife of a Bondsman

In contrast to the slave wife of a free man treated by vv. 8-11, the slave wife of a slave mentioned in v. 4 does appear to be her master's chattel. The law of the Hebrew slave tells us almost nothing about this woman. We do not know if she is freeborn or slave-born, Israelite or foreign, or whether she could be an enslaved daughter. She is simply her master's possession whom he may give to the bondsman. The law seeks to establish that the master, not the bondsman maintains ownership of her

40. Paul, *Studies*, p. 59, cites a Neo-Babylonian document that suggests slaves had a right to food, oil and clothing.

41. The point is stressed by Turnbam, 'Male and Female Slaves', p. 547.

42. The distinction between slave wives of free men and other female slaves has yet to be thoroughly investigated. Presumably the slave wife's offspring would be counted as her master's children. Presumably he maintained exclusive rights to her sexuality, thus protecting her from sexual abuse by anyone besides her master.

and of any children that she might bear. A hint of an alternative perspective is found in v. 6; the Hebrew slave's motivation for choosing permanent bondage is that he loves his wife and children. His perspective differs from that of the master. Apart from this slight hint, the law treats the bondman's slave wife as an object.

6. *Do 'Master', 'Father', and 'Bondsman' include 'Mistress', 'Mother' and 'Bondswoman'?*

Exodus 21.2-11 explicitly names women in four capacities: wife, daughter, slave wife of a free man and slave wife of a bondsman. The roles explicitly mentioned do not exhaust the roles played by women in early Israel. The wife, the daughter, and the slave wives are all under the authority of a husband, father or master. It was surely normative for a woman to have such a place within a male-headed household. In practice, however, there would have been women who were not under male authority, with its restrictions and its security. There would have been widows or abandoned wives (cf. v. 11) without male protectors and without property. There would also have been widows who managed property left for their sons, or who possessed dowries. These laws tell us nothing about such women. Nonetheless, one may suspect that references to the master, father and Hebrew bondsman may implicitly include at least some female counterparts.

Mistresses and Mothers

It is likely that the terms 'master' and 'father' were understood as including 'mistresses' and 'mothers' in some circumstances. A comparison of Middle Assyrian and Neo-Babylonian private legal documents with the corresponding law codes shows that at least in some cases, drafters of laws could use masculine language generically rather than restrictively. The Middle Assyrian Laws having to do with pledges and debt consistently refer to the creditor as a man (MAL A.39, 44 and 48 [Roth, *Law Collections*, pp. 167, 170 and 173]). In contrast, a tablet from Assur cited by Driver and Miles show that an Assyrian woman could in fact offer a loan in exchange for a pledge.[43] 'Father' also

43. G.R. Driver and John C. Miles (*The Assyrian Laws* [Oxford: Clarendon Press, 1935], p. 288) refer to a document that states 'a certain man's wife has lent 40 talents 20 manehs of lead to a debtor and... this lead has been given to him "for the price of one woman" '. Similarly, the one Neo-Babylonian law that has to do with debt slavery (LNB 6, Roth, *Law Collections*, p. 145) refers to the creditor with

appears to have been used in a generic way in some cuneiform laws. For example, Neo-Babylonian marriage laws consistently refer to the bride's agent as her 'father'.[44] Yet the bride's father serves as her agent in only thirteen out of thirty-nine Neo- and Late Babylonian marriage contracts where the agent is known.[45]

Obviously the master who takes a slave wife in vv. 8, 10 and 11 is male. The 'you' who is to let the Hebrew slave go free after six years and the master who purchases a slave wife for a son could have been a woman. Biblical evidence suggests that early Israelite women could own or manage property, including slaves.[46] It appears likely that widows who had borne sons helped to manage their deceased husbands' households (including the households' slaves) at least until their sons grew up.[47] That women could own property, including slaves, is also suggested by evidence from surrounding cultures. Cuneiform documents demonstrate that women from a variety of ancient Near Eastern cultures owned freeborn slavegirls and bondsmen. Documents from Nuzi, Assyria and Neo-Babylonia record instances where women 'adopted' young girls in order to give them in marriage, or where women received freeborn persons as pledges.[48]

Similarly, it seems likely that the term 'father' (v. 7) could implicitly include the mother. In the absence of the father, an Israelite mother

male language while private documents cited by Dandamaev (*Slavery in Babylonia*, pp. 211, 221, and *passim*) establish that women could own bondsmen.

44. LNB 8–10 Roth, *Law Collections*, pp. 146-47.

45. Martha Roth, 'Age at Marriage and the Household: A Study of Neo-Babylonian and Neo-Assyrian Forms', *Comparative Studies in Society and History* 29 (1987), pp. 715-47.

46. See Judg. 1.14-15, 17.2-4; 2 Kgs 4.8; 8.1-6; Job 42.15; Ruth 4.3 and Num. 27.1-11 for evidence that women could own property during widely differing periods of Israel's history. See Gen. 16.1-15; 21.1-13; 29.24, 29; 1 Sam. 25.42 for references to maidservants owned by women.

47. See, for example, the story of the wooing of Rebekah (Gen. 24), in which Rebekah's mother and brother appear to manage the household, and in which the household is referred to as the *bêt 'am*. While Rebekah's father, Bethuel, is referred to in v. 50, he plays no integral part in the story. The reference is probably secondary.

48. See 'daughter and daughter-in-law' contracts XXXIV and FL 31 cited by Cyrus Gordon in 'The Status of Women Reflected in the Nuzi Tablets', *ZA* 43 (1936), pp. 146-69; Driver and Miles (*Assyrian Laws*, p. 288); and cases of Neo-Babylonian women who owned bondsmen cited by Muhammad Dandamaev (*Slavery in Babylonia*, pp. 211, 221, and *passim*).

appears to have had the authority to sell or surrender her children into slavery (cf. 2 Kgs. 4.1). A range of cuneiform documents also record the sale of children by mothers.[49]

Bondswomen

The terms 'master' and 'father' frequently appear to have a generic meaning in the cuneiform and biblical legal collections. I would argue that the *'ebed 'ibrî* also implicitly includes some bondswomen. It is clear from vv. 3 and 7 that the law of release does not directly apply to wives and daughters. Wives follow their husbands; daughters are not released. But there would be women who did not fall into either category. Widows, abandoned wives, and other women deprived of male protection would often be particularly economically and socially vulnerable (see the appeals for just treatment of widows and fatherless children). They would thus be especially vulnerable to forced enslavement. The question is whether the seventh year release of freeborn slaves would pertain to such women.

It seems most likely that it would. Elsewhere the *mišpāṭîm* treat the bondsman and bondswoman exactly alike. The bondswoman who is injured by her master must be manumitted—just like her male counterpart (21.26, 27). A bondswoman—like a bondsman—who is killed by the master is to be avenged (21.20). There are reasons that the law of release does not apply directly to the wife (she is under the authority of her husband and her status follows his) or the daughter (one would not expect a daughter to be released from male authority; moreover, she would have been sold for sexual and breeding purposes that would be frustrated were she emancipated). These reasons do not apply in the case of a widow or rejected wife. Given the evenhanded treatment of bondsmen and bondswomen elsewhere in the *mišpāṭîm*, one does not expect an arbitrary difference in treatment of them here. We would expect a widow, abandoned wife or the like who sells herself as a general household slave to be treated like the male slaves, and released.

There are several references to the release of freeborn slaves in cuneiform documents and biblical law. In every case apart from Exod.

49. A daughter is sold to an 'adopter' by her mother and grandmother in the 'daughter and daughter-in-law' contract referred to above (n. 48). In the nine contracts from Nippur recording the sale of children by their parents cited above (n. 35), the sellers were a father in one case, a father and a mother in a second case, and the mother in seven cases.

21.2-11, the release includes both males and females. In the prologue to Lipit Ishtar's legal collection, he brags, 'I procured the freedom of the sons and daughters of [Nippur] (etc.)'. LH 117 (Roth, *Law Collections*, p. 103) and the Edict of Ammiṣaduqa seek the release of wives, daughters and sons. Deuteronomy 15.12-18, Jer. 34.8-16 and Lev. 25.39-41 all try to prevent the permanent enslavement of women and of men. The consistent inclusion of the bondswoman in releases mandated or proclaimed elsewhere in the biblical and cuneiform materials suggests that the burden of proof lies with those who believe that the law of release excludes all women, not just daughters or wives.

The reasons commentators give for assuming that women are excluded from the law of release are not finally compelling. First, commentators often interpret v. 7 as excluding all female slaves from the seventh year release. This interpretation ignores that wording of the verse. The law excludes daughters, that is, unbetrothed girls, who are sold into slavery from release. It does not speak about women in other roles.

Secondly, commentators often argue that the word *'ebed* is exclusively male. Cuneiform and biblical slave laws often do refer explicitly to both bondsman and bondswoman (cf. Exod. 21.20-21, 26-27, 32). At first glance, this would suggest that a law that does not specifically refer to the bondswoman excludes her. A closer examination of the biblical and cuneiform legal materials, however, shows that it is not unusual for the term 'bondsman' (or even 'bondswoman') to be used generically in the midst of a collection where other slave laws explicitly refer to both sexes.

The overwhelming majority of the Deuteronomic slave laws, for example, refer to both *'ebed* and *'āmâ*. Yet Deuteronomy includes one law, the law of the fugitive slave (23.16-17), which refers only to the bondsman. It is quite unlikely that the law was understood as applying only to male slaves; the cuneiform laws do not treat male and female fugitive slaves differently. Rather, 'bondsman' should be understood generically in this instance.[50]

50. In the Book of the Covenant, the sabbath law (23.12) appears to use the phrase *ben 'ᵃmātᵉkâ*, 'son of your slave woman', generically. Elsewhere the bondswoman is included in the Sabbath commands. Cuneiform laws pertaining to slaves usually refer to both the bondsman and the bondswoman, but either term can be used generically. LE 22 and 23 (Roth, *Law Collections*, p. 62), for example, treat cases where a slave girl has been illegally distrained. The use of a gender-specific

Indeed, in two other passages in the Hebrew Bible, laws that attempt to prohibit the permanent enslavement of Hebrews are couched in male language that the context shows is generic rather than exclusive. The well-known prophecy against Jerusalemites for re-enslaving those whom they had released (Jer. 34.8-16) refers explicitly to bondsmen and bondswomen. However, the law of release cited (or paraphrased) in Jer. 34.14 uses masculine language: 'each of you must let go his kinsman, the Hebrew (*'āḥîw hā'ibrî*)'. Given the context, *'āḥîw hā'ibrî* must be interpreted generically. Similarly, Lev. 25.39 prohibits treating a kinsman (*'āḥîkâ*) forced to become a hired laborer as a bondsman (*'ebed*). The clause a few verses later that male and female slaves may be acquired from the surrounding nations (Lev. 25.44) makes it clear that the language of Lev. 25.39 is generic.[51]

It seems likely that the drafters of Exod. 21.2-11 used the masculine terms 'master' and 'father' because normatively the one who headed a household and controlled its economic assets (slaves) and its dependent minors (daughters) would be male. *'Ebed 'ibrî* can also be explained as a generic term that was chosen because normatively the released slave would have been male. Normatively, free women were under the authority of either their fathers or their husbands. The law envisions that the daughter is excepted from release and that the wife follows her

term cannot be explained by suggesting that male slaves would not have been distrained; they clearly were (cf. LH 116 [Roth, *Law Collections*, p. 103]). Nor is there anything about the penalty that is gender specific. The penalty is not a fixed price (which would differ in the case of a male); the distrainer is to replace the slavegirl with one (LE 22) or two (LE 23) others. That penalty could hold equally well for illegally distrained male slaves. Rather, it seems likely that the drafters used the female term generically, either because bondswomen were more frequently distrained or pledged than bondsmen, or because the paragraph evolved from an actual case involving a slavewoman. LNB 6 (Roth, *Law Collections*, p. 145) deals with the case of a female slave who had been sold and who, after the sale, was taken by a creditor who had a claim against her. The seller is required to compensate the purchaser. The law goes on to establish the amount of compensation which the seller owes the purchaser for any children whom the slave woman bore. Here, the main case would apply to bondsmen as well as bondswomen; the drafters have used the female term because the subcase is gender specific. Cases refer to the bondsman in a generic sense in paragraphs where a law that had explicitly referred to male and female slaves had been revised (e.g. HL 8, 12, 14, 16 [Roth, *Law Collections*, pp. 218-19]) or in subcases where the main case names both bondsman and bondswoman (e.g. LL 12-13; LH 17-20 [Roth, *Law Collections*, pp. 28; 84-85]).

51. Deut. 15.12-18 is discussed below.

husband in and out of slavery. The case where a woman was not under male authority would be non-normative.[52] Yet such women undoubtedly existed and cuneiform records suggest that they could have given themselves into bondage in order to survive or been forced into slavery because of debt.[53] Unless she had sold herself into concubinage, we would expect that such a bondswoman would be implicitly covered by v. 2.

A later Deuteronomic version of the law of the Hebrew slave is often cited as a third reason for assuming that Exod. 21.2 excluded all bondswomen from release. The Deuteronomic law (Deut. 15.12-18) pointedly includes the *'āmâ* in the seventh year release. Verse 12 mandates that 'your brother (*'āḥîkâ*), a Hebrew male or female (*hā 'ibrî 'ô hā'ibriyyâ*)' who is sold into slavery is to be freed after six years of servitude. A provision drafted in third-person masculine that allows the slave to choose lifelong bondage (vv. 16-17) is followed by the clause 'and do the same for your bondswoman' (v. 17b). While the reference to the male or female Hebrew in v. 12 could be an example of typical Deuteronomic rhetoric, the clause in 17b appears to be a deliberate redactional addition.[54] Moreover, the Deuteronomic law does not include the provision excepting the enslaved daughter from release.

Many scholars interpret these additions and deletions as evidence that the Exodus law of release excluded all bondswomen and the Deuteronomic law was revised to include them. The explicit reference to the *hā'ibriyyâ*, however, may be accounted for in other ways. The

52. Chirichigno (*Debt-Slavery*, p. 246) suggests that the omission of the bondswoman in v. 2 is explained by the structure of Exod. 21.2-11, which balances attention to the marital rights of the male slave (vv. 2-6) on the one hand, and the female slave (vv. 7-11) on the other. It is possible that the generic masculine in the main case was chosen because of the gender-specific subcases. The drafters of LNB 6 (Roth, *Law Collections*, p. 145) appear to have used 'bondswoman' in a main case that would apply to males or females because of a gender–specific subcase (see n. 51). An explanation that accounts for the generic male language in Jer. 34.14 and Lev. 25.39 is preferable, however.

53. Bernard Jackson ('Some Literary Features of the Mishpatim', *'Wunschet Jerusalem Frieden': Collected Communications to the XII Congress of the International Organization for the Study of the Old Testament* [Frankfurt: Peter Lang, 1986], pp. 235-42) states that the evidence suggests that women in the ancient Near East were more frequently sold to be debt-slaves than were men.

54. See Phyllis Bird, 'Translating Sexist Language as a Theological and Cultural Problem', *USQR* 42.1-2 (1988), pp. 89-95.

increase in the number of laws intended to help the widow and the fatherless and the references to divorce (Deut. 22.19, 29; 24.1-4) suggest that war and other social disruptions had led to an increase in the number of women outside of the protection of a male headed household and thus economically vulnerable. The enslavement of women in the time of Deuteronomy (or of the Deuteronomistic redactions) may have been correspondingly more frequent than it was in the time the *mišpaṭîm* were compiled.

The absence of the exception found in Exod. 21.7 may reflect resistence on the part of the Deuteronomic compilers to applying the language of slavery to concubines. Some (albeit inconclusive) evidence for this is found in the law of the captured bride, Deut. 21.10-14. This law, like Exod. 21.7-11, prohibits the master from selling a woman with whom he has cohabited. As in Exod. 21.7-11, the woman's status is precariously slave-like; she is a captive of war. Unlike Exod. 21.7-11 the compilers refer to the woman using the language of marriage, not the language of slavery. It seems plausible that Deut. 21.10-14 reflects the compilers' rejection of slave-wifery.[55]

It is also possible that the Deuteronomic redactors did have different assumptions or values concerning daughters. It is clear, though, that any differences in the way the Deuteronomic law of release treats women from their treatment by the Exodus law of release is limited to the case of the enslaved daughter, not to all bondswomen. It is very doubtful that the wife of a free man would enter into slavery on her own initiative. The later Jubilee laws take it for granted that the wife's status depends upon that of her husband. She follows him in and out of servitude (Lev. 25.39-46). Moreover, given the subordination of wives to their husbands presupposed by other Deuteronomic laws, it is unthinkable that the Deuteronomic (or Deuteronomistic) redactors would give a free man's wife the right to opt for lifelong enslavement independently of her husband.

If my reasoning is correct, the explicit reference to bondswoman in the Deuteronomic law of release should be taken as evidence that

55. The suggestion that concubinage may not have existed by the Deuteronomic period was made by S.R. Driver (*A Critical and Exegetical Commentary on Deuteronomy* [Edinburgh: T. & T. Clark, 1951], p. 182) as early as 1895. I do not argue that concubinage was no longer practised in Israel; rather the Deuteronomic compilers may have considered it incompatible for a woman to be at the same time a man's 'wife' and his 'slave'.

increasing numbers of women were without male protection, and were forced to enter into slavery. That daughters were not explicitly excepted from the release may signal a change in assumptions or attitudes toward daughters; it may, however, reflect the view that 'slave' and 'wife' were incompatible statuses. The differences between Deut. 15.12-18 and Exod. 21.2-11, then, should not be taken as evidence that the Exodus law was intended to exclude widows and other women not under male authority and protection from release.

7. *Conclusion*

The exclusion of the enslaved daughter from the law of release in Exod. 21.2 has often been taken as the basis for sweepingly general statements about the status of women in the earliest period of Israelite history. That women were property, that women could not own property, that women were not part of the covenant community, or, at the least, that all slave women were concubines and therefore permanently bound to their masters. Recent discussions of women and the slave laws, perhaps partly in reaction to such negative generalizations, argue that the bondsmen and bondswomen were treated with marked parity; the bondswoman would either be freed under the law of release (v. 2) or by becoming the free wife of her master.

The evidence does not justify either such negative or such positive generalizations. The wife's status follows that of her husband. The daughter is under her father's extensive control. Her ultimate status depends upon his decisions; still, she has some customary rights. The slave wife of a free man does not have the status of a free wife, but neither is she merely a chattel. The legal status of the slave wife of a bondsman does appear to be as a chattel, though even in her case there is a hint of her humanity in the bondsman's motivation for choosing permanent servitude.

The women named in the slave laws have differing roles and statuses, depending upon generation and class as well as gender. In fact, in these laws the woman's gender does not directly determine her status, nor does it directly determine whether or not the law of release (v. 2) applies to her. Rather, the woman's gender determines that normatively she will be under the authority and protection of a man. Her status depends on that relationship. Whether or not she is implicitly included in the law of release (v. 2) depends upon whether or not she was under male authority when she became enslaved.

GENDER AND LAW: A CASE STUDY FROM ANCIENT MESOPOTAMIA

Martha T. Roth

*Introductory Remarks**

Can we recover gender assumptions in the surviving legal documents and the reflexes of legal actions in ancient Mesopotamia? Can such a possible recovery aid our understanding of the documents and the legal system? First we must be clear about how we understand the construct 'gender' and how that construct impacts upon roles or statuses recognized by the legal mechanisms.[1]

Although discussions of social and legal categories tend to focus on

* This paper reproduces part of my remarks to the session on 'Gender and Law' at the Society of Biblical Literature meetings in November 1995 in Philadelphia. I thank especially Bernard Levinson, who invited me to participate in that session, and I am grateful to the participants and audience for their questions and insights.

1. The term 'gender' is used for the social categories of feminine and masculine; the term 'sex' is reserved for the biological categories of female and male. The literature of gender studies is vast and sophisticated today, and my own readings in the field are certainly not comprehensive, but weighted to works involving legal assumptions. Diverse recent bibliographies (and many provocative points demanding more sophisticated attention than possible here) are found in the essays collected in Katherine T. Bartlett and Rosanne Kennedy (eds.), *Feminist Legal Theory: Readings in Law and Gender* (Boulder, CO: Westview Press, 1991); Leonore Davidoff, *Worlds Between: Historical Perspectives on Gender and Class* (London: Routledge, 1995); Catharine A. MacKinnon, *Feminism Unmodified: Discourses on Life and Law* (Cambridge, MA: Harvard University Press, 1987); Fatma Müge Göçek and Shiva Balaghi (eds.), *Reconstructing Gender in the Middle East: Tradition, Identity, and Power* (New York: Columbia University Press, 1994). Robin West, 'Jurisprudence and Gender', *The University of Chicago Law Review* 55 (1988), pp. 1-72, presents summaries of some major trends in feminist jurisprudence theory.

polar or binary pairs (parent–child, slave–free, brother–sister, old–young,[2] citizen–foreigner, inside–outside, public–private, shame–honor,[3] rich–poor, etc., as well as male–female and masculine–feminine) the relational statuses are more nuanced in the daily operations of social interactions. Any construct of a dyad obscures both the gradations between the polar elements of the pair, and the multiple roles that are simultaneously in play. For example, 'freedom' of person includes a variety of roles—fully free land-owning, free non-land-owning, indentured, servant, slave with and without possibility of redemption; 'age' categories include minor and major, infant, child, young and mature adult, elderly; 'nationality' and 'citizenship' include native-born, naturalized, resident alien, guest alien, hostile alien; so, too, 'race' or 'ethnicity' or 'religious affiliation' and a host of other possible acquired or innate factors, many of which may be difficult to fathom outside of their particular social contexts. The combinations of such defining factors might condition the way the individual is perceived in the law. Equally, 'gender' involves a number of classifications recognizable in and by the law, and not only the obvious two of female and male, but also a series of often paired socially constructed and biological categories. Thus, in addition to male and female, there might be not-male and not-female (i.e. homosexual, with further subcategories); fertile and infertile; married, unmarried, never-married, divorced, or widowed; primagravid and multigravid; nursing mother and one who entrusts her newborns to a wetnurse; warrior and scholar; premenarchic and postmenapausal, and so on. I deliberately bring in so many alternative categorizations in order to stress that to assess the standing of a person before the law, to arrive at a systemic valuation of the individual, it is necessary to know much more than simply whether the person is female or male. A wide range of tangible and intangible factors such as citizenship, wealth, age, family position, as well as gender, combine in often subtle and unexamined ways to produce an individual's standing in the law as a 'legal subject'.

Bearing in mind just some of the multiple factors and assumptions that one should take into account in an assessment of the realities of

2. See M.T. Roth, 'Age at Marriage and the Household: A Study of Neo-Babylonian and Neo-Assyrian Forms', *Comparative Studies in Society and History* 29 (1987), pp. 715–47.

3. See M.T. Roth, 'Mesopotamian Legal Traditions and the Laws of Hammurabi', *Chicago–Kent Law Review* 71.1 (1995), pp. 13–39, especially pp. 25-37.

social categories and their interplay in a legal system, it should be obvious to a student of the ancient Near East that the available documentation will never adequately reveal most of what we want to know. The absence of adequate answers is, of course, attributable not only to the usual constraints of the accidents of preservation, recovery, and publication. More important, the social categories themselves almost certainly were assumed and unexamined by the subject populations and certainly were never made explicit in the written records. But our questions do inform the ways we interpret those records, and can help uncover those assumptions. In what follows, then, I present one case study in which the evaluation of legal personhood involves some gender-determined questions.

The Nippur Homicide Trial

The famous 'Nippur Homicide Trial' records the outcome of the trial in which the defendants were three men and the widow of the victim. The record of the 'trial' is found in at least three manuscripts, written in the early part of the second millennium BCE, in Sumerian on cuneiform clay tablets. The earliest was published in 1922 and is found on a partially damaged tablet; both the second, also a single-trial tablet, excavated in 1950, and the third, a multi-trial record,[4] excavated in 1952, remain unpublished in copy or photograph.[5] I quote the record in full

4. Summaries of the cases recorded on this Sammeltafel are found in M.T. Roth, 'The Slave and the Scoundrel', *JAOS* 103 (1983), pp. 279–82.

5. Casts were made available to me at the Oriental Institute by courtesy of John A. Brinkman, Curator of the Oriental Institute Tablet Collections. The joined tablet made up of fragments from the University Museum and the Oriental Institute collections (ms. c+d) has been examined and edited by courtesy of Åke W. Sjöberg and Miguel Civil. *Manuscripts*: (a) CBS 7178, published in E. Chiera, PBS 8.2 No. 173; single-trial tablet; (b) 2N-T 54 (= IM 58943, cast in the Oriental Institute), see OIP 78 p. 75, found in TB level II.1, in the 'scribal quarter' during the second season of the joint Oriental Institute and University Museum excavations, in room TB 10 (early Rim-Sin of Larsa); single-trial tablet; (c) 3N-T 273 (cast in the Oriental Institute) + 3N-T 340 + 3N-T 403 (all = UM 55–21–436), see OIP 78 p. 116, and (d) + 3N-T 426 (= A 30240) (cast in the Oriental Institute), all 3N-T texts found during third season of the joint Oriental Institute and University Museum excavations, later copies dating from time of Samsu-iluna; multi-trial tablet recording trials held before the Assembly of Nippur. *Treatments*: E. Chiera, PBS 8.2 pp. 172-73; S.N. Kramer, *From the Tablets of Sumer* (Indian Hills, CO: Falcon's Wing Press, 1956), pp. 52–55; Th. Jacobsen, 'An Ancient Mesopotamian Trial for

before turning to an examination of some of its gendered assumptions.

(1–5) Nanna-sig, son of Lu-Suen; Ku-Enlilla, son of Ku-Nanna, the barber; and Enlil-ennam, servant of Adda-kalla, the orchard man—killed Lu-Inanna, son of Lugal-uru-du, the *nešakku* (official of the Enlil cult in Nippur). (6–12) When Lu-Inanna, son of Lugal-uru-du, the *nešakku*, had been killed, they told Nin-Dada, daughter of Lu-Ninurta, wife of Lu-Inanna, that her husband Lu-Inanna had been killed. (13–14) Nin-Dada, daughter of Lu-Ninurta, did not open her mouth, she covered it with a cloth.[6]

(15–19) Its case was taken to Isin (for a hearing) before the king. King Ur-Ninurta ordered its case accepted for trial in the Assembly of Nippur.

(20–29) Ur-Gula, son of Lugal-ibila; Dudu, the bird catcher; Ali-ellati, the *muškēnu*; Puzu, son of Lu-Suen; Eluti, son of Tizkar-Ea; Shesh-kalla, the potter; Lugal-kam, the orchard man; Lugal-azida, son of Suen-andul;[7] and Shesh-kalla, son of Shara-har,[8] addressed (the Assembly). (30–34) They declared: 'As men who have killed men, they should not be allowed to live. Those three males[9] and that woman shall be killed before the chair[10] of Lu-Inanna, son of Lugal-uru-du, the *nešakku*'.

(35–37) Shuqallilum, the chief of the troops, the soldier of Ninurta; and Ubar-Suen, the orchard man, addressed (the Assembly). (38–41) They declared: 'Given even that Nin-Dada, daughter of Lu-Ninurta,[11]

Homicide', *AnBib* 12 (1959), pp. 130–50, republished in *Toward the Image of Tammuz and Other Essays on Mesopotamian History and Culture* (Harvard Semitic Series, 21; Cambridge, MA: Harvard University Press, 1970), pp. 193–204.

6. Probably an idiom suggesting a refusal to speak, or, more metaphorically, a covering up of the deed. See futher below.

7. Variant: Lu-Suena.

8. Variant: Harabi.

9. The term used here, *nita* (rather than *lú*, 'man', the term used in the previous sentence) is that used in the law collections (Laws of Ur-Namma, Laws of Lipit-Ishtar, and cf. LH) to identify the outsider male who violates a husband's marital rights; see Roth, *Law Collections from Mesopotamia and Asia Minor* (Writings from the Ancient World, 6; Atlanta: Scholars Press, 1995), p. 35 n. 2. The use of this term here emphasizes the awareness of the court of the differences between the deed of the three men and the deed of the woman.

10. The significance of the execution before the 'chair' of the victim is not clear. In that the victim was an official of major importance in the Enlil cult in Nippur, the 'chair' might have some profession-specific implication and one should be cautious about assigning any generalized symbolism here.

11. Variant adds: 'and wife of Lu-Inanna'.

might have killed her husband—but a woman, what can she do, to warrant that she be killed?'

(42–43) The Assembly of Nippur addressed them. (44–48) They declared: 'A woman who does not value her husband might surely know[12] his enemy; he might kill her husband; he might then inform her that her husband has been killed. (49) Why should he not make her keep her mouth shut about him?[13] (50–52) It is she who (as good as) killed her husband; her guilt exceeds even that of those who (actually) kill a man'.

(53–59) The Assembly of Nippur resolved the matter: Nanna-sig, son of Lu-Suen; Ku-Enlilla, son of Ku-Nanna, the barber; and Enlil-ennam, servant of Adda-kalla, the orchard man; and also Nin-Dada, daughter of Lu-Ninurta, wife of Lu-Inanna—were delivered up to be killed.

(60) Case accepted for trial in the Assembly of Nippur.

In his excellent commentary on this text, Thorkild Jacobsen explicated a number of philological, lexical, and legal points of interest. What concerns us here is specifically the challenge to the majority opinion that sought to defend the widow Nin-Dada,[14] formulated in direct speech:

> Given even that Nin-Dada, daughter of Lu-Ninurta, might have killed her husband—but a woman, what can she do, to warrant that she be killed?

and the majority's response to that challenge, reiterating its condemnation of her, again in direct speech:

> A woman who does not value her husband might know his enemy; he might kill her husband; he might then inform her that her husband has been killed. Why should he not make her keep her mouth shut about him? It is she who (as good as) killed her husband; her guilt exceeds even that of those who (actually) kill a man.

These statements, most clearly among all our surviving cuneiform sources, demonstrate a Mesopotamian probing of what the modern

12. On this term, 'know', see further below.

13. a-na-aš-àm k[a$^{?}$] ugu-na li-bí-in-si. Jacobsen translates, 'Why should he not thus make her keep silent about him?'; PSD A/1 122a s.v. a-na-aš, reads a-na-aš-àm si ugu-na (etc.) and translates 'why is it (that) he should not make her keep silent about him?' The copy of CBS 7178 in PBS 8/2 No. 173 has: a-na-aš-à[m x] ugu-na (etc.); 3N-T 426:17 shows giš ba-an-tuku-àm a-na-aš-àm x-[...], where the final sign, broken, begins with two short horizontals (hence perhaps the /si/ of PSD?), read here as the beginning of the sign /ka/; other manuscripts broken here.

14. Or Nin-adda in some manuscripts.

English and American legal systems call the 'rational person', that hypothetical person who sets the standard for how an individual could or should respond to a given set of circumstances. Clearly, in Mesopotamia (as still most commonly in the English and American judicial systems) the applicability of the rational person standard presupposes the perspectives of males rather than those of females.

In seeking to defend Nin-Dada against the charge of homicide, her defenders are faced with a decidedly modern dilemma: do they, as her defenders, take the practical but short view, ceding her 'diminished capacity' as a woman easily intimidated by the three males, and thus try to get her off, or at least to get a lesser sentence imposed? Or do they take the morally more commendable long view, arguing that Nin-Dada should be accused, judged, and if appropriate condemned only by the same standards and with the same rights as would any male charged with a comparable offense?

Remember that Nin-dada was not accused of having participated in the actual manslaughter. Her offense, as presented in the summation with which this text, like all Mesopotamian trial records, begins, is that she had knowledge of the murder but did not bring the deed to the attention of the authorities and did not name names: she 'did not open her mouth, she covered it with a cloth'. Her defenders, in turn, did not try to get her off by resorting to these 'facts'; these details—no first hand involvement in the slaying, no participation in the actual deed—presumably were irrelevant. Instead, her defenders took the short view and pleaded the weakness of the fairer sex: Even if she had participated, even she had put her hand to the bloody act, even then, they argue, she is but a woman; and what, after all, can a mere woman do to prevent the crime? Or even to bring its perpetrators to justice? Surely, she kept silent out of fear for her own life. And for this act of self-preservation, a concern for the welfare of her children perhaps, must she be executed? The Mesopotamian defenders, in other words, try to play upon the sympathies of the Assembly, drawing upon their unchallenged perceptions of female attributes and responses.

There is an important assumption behind the defense of Nin-Dada: anyone who has knowledge of a crime is obligated to report it to the suitable authorities. Further, perhaps, there is also the assumption that the failure to do so incurs graves penalties. This is so in the case in the LH §109 in which a woman innkeeper harbors wanted persons:

> If there should be a woman innkeeper in whose house criminals congregate, and she does not seize those criminals and lead them off to the palace authorities, that woman innkeeper shall be killed.[15]

Is it no coincidence that in both the Nippur Homicide Trial and LH §109 the person whose concealment of a crime risks the death penalty is a woman? And therefore is there an underlying assumption that women are more easily intimidated into collusion than are men? If so, the law emphasizes that women are as liable as men in this area; or, to put it another way, that if even a woman is obliged to reveal the crime, it is even more incumbent upon a man to do so.

The majority on the court, however, does not accept a 'diminished capacity' or 'weaker sex' defense. No, they take the hard line, and not only do they disallow the defense, but they condemn her by a different and harsher standard than applied to the male defendants. They do not try to argue that she did participate in committing the physical act. In fact, the Mesopotamian Assembly four millennia ago probably dismissed the notion that a woman could kill her husband as easily and unreflexively as did Thorkild Jacobsen just four decades ago when he commented, 'it is quite obviously unlikely that as a woman she could have participated directly in the physical act of killing'.[16]

The majority then proceeds to spin what might appear to be a paranoid and prejudicial series of escalating offenses. First, it is assumed that a woman—Nin-Dada in this case, but more universally perhaps any woman—does not 'value' her husband. By this is implied a whole range of culturally appropriate behaviors expected of a wife by a husband, the most important of which are his exclusive sexual access and exclusive procreative rights. There is no unambiguous statement charging Nin-Dada with adulterous activities; nonetheless, the language employed by the Assembly suggests the possibility: 'A woman who does not value her husband might surely know his enemy'. Recall that in the original setting forth of the details it is said that the manslayers 'told' Nin-Dada (employing the common Sumerian *marû* verb /e/, Akkadian *qabû*, 'to speak'); thus she is in possession of simple information and not of carnal knowledge. But the Assembly's use of the

15. Cf. MAL, A §40, in which a man who does not turn in a veiled prostitute or slave woman to the authorities is subject to fifty blows and public humiliation; see also MAL A §53, referring to concealment of an abortion; all in Roth, *Law Collections*, pp. 101, 167ff., 174.

16. Jacobsen, *Tammuz*, p. 210.

verb /zu/ (Akkadian *idû*, 'to know' but also *lamādu*, 'to learn', or 'to know carnally', as in the biblical use of the term) serves as a double entendre to trigger the second assumption in this series of offenses: the wife's adultery.

The third stage in this fantasy is then reached: an adulterous woman's lover—the husband's 'enemy' (lú-kúr)[17]—could easily progress to the next treachery, that of killing the husband. Again, the culpability of the woman (by now presumed a seductress or instigator and not an innocent victim) is obvious to the Nippur Assembly. As Jacobsen and others have noted, the underlying assumption is also present in the LH, in which the hypothetical case in §153 outlines:

> If a man's wife has her husband killed on account of (her relationship with) another man,[18] they shall impale that woman.[19]

The fourth step in this increasingly paranoid fantasy is that, for whatever reasons of control and manipulation, the homicidal lover would tell the woman that he did indeed murder her husband, making her an accessory after the fact. This deepens the presumed intimate relationship they secretly enjoyed before, and strengthens their emotional ties to one another.

Finally, then, the men of the Assembly allow the fantasy to reach its crescendo: it does not matter whether or not she personally participated in the slaying. 'It is she who killed her husband', they conclude. And furthermore, *because* she is a woman who violated the marital trust, it is even worse: 'her guilt *exceeds* even that of those who (actually) kill a man'.

A similarly escalating series of offenses is enumerated in the Sumerian adultery trial first published by van Djik and explicated by Greengus.[20] There, the adulterous wife's offense is the culmination of a series

17. The characterization of the hypothetical man as lú-kúr 'enemy' is odd, presuming a prior history of enmity between the two men rather than a current relationship of intimacy between the man and the married woman. It is possible, therefore, that lú-kúr designates not Akkadian *nakru*, 'enemy, foe', but *šanû*, 'another, someone else'; compare the designation of the three murderers as nita, and see above n. 9. Thus the line could be translated, 'A woman who does not value her husband might surely (carnally) know her "other man"'.

18. *aššum zikarim šanîm*, compare previous note.

19. Roth, *Law Collections*, p. 110.

20. S. Greengus, 'A Textbook Case of Adultery', *HUCA* 40-41 (1969–70), pp. 33-44.

of increasingly 'unwifely' actions, also presented for the judgment of the Assembly: 'Firstly, she burglarized his storeroom; secondly, she made a breach in his oil jar and concealed it with a cloth; thirdly, he seized her upon a man'. The underlying premises are similar in the two trial records: a woman's marital infidelity—in which is included sexual infidelity, but not exclusively so—is so much a threat to the status quo that even a hint of impropriety (such as pilfering supplies from the storeroom) is viewed as the first step on the road to inevitable total breakdown of the social bonds.

Concluding Remarks

The gendered assumptions about legal personality that emerge from the Nippur Homicide Trial are not, of course, unique to that one text in the vast Sumerian and Akkadian legal corpus. There is ample evidence that in the legal spheres the natural, neutral, unmarked perspective is that of male interests and characteristics. In fact, one could go beyond seeing just gendered nuances in the law, and recognize also that the law texts take as their assumed legal subject not just the male, but the adult male rather than the child, the native resident rather than the foreigner, the established class (whatever that entailed) rather than the subservient ones—the lú and *awīlum*, in other words, of the Sumerian, Babylonian, and Assyrian law collections is the Mesopotamian equivalent of the nuanced use in very recent English of the term 'man' (as in 'all men are created equal'): male and not female; of European and not African, Asian, or native American descent; Protestant and not Catholic, Jewish, Islamic or Buddhist; adult and not minor; property-owning and solvent and not indentured.

We should not be too hasty in condemning Mesopotamian women to lives less 'liberated' than they really experienced, however. There are indications that, although the *presupposition* of the legal system was of the male legal subject, the system did not necessarily always reinforce the status quo. For example, in direct contradiction of the common law concept of coverture, 'the husband and wife are one, and that one is the husband',[21] the Middle Assyrian Laws set out guidelines for spouses' mutual and separate liabilities and benefits, as in MAL A §35:

21. William Blackstone, *Commentaries on the Laws of England.* I. *Of the Rights of Persons (1765)* (Chicago: University of Chicago Press, 1979), p. 430: 'By marriage, the husband and wife are one person in law'.

> If a widow should enter into a man's house, whatever she brings with her belongs to her (new) husband; and if a man should enter into a woman's house, whatever he brings with him belongs to the woman.

Many features of the law and legal consequences differ for women and men, as they also differ for various class, racial, ethnic, and age categories. But the rationales or motivations for these different constructs cannot always be attributed exclusively to the cultural assumptions of one category or another. For example, a woman in the Neo-Babylonian period generally is represented by an agent in contracting her marriage, while a man most commonly acts independently.[22] But is this phenomenon a consequence of the categories of *gender*—bride versus groom, female versus male, legal dependency versus legal autonomy? Or is it rather one of *age*? For we know that Neo-Babylonian wives tended to be younger than their spouses by about a decade, and thus the bride was more likely than the groom to have a living parent (by which I mean female as well as male parent—mothers acted to arrange their daughters' marriages, too[23]). So we find that age categories rather than or in addition to gender categories inform the cultural assumptions behind the phenomenon of differential contracting agents that appears to us as brides having agents acting for them while grooms act independently.

Equally, gender considerations might not necessarily play a major or defining role in understanding the graphic and dramatic means of execution or infliction of corporal punishments for women (and not only adulterous wives) in the law collections and contracts. The punishments are, in fact, matched by an array of equally creative solutions for disposing of male offenders. Both women and men are subject to mutilations resulting in the loss of a body part—such as an eye, ear, finger, lip, tongue, hand, foot—while more gender-specific mutilations such as cutting off of the breast or shaving off half the beard are restricted to the appropriate recipients. Most of these penalty choices have a fairly obvious sympathetic association with the designated offense (cutting off the breast of the wetnurse, cutting off the hand of the thief, cutting out the tongue of the impudent slave, etc.). But we should be cautious

22. See Roth, 'Age at Marriage', pp. 723–27, and M.T. Roth, *Babylonian Marriage Agreements, 7th–3rd Centuries* BC (AOAT, 222; Kevelaer: Butzon & Bercker, 1989), pp. 5-6.

23. Roth, 'Age at Marriage', p. 724 with Table 1.

about assigning any particular value to the female-specific punishments since our sample is heavily skewed by the Middle Assyrian Laws Tablet A, most of whose fifty-nine provisions are dedicated to regulating women's behavior and offenses, and which concludes: 'In addition to the punishments for [a man's wife] that are [written] on the tablet, a man may [whip] his wife, pluck out her hair, mutilate her ears, or strike her, with impunity'[24]—or, in modern terms, 'spousal abuse is not actionable'.

Also, when we examine the disparate nature of the penalties envisioned for the adulterous wife on the one hand and for her lover on the other, the gendered nuances are not necessarily nor exclusively dictated by the woman and man's differential standing in the law. While the adulterous wife is subject to being thrown from a tower, to being tied up and thrown into the river, to facial or genital mutilation, or to debasement of status to slavery (usually at her husband's discretion), her lover's fate *maximally* matches her own, but might be negligible, and never exceeds it in severity. But is this disparity because one offender is female and the other male? Or is it weighted by the fact that one (the adulterous wife) is an *insider*, a spouse who violates a marital contractual obligation and trust, and the other (her lover) is an *outsider*, a stranger and non-family member who is, finally, only a thief? Thus, is the legal person of the offender defined exclusively by gender or also by an insider–outsider dyad?

There is no doubt that women and men stand differently in their interactions with the law. This discussion should illuminate some of the ways in which the constructs of gender are assumed in Mesopotamian legal actions. Rather than providing any answers however, this discussion must raise more questions, with one of which I will close. We observe that in our surviving records, the cases in which women appear as participants in the legal systems tend to be cases in which *reproductive rights* figure directly or indirectly, that is, cases involving marriage, adultery, miscarriage, inheritance rights, wetnursing, and so on. This observation leads to the question: Do the reproductive concerns override other potential considerations and result in a more pronounced gendered differential than we might find in, for example, cases involving real estate transfer or tax payments (although even those cases also might not be immune to the gendered nuances)? Although it is clear

24. MAL A §59, in Roth, *Law Collections*, pp. 175-76.

that gender is one factor that must be kept in mind in exploring Mesopotamian legal institutions, it is not always fully clear *how* gender itself was socially constructed. No social or legal system, in other words, is monolithic or consistent in the assessments and applicabilities of its social categories.

'LEST HE DIE IN THE BATTLE AND ANOTHER MAN TAKE HER': VIOLENCE AND THE CONSTRUCTION OF GENDER IN THE LAWS OF DEUTERONOMY 20–22

Harold C. Washington

L'humanité ne progresse pas lentement de combat en combat jusqu'à une réciprocité universelle, où les règles se substitueront, pour toujours, à la guerre; elle installe chacune de ces violences dans un système de règles, et va ainsi de domination en domination.

Humanity does not gradually progress from combat to combat until it arrives at universal reciprocity, where the rule of law finally replaces warfare; humanity installs each of its violences in a system of rules and thus proceeds from domination to domination.

Michel Foucault, 'Nietzsche, la généalogie, l'histoire'.

Introduction

In the summer of 1995, Circuit Court Judge Albert Mestemaker of Hamilton County, Ohio, gained notoriety for ordering a man convicted of assaulting his female companion to marry the woman as a condition of his probation. News reports characterized the ruling as egregious judicial misconduct. Dismayed by the global headlines, the judge reversed himself, commenting that 'to order a woman to marry her abuser would be the same thing as ordering a woman to marry a man who had raped her, no more, no less'.[1] Judge Mestemaker's original ruling was no mere aberration, however. Despite decades of activism and critical legal scholarship, still the US courts rarely address violence against women adequately.[2] The judge's example can be multiplied by

1. Annie Groer, 'Court and Sparks in Cincinnati: Judges Reverses Self and Drops Marital Punishment', *Washington Post*, 21 July 1995.

2. See for example Kathleen Waits, 'The Criminal Justice System's Response to Battering: Understanding the Problem, Forging the Solutions', in Patricia Smith

many others in which violent behavior appears, in the eyes of the law, paradoxically to legitimate rather than to diminish a man's claim to authority over a woman.[3] Despite Judge Mestemaker's disclaimer, the requirement that a woman marry the rapist has precedents extending all the way back to the book of Deuteronomy.

My aim in this essay is to contribute to the genealogy of this peculiar legal subject who appears in the courts even today—the man who by 'virtue' of his violence confirms his control of a feminine object.[4] I maintain that biblical law (en)genders violence, and I interpret the Deuteronomic laws governing warfare and sexual assault (Deut. 20.1-20; 21.10-14; 22.23-29) as a discourse of male power. My interest is not in the juristic application of these laws in ancient Israel. The question of enforcing many of the laws was moot for the greater part of the biblical period. Instead I am concerned with the discursive capacity of these laws to construct gender. In the ancient cultural milieu where the Deuteronomic law was produced, violence against a feminine object was central to the consolidation of masculine identity. These laws, grounding male subjectivity in the violent relation to a female object, create a field of power where social relations based on a violent masculine prerogative come to appear inevitable.

While many readers have regarded the Deuteronomic laws of war and sexual assault as salutary attempts to curb violence or to protect people from its effects, I propose that the laws are productive of

(ed.), *Feminist Jurisprudence* (New York: Oxford University Press, 1993), pp. 188-210.

3. See the harrowing accounts of women's experience in rape trials documented by Z. Adler, *Rape on Trial* (London: Routledge & Kegan Paul, 1987); and Susan Estrich, *Real Rape* (Cambridge, MA, Harvard University Press, 1987); as well as the analysis of Carol Smart, *Feminism and the Power of Law* (Sociology of Law and Crime; London: Routledge, 1989), pp. 26-49. The common law tradition entitled a husband to 'chastize' his wife (i.e. to beat her), to rape her, and to keep her in his home by force. Blackstone distilled the principle in his assertion that a wife's legal existence is suspended during marriage (Frances E. Olsen, 'The Family and the Market: A Study of Ideology and Legal Reform', *Harvard Law Review* 96 [1983], pp. 1497-1578 [1536-37]). Efforts at reform of the US law codes have had mixed success: by 1982 ten states had eliminated the spousal exemption from their rape laws, but meanwhile thirteen had extended the exemption to unmarried cohabitants (Olsen, 'The Family and the Market', p. 1536 n. 150).

4. By 'genealogy' I mean not simply a tracing of origins, but rather a critical account of how power—in this case the power of male domination—works to make certain contingent historical effects seem necessary and normal.

violence: they render warfare and rape intelligible and acceptable, providing a means for people both to justify and endure violence. These laws valorize violent acts, construe them as essential to male agency, and define licit conditions for their exercise. As foundational texts of Western culture, these laws authenticate the role of violence in the cultural construction of gender up to the present day.

Theoretical Perspective

Critical Legal Studies and Biblical Law

In 1988 Peter J. Haas presented a paper to the SBL Biblical Law Group tracing parallels since the early nineteenth century between methodological developments in critical study of the Hebrew Bible and in Anglo-European legal theory.[5] He argued that new departures in the academic study of law (and in other humanistic disciplines), regularly presaged changes in the view of the biblical text. Thus, for example, the great German jurist and legal historian Friedrich Karl von Savigny (1779–1861), opposing a view of law as the result of a transhistorical rationality, developed a Romantic conception of law as the culturally embedded expression of a particular *Volksgeist*. Meanwhile W.M.L. de Wette (1780–1849) described biblical law as the product of ancient Israel's innate religious spirit, opposing the traditional view of Mosaic law as divine revelation. Subsequently in nineteenth-century Germany, Haas observes, nationalist reaction to the liberal legal reforms imposed by Napoleon stirred an attempt to recover an authentic Teutonic legal tradition. Legal scholarship became committed to the historicist project of relating law to the concrete circumstances of the nation, and to a positivist conception of law as 'the result of some kind of self-conscious legislation, that is, as the outcome of specific political activity carried out by people in a certain time and place'.[6] Similarly, Vatke's *Biblische Theologie* (1835) attempted to trace the development of Hebrew law in relation to the stages of ancient Israelite nation-building.

5. 'From Savigny to CLS: Legal Thought and the Biblical Text', paper presented to the SBL Biblical Law Group, November, 1988. My thanks to Professor Haas for providing me a copy of his paper. On parallels between the development of modern legal theory and biblical studies, see also Peter J. Haas, '"Die He Shall Surely Die": The Structure of Homicide in Biblical Law', *Semeia* 45 (1989), pp. 67-87 (71-73).

6. Haas, 'From Savigny to CLS', p. 8.

Bringing his analysis up to the present, Haas suggests that the study of biblical law might tend toward developments similar to those of the Critical Legal Studies (CLS) movement, where law is viewed not as an objectively intelligible moral order, but rather as a site of contested power.[7] CLS emerged in law schools in the United States in the 1970s, more a political movement inspired by the American New Left than a unified intellectual program, although the poststructuralist views of language and subjectivity advanced by Foucault, Derrida, and Lacan eventually figured prominently in CLS writing. Lacking a common method, the diverse proponents of CLS shared an opposition to hierarchy in the legal profession and to various forms of social domination. They were committed to egalitarian political goals and suspicious of the presumed neutrality, objectivity, and rationality of conventional legal doctrine. As deconstruction became influential in literary studies, CLS scholars applied the notion of radical indeterminancy to legal interpretation, 'trashing' legal doctrine by showing that arguments advocating a particular rule can just as readily be used in support of its opposite.[8] 'Legal consciousness' for CLS scholars refers to the self

7. 'From Savigny to CLS', pp. 18-21. Haas refers to Roberto Mangabeira Unger, *The Critical Legal Studies Movement* (Cambridge, MA: Harvard University Press, 1986). For surveys of the movement and examples of CLS scholarship, see *Critical Legal Studies: Articles, Notes and Book Reviews Selected from the Pages of the Harvard Law Review* (Cambridge, MA: The Harvard Law Review Association, 1986); Mark Kelman, *A Guide to Critical Legal Studies* (Cambridge, MA: Harvard University Press, 1987); Peter Fitzpatrick and Alan Hunt (eds.), *Critical Legal Studies* (Oxford: Basil Blackwell, 1987); Allan C. Hutchinson (ed.), *Critical Legal Studies* (Totowa, NJ: Rowman & Littlefield, 1988); David Kairys (ed.), *The Politics of Law: A Progressive Critique* (New York: Pantheon, rev. edn, 1990); James Boyle (ed.), *Critical Legal Studies: Selected Readings* (International Library of Essays in Law and Legal Theory; New York: New York University Press, 1992); Neil Duxbury, *Patterns of American Jurisprudence* (New York: Oxford University Press, 1995), pp. 421-509; Gary Minda, *Postmodern Legal Movements: Law and Jurisprudence at Century's End* (New York: New York University Press, 1995), pp. 106-27; and Richard W. Bauman, *Critical Legal Studies: A Guide to the Literature* (Boulder, CO: Westview Press, 1996).

8. Bauman, *Critical Legal Studies*, p. 35; Minda, *Postmodern Legal Movements*, p. 111. Mark Kelman describes the approach in this way: 'take specific arguments very *seriously* in their own terms; discover they are actually *foolish* ([tragi]-*comic*); and then look for some (external observer's) *order* (not the germ of truth) in the internally contradictory, incoherent chaos we've exposed' (quoted in

delusion inherent in the legal profession's unreflective attitude toward questions of interpretation and the politics of law.[9] CLS seeks constantly to uncover the contending interests at work in legal reasoning, hence it rejects the confidence of conventional legal theory that the rule of law can be depended upon to constrain power and protect people from its abuses. 'For CLS', observes Allan Hutchinson, 'the Rule of Law is a mask that lends to existing social structures the appearance of legitimacy and inevitability; it transforms the contingency of social history into a fixed set of structural arrangements and ideological commitments'.[10] Hence CLS maintains that often 'the very idea of the rule of law serves as an instrument of oppression and domination'.[11]

Reaching its height in the 1980s, by the early 1990s CLS had more or less dissipated as a movement.[12] The critical impulse of CLS, however, has been carried forward by feminist jurisprudence and critical race theory, and deconstructive strategies remain useful for contesting the hegemonic grip of conventional legal doctrine.[13] Admittedly it is a long way from Iron Age Israel and Judah, where the Deuteronomic law originated, to the world of postmodern legal theory. Yet biblical scholars have often acknowledged a degree of continuity between biblical law and the Western juridical tradition. Dale Patrick, for example,

Hutchinson [ed.], *Critical Legal Studies*, p. 209; for Mark Kelman's full discussion, see 'Trashing', *Stanford Law Review* 36 [1984], pp. 293-348).

9. Boyle, 'Introduction', in *Critical Legal Studies*, p. xxi.

10. Hutchinson, *Critical Legal Studies*, p. 3.

11. Andrew Altman, *Critical Legal Studies: A Liberal Critique* (Studies in Moral, Political, and Legal Philosophy; Princeton, NJ: Princeton University Press, 1990), p. 15.

12. Minda, *Postmodern Legal Movements*, p. 126; Duxbury, *Patterns of American Jurisprudence*, p. 468.

13. For orientation to the field of feminist legal scholarship, see Mary Joe Frug, 'A Postmodern Feminist Legal Manifesto', in *idem*, *Postmodern Legal Feminism* (London: Routledge, 1992), pp. 125-53; Carol Smart, 'Law's Truth/Women's Experience', in Regina Graycar (ed.), *Dissenting Opinions: Feminist Explorations in Law and Society* (London: George Allen & Unwin, 1990), pp. 1-20; Patricia Smith, 'Introduction: Feminist Jurisprudence and the Nature of Law', in Smith (ed.), *Feminist Jurisprudence*, pp. 3-16; Minda, *Postmodern Legal Movements*, pp. 128-48; Frances Olsen, 'The Sex of Law', in Kairys (ed.), *The Politics of Law*, pp. 453-67. On critical race theory, see Minda, *Postmodern Legal Movements*, pp. 167-88; and for more recent engagement with deconstruction, Costas Douzinas, Peter Goodrich, and Yifat Hachamovitch (eds.), *Politics, Postmodernity, and Critical Legal Studies: The Legality of the Contingent* (London: Routledge, 1994).

asserts that in comparison with biblical law, 'most Western legal traditions are as much descendants as rivals'.[14] Perhaps at present, as critics assert the radical contingency of interests borne in Western legal doctrine, it is appropriate to raise similar questions about biblical law, an ancestor of the received tradition. The oppositional stance of CLS is certainly appropriate for a gender-critical project like the present one, given the continuities in the oppression of women from the laws of biblical antiquity up to those of the contemporary West.

Discourse and the Subject: Genealogy as Critique

Michel Foucault asserts that the conditions for the appeal to 'truth' in any society are created by that culture's authoritative discourses:

> Each society has its régime of truth, its 'general politics' of truth: that is, the types of discourse which it accepts and makes function as true; the mechanisms and instances which enable one to distinguish true and false statements, the means by which each is sanctioned; the techniques and procedures accorded value in the acquisition of truth; the status of those who are charged with what counts as true.[15]

Authoritative discourses give social constructs their appearance of naturalness. Discourse does not therefore simply reflect social reality, but is productive of social formations in complex, reciprocal ways. In the words of Elizabeth Castelli, 'discourse "invents" social relations and is reinscribed by them'.[16] Discursive formations complement their productive power by suppressing possible alternatives, so that as discourse produces the social forms within which people live, it also

14. Dale Patrick, 'Studying Biblical Law as a Humanities', *Semeia* 45 (1989), pp. 27-47 (43); cf. especially J. J. Finkelstein, *The Ox That Gored* (Transactions of the American Philosophical Society, 71; Philadelphia: American Philosophical Society, 1981).

15. Michel Foucault, 'Truth and Power', in Colin Gordon (ed.), *Power/ Knowledge: Selected Interviews and Other Writings 1972–1977* (New York: Pantheon, 1981), p. 131. Foucault's writings have been rarely engaged by Hebrew Bible specialists, but that is beginning to change. For a Foucauldian approach to the problem of violence in the book of Joshua, see Lori L. Rowlett, 'Inclusion, Exclusion and Marginality in the Book of Joshua', *JSOT* 55 (1992), pp. 15-23; and *Joshua and the Rhetoric of Violence: A 'New Historicist' Analysis* (JSOTSup, 226; Sheffield: Sheffield Academic Press, 1996).

16. Elizabeth A. Castelli, *Imitating Paul: A Discourse of Power* (Literary Currents in Biblical Interpretation; Louisville, KY: Westminster/John Knox Press, 1991), p. 56.

determines what it is possible to think of or to speak of at a given historical moment.

In Foucault's view, both what we might call the exteriority of social forms and the interiority of human subjectivity are produced through the power relations effected in discourse. For Foucault, as for other poststructuralist thinkers, the stable, unified subject of Western humanism is displaced by an understanding of subjectivity as a transitory, contingent effect of differential relations (power relations in a Foucauldian perspective). This radical historicizing of the subject opens the possibility for critique and change, for even though people are, in this view, inescapably subject to the various discourses that constitute even their interior experience (hence the impossibility of the Enlightenment ideal of the autonomous subject), localized resistance can alter the discursive forms in which power is circulated. As the assumption of an essential human nature fades, possibilities for new forms of the self emerge. Caroline Ramazanoğlu summarizes this perspective:

> People are, therefore, social selves, and these social selves are not essential, but historically variable. They are also produced in power relations. People are constituted as subjects in discourses and disciplinary practices, and also (whether knowingly or not) contribute themselves to the process of turning themselves into particular kinds of subjects.[17]

'Genealogy' is the name Foucault (following Nietzsche) gives to the critical procedure by which the exercise of power in normative discourse is exposed, thereby creating the possibility of alternative formations.[18] As a philosophical strategy, Foucauldian genealogy is an 'exercise in exposing and tracing the installation and operation of false universals'.[19] As an approach to the human past, genealogy aims 'to

17. 'Introduction', in Caroline Ramazanoğlu (ed.), *Up against Foucault: Explorations of Some Tensions between Foucault and Feminism* (London: Routledge, 1993), p. 24.

18. See Foucault's essay, 'Nietzsche, la généalogie, l'histoire', in *Hommage à Jean Hyppolite, Epiméthée: Essais philosophiques* (Paris: Presses Universitaires de France, 1971), pp. 145-72; ET 'Nietzsche, Genealogy, History', in Donald Bouchard (ed.), *Language, Counter-Memory, Practice: Selected Essays and Interviews by Michel Foucault* (Ithaca, NY: Cornell University Press, 1977), pp. 139-64. See also Rudi Visker, *Michel Foucault: Genealogy as Critique* (London: Verso, 1995).

19. Judith P. Butler, *Bodies That Matter: On the Discursive Limits of 'Sex'* (London: Routledge, 1993), p. 282 n. 8.

historicize what is thought to be immutable'.[20] The contingency of false universals such as 'human nature', 'freedom', and 'rationality', Foucault asserts, needs to be disclosed through genealogical critique. Feminists have urged the same for normative notions of 'masculinity' and 'femininity'.[21]

Discourse and Gender

Michel Foucault was no feminist, as many have noted.[22] But a poststructuralist view of gender as a discursive product is a powerful tool for the critique of gender norms, because it radicalizes the basic feminist-critical contention that gender is a social construct.[23] This view stresses the gravity of the fact that the contingent (and disparate) categories of masculine and feminine give structure both to the social domain and to the realm of 'private' experience. A discursive theory of gender would, for example, problematize the notions of consent applied in most rape laws. Indeed, all forms of physical violence against women would be seen as part of a broader discursive field that circulates the power of male domination. As Teresa de Lauretis insists:

> The historical fact of gender, the fact that it exists in social reality, that it has concrete existence in cultural forms and actual weight in social relations, makes gender a political issue that cannot be evaded or wished away, much as one would want to, be one male or female. For even as we agree that sexuality is socially constructed and overdetermined, we cannot deny the particular specification of gender that is the issue of that

20. Steven Best and Douglas Kellner, *Postmodern Theory: Critical Interrogations* (Critical Perspectives; New York: Guilford Press, 1991), p. 46.

21. Judith P. Butler, *Gender Trouble: Feminism and the Subversion of Identity* (Thinking Gender; London: Routledge, 1990); see especially pp. 5, 33.

22. Teresa de Lauretis, 'The Violence of Rhetoric: Considerations on Representation and Gender', in Nancy Armstrong and Leonard Tennenhouse (eds.), *The Violence of Representation: Literature and the History of Violence* (Essays in Literature and Society; London: Routledge, 1989), pp. 239-58 (244-45); and *Alice Doesn't: Feminism, Semiotics, Cinema* (Bloomington: Indiana University Press, 1984), p. 94; see also the essays collected in Ramazanoğlu (ed.), *Up Against Foucault*; Jana Sawicki, 'Foucault and Feminism: A Critical Reappraisal', in Sawicki (ed.), *Disciplining Foucault: Feminism, Power, and the Body* (Thinking Gender; London: Routledge, 1991), pp. 95-109; Butler, *Gender Trouble*, pp. 91-106.

23. For critical legal pursuit of this point, see the editorial 'Patriarchy is Such a Drag: The Strategic Possibilities of a Postmodern Account of Gender', *Harvard Law Review* 108.8 (June 1995), pp. 1973-2008.

> process; nor can we deny that precisely such a process finally positions women and men in an antagonistic and asymmetrical relation.[24]

In many cultures, including those that produced the Hebrew Bible, violence and domination are central to the discursive production of the gendered subject. Intensely debated claims about the 'universality' of female subordination in human cultures have been qualified by ethnographic accounts of societies where male dominance is not determinative.[25] But across the cultural spectrum male domination remains almost ubiquitous, and despite the demonstrated variability in forms of masculinity, violence is most often construed as a masculine attribute.[26] In such cultural situations, gender becomes a crucial articulator of the experience of violence.[27] Perception of the rightness or wrongness of violence is shaped by normative gender discourses: violent acts bolster masculine identity while a woman's role, in many cultures, is properly to endure (i.e. receive) violence.

The power of male domination circulates through language that regularly positions the feminine as the lesser of two opposed values. Male and female are aligned with binary sets such as dominant–subordinate,

24. De Lauretis, 'The Violence of Rhetoric', p. 245.

25. Sherry B. Ortner asserted 'the universality of female subordination, the fact that it exists within every type of social and economic arrangement and in societies of every degree of complexity', in a 1972 essay ('Is Female to Male as Nature is to Culture?', in Sherry B. Ortner (ed.), *Making Gender: The Politics and Erotics of Culture* [Boston: Beacon Press, 1996], p. 21; originally published in *Feminist Studies* 1 [1972], pp. 5-31; and reprinted in Michelle Z. Rosaldo and Louise Lamphere (eds.), *Woman, Culture and Society* [Stanford: Stanford University Press, 1974], pp. 67-88). In her more recent work, Ortner summarizes two decades of debate and acknowledges the significance of societies like the Andaman Islanders, whose gender formations are 'hegemonically egalitarian' (*Making Gender*, p. 171).

26. See Sherry B. Ortner and Harriet Whitehead (eds.), *Sexual Meanings: The Cultural Construction of Gender and Sexuality* (Cambridge: Cambridge University Press, 1981); Henrietta Moore, 'The Problem of Explaining Violence in the Social Sciences', in Penelope Harvey and Peter Gow (eds.), *Sex and Violence: Issues in Representation and Experience* (London: Routledge, 1994), pp. 138-55; and Andrea Cornwall and Nancy Lindisfarne, 'Dislocating Masculinity: Gender, Power, and Anthropology', in *idem* (eds.), *Dislocating Masculinity: Comparative Ethnographies* (Male Orders; London, Routledge, 1994), pp. 11-47.

27. I borrow this phrase from Edith Hall, 'Asia Unmanned: Images of Victory in Classical Athens', in John Rich and Graham Shipley (eds.), *War and Society in the Greek World* (Leicester–Nottingham Studies in Ancient Society, 4; London: Routledge, 1989), pp. 109-10.

active–passive, complete–deficient, important–trivial, and honorable–shameful. The use of the masculine as a false generic, both in languages that exhibit grammatical gender and in those that do not, likewise positions the feminine as secondary and derivative. In certain figurative expressions, the feminine signifies an object of violence in opposition to male violent agency. For example, the Western press described a 1991 military invasion by Iraq as 'the rape of Kuwait'.[28] The figure of an invaded country as a raped woman derives its meaning from the prior signification of 'female' as 'object of (male) violence'.[29] These broader discourses of power that draw on the categories of gender are 'not always literally about gender itself'.[30] Yet they nonetheless reinscribe the female as 'essentially' an object of violence, rendering the associated gender roles more ostensibly 'natural', thus completing the discursive cycle of gendered violence. The biblical texts I will consider below exemplify this circulation of male violent power. As authoritative (scriptural) discourse, they are not simply records of the social conditions of ancient Israel; rather they have participated in the exercise

28. This figure has a long history of use, for example, the 'rape of Nanking' in the Second World War, Hitler's 'rape of Poland', etc. Cf. Susan B. Thistlethwaite, '"You May Enjoy the Spoil of Your Enemies": Rape as a Biblical Metaphor for War', *Semeia* 61 (1993), pp. 59-75 (59-60). For the masculinist rhetoric of the US military establishment, see Carol Cohn, 'Wars, Wimps, and Women: Talking Gender and Thinking War', in Miriam Cooke and Angela Woollacott (eds.), *Gendering War Talk* (Princeton, NJ: Princeton University Press, 1993), pp. 227-46. On popular representations of the US Gulf War, see James McBride, 'America's War in the Gulf: Phallic and Castration Imagery in the Rhetoric of Combat', in *War, Battering, and Other Sports: The Gulf Between American Men and Women* (Atlantic Highlands, NJ: Humanities Press, 1995), pp. 35-76.

29. Cf. de Lauretis, 'The Violence of Rhetoric', pp. 245-50. De Lauretis acknowledges that male-to-male violence also has a distinct semiotic value (e.g. in René Girard's category of 'violent reciprocity'). But this configuration derives its notion of reciprocity from the assumption that violence is intrinsically masculine, thus it is already based on the opposition of violent agency to a feminine object. De Lauretis's example of this primary opposition is ' "nature", as in the expression "the rape of nature", which at once defines nature as feminine, and rape as violence done to a feminine other (whether its physical object be a woman, a man, or an inanimate object)' (p. 249).

30. Joan W. Scott, 'Gender as a Useful Category of Historical Analysis', in *Gender and the Politics of History* (New York: Columbia University Press, 1988), pp. 28-52 (42); cf. Louis Montrose, 'The Work of Gender in the Discourse of Discovery', *Representations* 33 (1991), pp. 1-41 (1).

of this power, both in biblical antiquity and during other eras, whenever the bible has been a culturally significant text.[31]

The Deuteronomic Laws of Warfare (Deuteronomy 20.1-20)

It is now known precisely how, or in some cases whether, biblical law was practically applied in antiquity. As with other extant ancient Near Eastern legal materials—law codes, scribal exercises, court case protocols, and royal edicts—one must constantly ask whether biblical laws are descriptive or normative, actual or ideal. Are the legal materials 'rules' of conduct, reflections of legal practice, instructions for magistrates, or popular propaganda?[32] By the time Deuteronomy reached its present form, much of the law it contains apparently had no juridical application. Deuteronomic law, rather, belongs to a larger authoritative discourse. Set within the context of a speech by Moses, the law codes of Deuteronomy 12–26 represent the 'culmination of the impulse toward homily in biblical law'.[33] This sermonizing appropriation of the legal tradition is directed more toward the inculcation of values and the creation of identity than the juristic imposition of rules.

Of all the Deuteronomic laws, the war code is among the most utopian, as it had no application for the latter half of the biblical period. For most of the time from the death of Josiah in 609 BCE until the Maccabean period, Judah had no army to speak of and thus 'the laws of war were defunct'.[34] Even during the Josianic period, when the war code

31. Cf. Lori Rowlett's account of a New Historicist view of the relation of text and society, *Joshua and the Rhetoric of Violence*, p. 2. Rowlett refers to Stephen Greenblatt, *Shakespearean Negotiations: The Circulation of Social Energy in Renaissance England* (The New Historicism: Studies in Cultural Poetics, 4; Berkeley: University of California Press, 1988), p. 6.

32. See, for example, Eryl Davies, 'Ethics of the Hebrew Bible: The Problem of Methodology', *Semeia* 66 (1994), pp. 46-47; and Henry McKeating, 'Sanctions against Adultery in Ancient Israelite Society, with Some Reflections on Methodology in the Study of Old Testament Ethics', *JSOT* 11 (1979), pp. 65-71. For the ancient Near Eastern materials, see Martha T. Roth, *Law Collections from Mesopotamia and Asia Minor* (SBL Writings from the Ancient World Series, 6; Atlanta: Scholars Press, 1995), pp. 4-7, and the literature cited there.

33. Dale Patrick, *Old Testament Law* (Atlanta: John Knox Press, 1985), p. 257. In von Rad's words: 'Deuteronomy is not divine law in codified form, but preaching about the commandments' (*Studies in Deuteronomy* [Studies in Biblical Thology, 9; Chicago: Henry Regnery, 1953], p. 15).

34. Alexander Rofé, 'The Laws of Warfare in the Book of Deuteronomy: Their

apparently reached its present form, the requirement for total extermination (*ḥerem*) applied only to towns occupied by Canaanite peoples (20.15-17), nations that were understood by the seventh century BCE no longer to exist.[35] Thus the *ḥerem* is not allowed for later wars; it is designed in its literary presentation to be a thing of the past. Lori L. Rowlett's study of the Deuteronomic rhetoric of violence concludes that under Josiah the discursive function of the *ḥerem* texts had nothing to do with actual Canaanites, but rather with the aim to intimidate Josiah's own subjects into submission.[36]

Despite its practical obsolescence, however, the Deuteronomic war code exerts a profound effect on gender as an organizing category for human experience in the Hebrew Bible. The language of war in the Hebrew Bible and other ancient Near Eastern literatures is acutely masculinist. Warfare is emblematically male and the discourse of violence is closely intertwined with that of masculine sexuality. Harry A. Hoffner, Jr gives an accurate, if uncritical, summary:

> The masculinity of the ancient was measured by two criteria: (1) his prowess in battle, and (2) his ability to sire children. Because these two aspects of masculinity were frequently associated with each other in the mind of the early Near Easterner, the symbols which represented his masculinity to himself and his society often possessed a double reference. In particular, those symbols which primarily referred to his military exploits often served to remind him of his sexual ability as well.[37]

Hoffner adduces from Hittite the example of the noun LÚ-*natar*, which denotes 'masculinity' both in the sense of 'military exploit' and 'male

Origins, Intent and Positivity', *JSOT* 32 (1985), p. 39. Cf. Moshe Weinfeld, 'Deuteronomy, Book of', in *ABD*, II, p. 179; Norbert Lohfink, *ḥaram; ḥerem*, *TDOT*, III, p. 197; Philip D. Stern, *The Biblical Ḥerem: A Window on Israel's Religious Experience* (BJS, 211; Atlanta: Scholars Press, 1991).

35. Norbert Lohfink, 'Der "heilige Krieg" und der "Bann" in der Bibel', *IKZ* 18 (1989), pp. 104-12 (111).

36. Rowlett summarizes: 'Although the Canaanites are the ostensible victims in Joshua, the goal is not to incite literal violence against a particular ethnic group... The purpose of the rhetoric of violence in the conquest narrative is to serve as a warning to the people of Josiah's kingdom that the post-imperial power of the central government could and would be unleashed upon any who resisted its assertion of control' (*Joshua and the Rhetoric of Violence*, p. 184).

37. Harry A. Hoffner, Jr, 'Symbols for Masculinity and Femininity: Their Use in Ancient Near Eastern Sympathetic Magic Rituals', *JBL* 85 (1966), pp. 326-34 (327).

genitalia'.[38] To this may be compared Hebrew יד, which, like Ugaritic *yd*, can denote both military might (Exod 13.3; Isa. 10.32) and the penis (Isa. 57.8).[39]

'Manhood', in such contexts, entails the capacity to exert violence. The Philistines, for example, facing the Israelite threat at Ebenezer, exhort one another with the words היו לאנשים, literally, 'become men...and fight' (1 Sam. 4.9).[40] Conversely, 'woman' signifies one who succumbs to violence; hence men who are defeated in combat are reckoned as women. A Hittite prayer to Ishtar of Nineveh says of an enemy army:

> Take from (their) men masculinity, prowess, robust health, swords(?), battle-axes, bows, arrows, and dagger(s)! And bring them to Hatti! Place in their hands the spindle and mirror of a woman! Dress them as women! Put on their heads the *kureššar* [women's headdress]. And take them away from your favor!

Similar are the self-maledictory oaths of the Hittite soldiers:

> Whoever breaks these oaths... let these oaths change him from a man to a woman! Let them change his troops into women, let them dress them in the fashion of women and put on their heads the *kureššar* headdress! Let them break the bows, arrows, (and) weapons in their hands and let them put in their hands distaff and mirror![41]

The Hebrew prophets use this language in their taunts of Israel's enemies:

> Look at your troops:
> they are women in your midst! (Nah. 3.13)
> The warriors of Babylon have given up fighting,
> they remain in their strongholds;
> their strength has failed,
> they have become women! (Jer. 51.30; cf. Jer. 50.37; Isa. 19.16)

38. Hoffner, 'Symbols for Masculinity and Femininity', p. 327 n. 4.

39. *HALAT*, II, p. 370; *UT*, no. 1072; Joseph Aistleitner, *Wörterbuch der ugaritischen Sprache* (Berlin: Akademie-Verlag, 3rd edn, 1967), no. 1139.

40. David J. A. Clines, 'David the Man: The Construction of Masculinity in the Hebrew Bible', in *idem*, *Interested Parties: The Ideology of Writers and Readers of the Hebrew Bible* (Gender, Culture, Theory, 1; Sheffield: Sheffield Academic Press, 1995), pp. 218-19.

41. Hoffner, 'Symbols of Masculinity and Femininity', pp. 331-32; see also *ANET*, III, p. 354.

Masculinity and femininity are mobile properties in this language, a complementary pair reciprocally determined by their relation to violence. Violent power belongs to the former; subjugation and defeat to the latter.

A key aspect of the gendered discourse of war in the Hebrew Bible is the figurative portrayal of a city under attack as a woman sustaining sexual assault. The city personified as a woman is a common motif in ancient Near Eastern literature.[42] The Hebrew prophets develop this personification into an elaborate metaphorical picture where the objects of military attack (cities and land) are depicted as feminine, the attack itself is figured as sexual assault, and the soldiers in their military advance (in some cases along with God, ultimate instigator of the punishing violence) are portrayed as rapists.[43] For example, Jer. 13.20-27 describes the Babylonian attack of Jerusalem as a rape. At the approach of 'those who go in' (הבאים 13.20),[44] God threatens Jerusalem with sexual violence:

42. See Chayim Cohen, 'The "Widowed" City', *JANESCU* 5 (1973), pp. 74-81; A. Fitzgerald, 'The Mythological Background for the Presentation of Jerusalem as a Queen and False Worship as Adultery in the OT', *CBQ* 34 (1972), pp. 403-16; and '*BTWLT* and *BT* as Titles for Capital Cities', *CBQ* 37 (1975), pp. 167-83; John J. Schmitt, 'The Motherhood of God and Zion as Mother', *RB* 92 (1985), pp. 557-69; and 'The Virgin of Israel: Referent and Use of the Phrase in Amos and Jeremiah', *CBQ* 53 (1991), pp. 365-87; Elaine R. Follis, 'The Holy City as Daughter', in *idem* (ed.), *Directions in Biblical Hebrew Poetry* (JSOTSup, 40; Sheffield: Sheffield Academic Press, 1987), pp. 173-84; Mark Biddle, 'The Figure of Lady Jerusalem: Identification, Deification, and Personification of Cities in the Ancient Near East', in B. Batto, W. Hallo, and L. Younger (eds.), *The Canon in Comparative Perspective* (Scripture in Context, 4; Lewiston, NY: Edwin Mellen Press, 1991), pp. 173-94; Julie Galambush, *Jerusalem in the Book of Ezekiel: The City as Yahweh's Wife* (SBLDS, 130; Atlanta: Scholars Press, 1992).

43. See Pamela Gordon and Harold C. Washington, 'Rape as a Military Metaphor in the Hebrew Bible', in Athalya Brenner (ed.), *A Feminist Companion to the Latter Prophets* (The Feminist Companion to the Bible, 8; Sheffield: Sheffield Academic Press, 1995), pp. 308-25; and F. Rachel Magdalene, 'Ancient Near Eastern Treaty-Curses and the Ultimate Texts of Terror: A Study of the Language of Divine Sexual Abuse in the Prophetic Corpus', in Brenner (ed.), *A Feminist Companion to the Latter Prophets*, pp. 326-52.

44. Or, 'the penetrators'; the sexual connotation of the phrase is clear; cf. W.L. Holladay, *Jeremiah 1: A Commentary on the Book of the Prophet Jeremiah Chapters 1–25* (Hermeneia; Philadelphia: Fortress Press, 1986), p. 414.

It is for the greatness of your iniquity
that your skirts are lifted up,
and your genitals are ravaged (13.22).[45]

I propose to take language of this sort as a context for interpreting the Deuteronomic laws of warfare.

As androcentric speech addressed for the most part to a generic masculine subject, Deuteronomic law already relegates women to a secondary status.[46] The female reader or hearer must constantly assess whether she is meant to be subsumed among the male-identified addressees of these texts.[47] Military orations frame the entire book of Deuteronomy (1.29-33; 2.24-25, 31; 3.21-22; 7.17-24; 9.1-6; 11.22-25; 31.1-6; cf. 20.1-4).[48] Ostensibly men and women alike are addressed by these speeches. For example, Deut. 9.1:

> Hear, O Israel! You are about to cross the Jordan today, to go in and dispossess nations larger and mightier than you, great cities, fortified to the heavens.

But the war code of Deut. 20.1-20 is addressed only to men. The noun העם (20.1, 2, 5, 8, 9), here denotes not 'the people' in an inclusive

45. Cf. Jer. 6.1-8; Lam. 1–2; Hos. 2.2-13; Isa. 47.1-4; Nah. 3.5-6. On the translation of the expression נחמסו עקביך in Jer. 13.22, cf. F. Rachel Magdalene, 'Ancient Near Eastern Treaty-Curses', pp. 328-29; and J.C. Exum, 'Prophetic Pornography', in *idem* (ed.), *Plotted, Shot, and Painted: Cultural Representations of Biblical Women* (Gender, Culture, Theory, 3; Sheffield: Sheffield Academic Press, 1996), pp. 101-28 (107).

46. On the consequences of the masculine as linguistic norm, see Dale Spender, *Man Made Language* (London: Routledge & Kegan Paul, 1980); and Deborah Cameron, *Feminism and Linguistic Theory* (London: Macmillan, 1985), pp. 28-71.

47. As de Lauretis observes: 'Studies in language usage demonstrate that, if the term "man" includes women (while the obverse is not true, for the term "woman" is always gendered, i.e., sexually connoted), it is only to the extent that, in the given context, women are (to be) perceived as non-gendered "human beings", and thus as man' ('The Violence of Rhetoric', p. 256 n. 5). Cf. Athalya Brenner, 'An Afterword: The Decalogue—Am I an Addressee?', in *idem* (ed.), *A Feminist Companion to Exodus to Deuteronomy* (The Feminist Companion to the Bible, 6; Sheffield, Sheffield Academic Press, 1994), pp. 255-58. Brenner raises the question: how is a woman meant to read commandments such as, 'You shall not covet your neighbor's wife' (Deut. 5.21)?

48. Moshe Weinfeld, *Deuteronomy and the Deuteronomic School* (Oxford: Oxford University Press, 1972), pp. 45-51.

sense, but the army.[49] The war laws properly address the adult male who is called to combat: 'when you go out to war against your enemies' (כי־תצא למלחמה על־איביך, 20.1). The fact that the war laws are addressed to men might seem so obvious as to be trivial. But in a discursive context where 'the subject of violence is always, by definition, masculine',[50] even vicarious identification with texts like these is problematic for a woman, because a female-identified reader soon finds herself aligned with the object of violence. The male is by definition the subject of warfare's violence and the female its victim.

For example, the language of the siege instructions of Deut. 20.10-20 is densely supplied with syntactical groups joining a masculine singular verbal subject with a city as (feminine) object of attack. The laws thus reinscribe the discursive positioning of the feminine as object of violence. Given a linguistic milieu where cities are so often portrayed in the figure of a woman—either mother (Isa. 66.8-13), queen (Isa. 62.3), or virgin daughter (Isa. 37.22), a woman married (Isa. 62.5), widowed (Isa. 47.8, 9; 54.4; Lam 1.1), or raped (Jer. 6.1-8; 13.22; Isa. 47.1-4; Nah. 3.5-6)—the concentration of feminine forms in Deut. 20.10-20 inescapably evokes the figuration of the city as an assaulted woman, a construct that supplies basic cultural meaning to the categories of male and female. The gendered rhetoric of violence in biblical Hebrew here has a cumulative discursive effect.[51] In issuing the command to draw near to a city 'in order to attack it', this text effectively enjoins the soldier 'to attack her' (להלחם עליה, 20.10). The description of the submissive city 'opening' to the warrior (ופתחה לך, 20.11) evokes an image of male penetration. Similarly, the law uses the verb תפשׂ to describe the military seizure of a city (להלחם עליה לתפשׂה, 20.19), the same term used for the forcible seizure of a woman in sexual assault (ותפשׂה ושכב עמה, 22.28).[52]

49. Cf. Num. 20.20, 31.32; Judg. 5.2; Ps. 3.7 (J.H. Tigay, *Deuteronomy* [JPS Torah Commentary; Philadelphia: Jewish Publication Society, 1996], p. 379).

50. De Lauretis, 'The Violence of Rhetoric', p. 250.

51. It is not necessary for the various figurative associations of the feminine noun עיר, 'city', to be explicitly invoked in Deut. 20 for this effect to be operative. On the effects of grammatical gender as opposed to intrinsic or metaphorically gendered associations in language, cf. Cameron, *Feminism and Linguistic Theory*, pp. 57-71.

52. Moshe Weinfeld argues that Deut. 22.28 does not refer to force, translating the verb תפשׂ as 'to hold' (*Deuteronomy and the Deuteronomic School*, p. 486). But as Carolyn Pressler points out, 'the verb *tpś* has to do with coercion or violence

Many commentators emphasize the elements of restraint imposed by the laws of Deut. 20.1-20. A. Rofé, for example, maintains that these laws express 'a humanitarian idealism that sought to hold in check military abandon, bestiality, destructiveness, and cruelty'.[53] Deuteronomy 20 has been regarded as a source of modern Western standards concerning the role of non-combatants during warfare.[54] But the law knows nothing of the neutrality of non-combatants, nor is the valorization of warfare as manly predation ever brought into question in these texts. The laws prescribe offensive warfare (20.10a), the aim of the campaign being the seizure of property and captives, male and female (20.11b, 14). To the extent that the war code regulates violence, it does so toward the aim of more efficient exploitation. Among the besieged populations, lives are preserved in order to enslave them. Only by identifying with the conquerors is it possible to ascribe the injunction against cutting fruit trees (20.19), to 'humanitarian and environmental concern'.[55] The stipulation not to apply the axe to a tree in the event that 'you may eat from it' (כי ממנו תאכל, 20.19) simply completes the instruction that 'you may consume all the spoil of your enemies' (ואכלת את־שלל איביך, 20.14).

The exemptions from combat in Deut. 20.5-8 disclose the motive for constraint of violence in the war code. The majority of commentators, who emphasize in their readings the humaneness of these provisions, identify with the warriors envisioned by the laws. How else could they characterize texts that authorize the liquidation or enslavement of entire

whenever its direct object is a human being' ('Sexual Violence and Deuteronomic Law', in Athalya Brenner (ed.), *A Feminist Companion to Exodus to Deuteronomy* [The Feminist Companion to the Bible, 6; Sheffield: Sheffield Academic Press, 1994], pp. 102-12 (104); cf. C. Pressler, *The View of Women Found in the Deuteronomic Family Laws* (BZAW, 216; Berlin: W. de Gruyter, 1993), p. 38. Weinfeld's example is Jer. 40:10, ושבו בעריכם אשר תפשתם, which he translates: 'and live in towns that you have held'. But the context in Jer. 40 is armed revolt (cf. v. 7). Gedaliah refers in v. 10 to the towns that the leaders of Judean armed forces have seized and occupied with their troops.

53. Rofé, 'The Laws of Warfare in the Book of Deuteronomy', p. 37; cf. Tigay, *Deuteronomy*, p. 185.

54. M. Walzer, *Just and Unjust Wars: A Moral Argument with Historical Illustrations* (New York: Basic Books, 1977), pp. 134-35, 170.

55. Ian Cairns, *Deuteronomy: Word and Presence* (International Theological Commentary; Grand Rapids: Eerdmans, 1992), p. 186; cf. Anthony Phillips, *Deuteronomy* (The Cambridge Bible Commentary; Cambridge: Cambridge University Press, 1973), p. 137.

populations as 'humanitarian'?[56] The law exempts from combat a man who might shrink from the fighting (האיש הירא ורך הלבב, 20.8; he can be conceived only as fearful and disheartened). This is not a compassionate discharge; the individual presumably incurs shame for withdrawing. The man is removed from combat lest he compromise the military effectiveness of his fellows (20.8b). In the remaining cases, exemption from combat is grounded in the anxiety that 'another man' (איש אחר) might enjoy the newly acquired house, vineyard, or wife of a soldier who dies in war (20.5-7; cf. 24.5, 28.30). The aim of a siege is the acquisition of spoils, and the motive for this exemption is, in Gerhard von Rad's words, 'the idea that these men have a right to property and its produce which ought not to be curtailed by a possible death in action'.[57]

Here are envisioned soldiers setting out to deprive another people of their homes, their property, and their lives. Death in battle is a regrettable fate, but presumably an honorable one for the warrior. What cannot be tolerated, however, is the prospect of dying in combat and leaving behind a wife or property upon which the soldier never asserted his possession. The man's participation in war is checked, but only to preclude another Israelite male's encroachment upon his unrealized right of ownership. The fundamental priorities of the law are demonstrated in the release from combat of the man who has just taken possession of a wife, 'lest he die in the battle and another man take her' (20.7). This is the misfortune that a male code of war cannot allow.

The War-Captive Woman (Deuteronomy 21.10-14)

As with the other Deuteronomic laws governing warfare, there is reason to doubt that this law was extensively applied. Robert Carroll, for example, asks:

56. See for example, A.D.H. Mayes, *Deuteronomy* (NCB; London: Oliphants, 1979), p. 291. Compare J.A. Thompson's commentary on Deut. 20.5-7: 'This humanitarian spirit is a feature of Deuteronomy... [He cites numerous examples, including kindness to animals, Deut. 5.14; 22.6-7; 25.4.] Such a picture is a noble one and portrays an attitude toward life that finds echoes in the New Testament (Mt. 5.43-45; Lk. 6.27-30; Rom. 12.20; Jas 2.1-13). It is altogether according to the Spirit of Christ' (J.A. Thompson, *Deuteronomy: An Introduction and Commentary* [TOTC; Leicester: Inter-Varsity Press, 1974], p. 221).

57. Gerhard von Rad, *Deuteronomy: A Commentary* (trans. D. Barton; OTL; Philadelphia: Westminster Press, 1966), p. 132. Von Rad is either unaware or unconcerned that the property he refers to here includes women.

> What evidence is there for the view that the Israelites went to war against the Egyptians, Syrians, Assyrians, Babylonians, Persians, Greeks, and even Romans and collected wives from these groups whenever they achieved a victory against them?[58]

Warfare for the purpose of seizing women, however, does appear in biblical narrative (Judg. 21.8-12), and in Ugaritic epic (*KTU* 1.14-16), where the hero Kirta stages a military expedition to capture a woman from a neighboring city.[59]

Rape has accompanied warfare in virtually every known historical era.[60] Hence biblical commentators sometimes regard Deut. 21.10-13 as a prohibition of rape on the battlefield.[61] This is not the case, however. Although the law addresses the soldier ('when you go out to battle against your enemies' 21.10a), it governs conduct after the victorious completion of combat: 'and the Lord your God gives them into your hands' (21.10b). The setting is one where a town has fallen and the conquering soldiers are assembling captives from among the survivors. The law does not curtail men's rape and subsequent killing or abandonment of women during combat (cf. 20.14).

If the law is not concerned with the problem of rape in battle, it does give sanction to sexual coercion in the aftermath of war. Carolyn Pressler argues that the conditional protasis of the law extends through the phrase והבאתה אל־תוך ביתך in 21.12a. Thus:

> *When* you go out to battle against your enemies and the Lord your God gives them into your hands, and you take them captive, *if* you see among the captives a beautiful woman whom you desire and want to marry and bring into your household, *then* she shall shave her head, and pare her nails.[62]

58. Robert Carroll, 'War in the Hebrew Bible', in John Rich and Graham Shipley (eds.), *War and Society in the Greek World* (Leicester–Nottingham Studies in Ancient Society, 4; London: Routledge, 1993), p. 39.

59. H. L. Ginsberg, *The Legend of King Keret: A Canaanite Epic of the Bronze Age* (BASORSup, 2-3; New Haven: American Schools of Oriental Research, 1946); Johannes C. de Moor, *An Anthology of Religious Texts from Ugarit* (Nisaba Religious Texts Translation Series, 16; Leiden: E. J. Brill, 1987), pp. 191-223.

60. On the prevalence of rape in warfare, cf. Susan Brownmiller, *Against Our Will: Men, Women, and Rape* (New York: Simon & Schuster, 1975), pp. 31-113.

61. For examples, see Pressler, *The View of Women*, p. 11 n. 4.

62. Pressler, *The View of Women*, p. 10 (italics mine). This appears to be the Massoretic reading (followed by RSV and NRSV), marking the syntactic break with an *athnaḥ* in v. 12. JPSV extends the conditional clause through v. 11b, which can also accord with Pressler's interpretation of the law.

This reading, Pressler suggests, accounts for the double reference to marriage in the passage. The first is anticipatory, 'whom you desire and want to take as your wife' (v. 11b); the second refers to the concluded marriage, 'you will marry her (ובעלתה) and she will become your wife' (v. 13b). This interpretation likewise recognizes the syntactic break marked by the transition from second person masculine address (vv. 10-12a) to third person feminine injunction (vv. 12b-13a). Construed in this way, the effect of the law is to validate a man's long-term possession of a woman whom he has captured by force. As Pressler describes it, a primary intent of the law is to provide the means for a man to marry a woman who, as a war captive, has no legally competent family representative to conclude the marriage contract.[63] The woman's parents are presumably dead or enslaved (she is expected to mourn them in v. 13).

I agree with Pressler's reading of the text, but I think it is important to notice that the woman might also have had a husband and children before her capture.[64] The woman whom the victorious Israelite will marry is identified only as an adult female whom the man finds attractive (אשת יפת־תאר, v. 11). It is not necessary that she be a virgin (בתולה)[65] or an unbetrothed young woman (נערה אשר לא־ארשה). The law respects such distinctions only within the Israelite community (as in the Deuteronomic laws of adultery and sexual assault, Deut. 22.13-30), where a woman's status as the wife of a husband, or a marriageable (unbetrothed) young woman, determines the degree of a man's offense in having unauthorized sexual intercourse with her. From the victor's perspective that this law adopts, the adult male's prerogative over dependent females (sexual access for the husband, right of disposal for the father or guardian), has no validity among defeated enemies.

Given that the woman in this passage attains her position in marriage

63. Pressler, *The View of Women*, pp. 13-14. Cf. Pressler, 'Sexual Violence and Deuteronomic Law', pp. 102-103 n. 2.

64. Modern commentators generally do not consider this possibility, but Josephus and the rabbinic sources assume that married women are covered by this law (see Tigay, *Deuteronomy*, p. 381 n. 27.)

65. Or perhaps 'girl of marriageable age', i.e., 'nubile young woman' (G.J. Wenham, '*Bětûlāh*, A Girl of Marriageable Age', *VT* 22 [1972], pp. 326-48), but cf. the critique of Alexander Rofé, 'Family and Sex Laws in Deuteronomy and the Book of Covenant', *Henoch* 9 (1987), pp. 131-59 (136); and Pressler, *The View of Women*, pp. 25-28.

as the victim of capture by military attack, how should we regard the sexual relation depicted here? The provision for treatment of the war-captive woman can be viewed as a prohibition of rape only under the premise that women possess no personhood or bodily integrity apart from the determination of men. The fact that the man must wait for a month before penetrating the woman (ואחר כן תבוא אליה, 21.13) does not make the sexual relationship something other than rape, unless one assumes that by the end of the period the woman has consented. Commentators sometimes entertain this notion, perhaps evoking the familiar psychological phenomenon of a captive's identification with her captor. But to assume the consent of the woman is to erase her personhood. Only in the most masculinist of readings does the month-long waiting period give a satisfactory veneer of peaceful domesticity to a sequence of defeat, bereavement, and rape.

There is some question among the commentators regarding the purpose of the waiting period stipulated in v. 13. The symbolic acts prescribed for the beginning of the period (shaving of the head, paring of nails, and exchange of garment) have been interpreted as mourning rituals.[66] While these actions may seem suggestive of mourning, however, they do not correspond in detail to mourning rituals attested elsewhere in the Hebrew Bible or the ancient Near East. Hence the more widely accepted view is that the actions mark the woman's transition from her native community to that of her captors.[67] This view is confirmed by anthropological studies that have shown that transition rituals typically incorporate dramatic bodily marking (shaving, painting, cutting) to symbolize the liminal status of the individual in transition from one social identity to another.[68] If this interpretation is correct, the woman's incorporation into her captor's household is marked by ritual physical degradation. The shaving of a woman's head would have had this value

66. Von Rad, *Deuteronomy*, p. 137 Peter C. Craigie, *The Book of Deuteronomy* (NICOT; Grand Rapids: Eerdmans, 1976), p. 281; Thompson, *Deuteronomy*, p. 228.

67. For details, see Pressler, *The View of Women*, pp. 12-13.

68. The basic study of liminality in ritual is Victor W. Turner, *The Ritual Process: Structure and Anti-Structure* (New York: Aldine, 1969). A similar social function should probably be attributed to the comparable actions of the war-captive woman in the Mari texts (shaving of head and putting off clothes); see M. du Buit, 'Quelques contacts bibliques dans les archives royales de Mari', *RB* 66 (1959), pp. 576-81; and Mayes, *Deuteronomy*, p. 303.

in any ancient Near Eastern or Eastern Mediterranean culture (cf. Isa. 3.24).[69]

The text asserts that the waiting period before the man assumes sexual access to the woman is intended to allow the woman to mourn her parents (ובכתה את־אביה ואת־אמה, v. 13), yet the purpose of this provision too is problematic. Nowhere else in biblical law is a specific period of mourning stipulated for an occasion of bereavement. A variety of traditional mourning periods, ranging from three and seven days after death to the first anniversary of death, is attested in narrative and prophetic texts.[70] The usual period of mourning would appear to be seven days (Gen. 50.10; 1 Sam. 31.13; 1 Chron. 10.12; Jdt. 16.24; Sir. 22.12). Only twice is a thirty-day mourning period attested, when all Israel mourns the deaths of Aaron and Moses. In these cases, however, the period is denoted by the number of days (שלשים יום, Num. 20.29; Deut. 34.8) in contrast to the present text, which refers to 'a full month' (ירח ימים, Deut. 21.13).

Why does the law require a specific period of time for mourning only here, where the bereaved is not yet a member of the Israelite community? Why the relatively long period of time? And why the unusual designation for the period, ירח ימים, rather than the expected שלשים יום? An obvious solution is that by waiting a 'full month', that is, long enough for the woman's menstrual cycle to be completed, the man is assured his paternity of any children resulting from intercourse with her. This would be considered especially relevant since the woman is non-Israelite, not presumed to be a virgin or of marriageable status, and possibly the wife of another man among the defeated enemy. The burden of this requirement, therefore, is not to give adequate time for the woman's mourning, but rather to prevent the man from engaging in intercourse until it is clear that the woman is not pregnant. In this instance male sexual aggression is constrained only to secure the claim to paternity, another element of male sexual control.

Most interpreters credit the final provision of the law for its generosity to the woman (v. 14). She cannot be sold as a slave, but must be

69. Akiba, Rashi, and other rabbinic commentators assume the purpose is to make the woman unattractive to her captor (Tigay, *Deuteronomy*, p. 194).

70. For a survey of periods of mourning in the biblical and rabbinic periods, see Julian Morgenstern, *Rites of Birth, Marriage, Death and Kindred Occasions Among the Semites* (Cincinnati: Hebrew Union College Press/Quadrangle Books, 1966), pp. 164-66.

released as a 'free Israelite' if the man decides he wishes not to keep her.[71] Granted, this provision limits the man's ability to exploit his captive economically: he may not sell her (ומכר לא־תמכרנה בכסף). But it seems to me a strange case of apologetic legal consciousness to describe the law as a sanction against abuse, when the motivation enunciated for the rule of v. 14 is the fact that 'you have abused her' (תחת אשר עניתה, v. 14b). What sort of abuse does the text refer to in the expression עניתה? Does this refer to the devasting circumstances of the woman's original capture, the destruction of her home, killing of her family, and forcible removal of her person? Or does it refer to the woman's subjugation to ritual denigration in the captor's household, followed by compelled sexual penetration? Is the woman humiliated by the decision to dismiss her after marriage, or perhaps by the man's choice not to go through with the marriage after bringing her to his household?[72] The law is typically considered to remedy the mistreatment, whatever it may have been, by stipulating that the woman must be divorced as a wife rather than sold as a slave. But what sort of remedy does this avail a non-Israelite woman, to be released as a 'free citizen' in a patriarchal society where a woman's safety depends on her secure attachment to a male head of household?

There is slight protection for the woman in this law. The primary effect of the law is to assure a man's prerogative to abduct a woman through violence, keep her indefinitely if he wishes, or discard her if she is deemed unsatisfactory, above all, perhaps, if she proves to be pregnant by another man. By authorizing the violent seizure of women, this law takes the male-against-female predation of warfare out of the battlefield and brings it to the home.[73] It has its discursive effects, I would argue, in the construction of gender even in households that have never been touched by war.

71. Phillips, *Deuteronomy*, pp. 140-41; Dennis T. Olson, *Deuteronomy and the Death of Moses: A Theological Reading* (Overtures to Biblical Theology; Minneapolis, Fortress Press, 1994), p. 97; Mayes, *Deuteronomy*, p. 303.

72. Cf. Mayes, *Deuteronomy*, p. 304; Pressler, *The View of Women*, p. 12; Tikvah Frymer-Kensky, 'Law and Philosophy: The Case of Sex in the Bible', *Semeia* 45 (1989), pp. 89-102 (100 n. 9) and *In the Wake of the Goddesses: Women, Culture, and the Biblical Transformation of Pagan Myth* (New York: Free Press, 1992), p. 274 n. 34.

73. Cf. Pressler: 'All of the actions commanded by the law take place within the household' (*The View of Women*, p. 11).

Sexual Assault (Deuteronomy 22.23-29)

The statutes of Deut. 22.23-29 are not 'rape laws'; they are not designed to protect persons from sexual violence.[74] Most observers today would recognize the two instances of force in the text (החזיק, v. 25; תפש, v. 28) as rape, that is, the violent crime of forcing another person to submit to sexual intercourse. Biblical law, however, has no category of sexual assault, nor does biblical Hebrew have a word for rape as such.[75] The verb עִנָּה (piel) is used to designate acts that some readers would call rape (such as Amnon's attack on Tamar, 2 Sam. 13.12-14), but the semantic field of this word extends to a rather broad category of 'mistreatment'. Even in sexual contexts, the offense denoted by עִנָּה does not necessarily coincide with modern definitions of rape (e.g. Ezek. 22.10-11).[76] In Deuteronomy 22 the word עִנָּה designates the sexual violation, or 'misuse of', a woman (vv. 24, 29), but this is different from a recognition of the crime as an act of sexual violence against a woman. Rather than rape laws, the rules of Deut. 22.23-29 are best classified as a subset of the general law of adultery preceding them in Deut. 22.22. All of these laws illustrate the gender asymmetry common to the adultery sanctions of ancient Near Eastern and Mediterranean cultures: only a man can be aggrieved by an act of adultery, because adultery is defined as one male's violation of another man's right to possess a woman.

The lack of a legal category or even a word for rape as such in the Hebrew Bible illustrates the fact that the cultural meaning of sexual violence against women is a complex social production that is inextricably tied up, in experience and in representation, with exchanges of power. Sexual experiences of pleasure or distress, of mutuality or coercion, are available to individuals only as discursive products, contingent upon the cultural forms through which they are realized. There is no unmediated experience of sexuality or of violence apart from the

74. See especially Pressler, 'Sexual Violence and Deuteronomic Law', pp. 111-12.

75. Cf. Lyn M. Bechtel: 'The problem lies in the fact that what modern society calls "rape" is described in several Hebrew Bible texts, but there is no specific term for "rape" in Hebrew' ('What if Dinah is not Raped? [Genesis 34]', *JSOT* 62 [1994], p. 20).

76. Frymer-Kensky, 'Law and Philosophy', pp. 93, 100 n. 9; and *In the Wake of the Goddesses*, pp. 192-94, 274 n. 34.

channels of meaning and power constructed in a particular culture.[77] By describing rape, like gender, as a discursive formation, I do not mean to de-emphasize the physical reality of sexual violence against women in patriarchal cultures. Rather I adopt this critical perspective to describe how texts like Deuteronomy 22 generate cultural meanings of rape that simultaneously silence women's experience of violence and authorize male force.[78] The fact that the biblical laws do not recognize rape as a crime against women indicates the centrality of violence for the construction of gender in the Hebrew Bible. A culture understands rape as a crime against women only to the extent that it denies the violent masculine prerogative, and only so far as women, along with men, are assumed to possess bodily integrity. Neither of these conditions attains in the Deuteronomic law.

For rape to be recognized as a crime of force, there must be an acknowledgment of a woman's capacity to consent to sexual relations. This means, of course, that she must also be assumed to be capable of

77. Michel Foucault, *The History of Sexuality*. I. *An Introduction* (New York: Vintage Books, 1978). Foucault maintains that the very notion of sexuality is a modern disciplinary construct. This is a helpful reminder of the need to historicize interpretations of sexual relations in antiquity. I hasten to add, however, that for pragmatic reasons I reject Foucault's controversial proposal to 'desexualize' rape in the criminal codes by making it an ordinary civil offense punishable by a fine (in his introduction to a debate on rape in the Change Collective publication *La Folie encerclée* [Paris: Seghers-Laffont 1977]). For critique and discusion of Foucault's views, see Monique Plaza, 'Our Costs and Their Benefits', *m/f* 4 (1980), pp. 28-39; and Winifred Woodhull, 'Sexuality, Power, and the Question of Rape', in Irene Diamond and Lee Quinby (eds.), *Feminism and Foucault: Reflections on Resistance* (Boston: Northeastern University Press, 1988), pp. 167-76.

78. In her interpretation of Rembrandt's paintings of the raped Lucretia, Mieke Bal examines the rhetoric responsible for the 'artificial construction of rape', 'the semiotics of rape itself', and the 'semiotic use of rape for other purposes': 'Visual Rhetoric: The Semiotics of Rape', in *Reading 'Rembrandt': Beyond the Word–Image Opposition* [Cambridge New Art History and Criticism; Cambridge: Cambridge University Press, 1991], pp. 60-93 [61]). 'Rhetoric', she asserts, 'by shaping meaning, constructs reality through the construction of the meanings it offers reality to work with. That is to say, the rhetorical analysis does not stand in opposition to the real issue of rape. Rather, it partakes of it, the rhetorical figurations helping to construct the views of rape dominant in the culture in which the rhetorical discourse or image functions, and to condition the responses to real rape' (p. 69). My aim in connecting rape to discursive formations is akin to Bal's use here of the categories of rhetoric and semiotics.

refusing consent.[79] Deuteronomic law ostensibly applies a standard of consent in the stipulation that a betrothed young woman who is assaulted in the open country is not culpable, as she presumably cried for help but was not heard (22.27). This standard of consent founders, however, in the treatment of sexual assault within a town. If a man illicitly penetrates a betrothed young woman within the confines of the community, the law presumes that she did not cry for help, and so must have consented to the intercourse (22.24). The law fails to countenance the reality that a cry for help may go unheeded, or that an attacker can violently silence his victim, or can subdue her through a combination of deceit and intimidation (cf. 2 Sam. 13).[80] Thus Deuteronomic law refuses to recognize that rape can take place in town or in the home (a notion of collective male honor may be at stake here). This creates an impossible contradiction in a woman's standing under the law: the culture defines masculine gender in terms of strength and domination, while the feminine is seen as intrinsically weak and dependent. A woman is not generally positioned as one with the capacity to consent (or not), yet here she is presumptively blamed (and in v. 24 executed), for having consented to imposed illicit intercourse.

The material issue of these laws is neither the consent of the woman nor the act of violence against her, but rather the man's status of ownership over the woman who is misused. The laws do not protect women against sexual violence; rather they secure men's property interests.[81] No consistent determination of force or of consent pertains to the laws of Deut. 22.22-29 as a group. A coherent principle, however, of negotiability of possession determines the gravity of the offense and severity of the penalty to the man in each case. If a man transgresses another man's right to exclusive sexual access to a woman—if, in other words,

79. Smart, *Feminism and the Power of Law*, pp. 32-34; *idem*, 'Law's Truth/ Women's Experience', p. 14.

80. Mieke Bal comments on the standard of consent in Deuteronomy 22: 'Evidence that the woman screamed for help is the only evidence that the man raped her. Although there are surely other means of establishing a lack of consent, this form of proof...sounds more convincing than it really is. Screams can be staged, while the capacity to scream can be eliminated practically (in an isolated location) or psychically (by paralysis)' ('Rape: Problems of Intention', in Elizabeth Wright (ed.), *Feminism and Psychoanalysis: A Critical Dictionary* [Oxford: Basil Blackwell, 1992], pp. 367-71 (368).

81. This also emerges clearly in Pressler's study, 'Sexual Violence and Deuteronomic Law', esp. pp. 103, 107.

he has intercourse with the wife or betrothed of another man—he is subject to the death penalty (22.22, 23, 25). If, however, a man illicitly penetrates a woman who is legally still available (namely, unbetrothed, thus still under the right of disposal of her father or guardian), he pays an amount comparable to what he would have paid for a properly negotiated marriage contract (22.29).[82]

Thus in the case of the rape of the unbetrothed woman of 22.28-29, the woman's bodily integrity is treated as what modern legal theory would call a fungible object, namely, something that is replaceable with money or other objects. This utterly effaces the woman's personhood. A fungible object properly 'can pass in and out of a person's possession without effect on the person'.[83] To treat the woman's bodily integrity as if it were this sort of exchangeable commodity erases her as a legal subject. An asset, moreover, is properly fungible when the possessor herself receives compensation in exchange for it. Here, however, it is not the woman but her father who receives the payment.

The Deuteronomic laws therefore protect a household against the theft of a marriageable woman without the paying of a brideprice, but they do not diminish the reality that women in this society are at men's disposal. The laws might be called 'rape laws', not because they provide sanction against sexual assault, but because they institute and regulate rape so that men's proprietary sexual access to women is compromised as little as possible. The laws do not interdict sexual violence; rather they stipulate the terms under which a man may commit rape, provided he pays reparation to the offended male party. Once again male violence is constrained not out of consideration for potential victims, but to secure a more fundamental form of male control.

The Deuteronomic laws offer none of the women envisioned in the various cases protection against violence. On the contrary, if a woman who is attacked is already the wife of another man, she will probably

82. Perhaps including an additional amount as a fine. Deut. 22.29 does not use the term מהר, 'brideprice'(cf. Exod. 22.16), and as Moshe Weinfeld observes, the amount of a brideprice appears to have been negotiated for each marriage according to the circumstances of the families (*Deuteronomy and the Deuteronomic School*, pp. 285-86). It is possible therefore that the sum of fifty shekels stipulated in Deut. 22.29 represents an average brideprice plus punitive damages (Tigay, *Deuteronomy*, p. 208).

83. Cf. Margaret Jane Radin's discussion of financial compensation for rape victims: 'Market Inalienability', in Smith (ed.), *Feminist Jurisprudence*, pp. 389-430 (399).

lose her life (v. 22). If a rape victim is still under the right of disposal of her father, the law validates rape as a means of transferring possession of a woman from the father's household to that of the rapist (v. 29). To regard the requirement that the offender marry the victim, along with the stipulation that he may not divorce her, as a 'reparative marriage' benefiting the woman, is to identify with the male power exercised by this text. It is to assume that the woman is somehow better off in the household of her attacker than she would be if she remained in the household of her father or guardian (cf. 2 Sam. 13.20b). This would be to endorse the process by which, as still happens in the courts today, the law places a woman even more securely in the grip of the man who assaulted her.

Conclusion

> *My point is not that everything is bad, but that everything is dangerous.*
> Michel Foucault, 'On the Genealogy of Ethics: An Overview of Work in Progress'

I have noted how frequently biblical commentators express their esteem for the 'humaneness' or 'universal compassion' of Deuteronomy, and even for the Deuteronomic laws of warfare and sexual assault when considered in their ancient Near Eastern context.[84] I have also made it clear that I find this optimistic reading difficult to sustain. Such an interpretation seems to me to be similar to the admiration that liberal political philosophers give to ancient Athens for its founding of the democratic principle of equality under the law.[85] These interpreters tend to downplay the fact that the provision of equality under law for citizens of the Greek polis excluded women, slaves, poor people, and foreigners; and similar disenfranchisements have, to varying degrees, characterized most Western societies throughout history.

A basic insight of Foucault's is that the ostensible regulation of power can be a means of legitimating and ensuring the effective exercise of domination and violence. When commentators write

84. For additional examples, see Moshe Weinfeld, *Deuteronomy and the Deuteronomic School*, pp. 282-97; and David Daube, 'Biblical Landmarks in the Struggle for Women's Rights', *Juridical Review* 23 (1980), pp. 177-80.

85. Cf. Altman, *Critical Legal Studies: A Liberal Critique*, pp. 22-23. Altman refers to Chester Starr, *Individual and Community: The Rise of the Polis* (New York: Oxford University Press, 1986), p. 90.

appreciatively of these biblical laws as constraints of force they overlook the fact that the laws neither protect victims from attack nor provide remedies for violence; they actually authorize the unleashing of violence. The Deuteronomic war code seems restrictive only to the reader who identifies with the perspective of the victor in offensive warfare envisioned by the laws, and only if one is not troubled by their reinscription of the masculinist ethos and rhetoric of ancient Near Eastern warfare. The laws of sexual assault secure men's possession of their wives and betrothed under pain of death, but if a man rapes an unbetrothed woman, the effect of the law is irrevocably to seal the rapist's control of his victim. In this perspective the laws function as a discourse of male power. Far from ameliorating male domination, they install it and circulate its force. The laws confirm, in other words, Foucault's claim that juridical power generates the desires it claims to regulate, producing the very subjects it purports to control.

From the perspective of women who cannot assume that society grants them their own bodily integrity, and of men as well as women whose lives are marred by the cultural validation of violence, these laws are more bane than benefit. Even if the station of women in Deuteronomy appears relatively advantageous in the ancient Near Eastern context, it remains important to recognize the enduring contribution of these laws to the construction of male gender as licitly violent, and thus their post-biblical role in the maintenance of the institutions of warfare and rape.[86]

86. Preparation of this essay was supported by research grants from the National Endowment for the Humanities and the Harry Frank Guggenheim Foundation. Portions of this essay also appear in slightly different form in my article 'Violence and the Construction of Gender in the Hebrew Bible: A New Historicist Approach', *BibInt* 5 (1997), pp. 324-63. I am grateful to the SBL Biblical Law Group for providing a forum for the initial presentation of this work, to Sherry Wright for research assistance, and to Pamela Gordon for critical suggestions and moral support.

THE FEMALE SLAVE

Raymond Westbrook

Introduction

In the legal systems of the ancient Near East, male and female slaves were for the most part subject to the same rules.[1] Of necessity, however, there were special rules for female slaves in respect of their sexuality and reproductive capacity. Regrettably, sources that deal with female slaves as a separate category are scattered and few. My interest in gathering them together is twofold. First, concentrating attention on material concerning females alone may throw new light on familiar sources that are usually considered only in their immediate textual context or from the viewpoint of slavery in general. Secondly, the rules that governed the condition of female slaves are of particular jurisprudential interest because they arose from a conflict between family law, which applied to slaves as persons, and property law, which applied to slaves as chattels. Sometimes the one institution prevailed, sometimes the other, and sometimes the rules represented a compromise between the two.

The legal framework for sexual relations between free persons was either concubinage or marriage.[2] Both applied to female slaves, but in differing measure.

1. Sigla such as Nbn. 682 refer to publications of copies of cuneiform texts. The full titles are given in the Provisional List of Bibliographical Abbreviations of the *Chicago Assyrian Dictionary*. The abbreviations for the cuneiform law codes are those used in M. Roth, *Law Collections from Mesopotamia and Asia Minor* (Atlanta: Scholars Press, 1995), where an English translation of the paragraphs cited may be found. All translations in this article are the author's.

2. A third possible framework was prostitution, but being a transitory arrangement it was obviously not relevant to relations between master and slave. Female slaves were used for prostitution with third parties, e.g. Nbn. 682.

Concubinage

Status of the Woman

Since a female slave was property, her owner could exploit or dispose of her sexuality like any other beneficial aspect of property. She could thus be made her owner's concubine or could be given in concubinage to another at her owner's behest. Where concubinage resulted in motherhood, however, the slave might be accorded some qualified protection from the consequences of her status as property. According to LH 171, a slave concubine who had borne her master children had to be freed by operation of law after his death. LH 146-47 discusses the case of a wife who gives her female slave to her husband as a concubine:

> If a man marries a *nadītu* and she gives a slave-woman to her husband and after she has borne children that slave-woman makes herself equal to her mistress, because she has borne children, her mistress shall not sell her; she may place the slave-mark upon her and count her among the female slaves. If she does not bear children, her mistress may sell her.

The slave's legal personality is split: she remains the slave of her mistress while becoming the concubine of the latter's husband. The mistress may therefore discipline her or sell her, at will. If the slave's concubinage results in offspring, however, the mistress's ownership rights are restrained; she may only discipline her slave by reducing her social status within the household.

A word of warning must be given about the effect of law code provisions such as the above. The ancient Near Eastern law codes were not legislation in the modern sense, and their provisions should not always be attributed with the absolute, peremptory character of modern laws. In my view, the paragraphs in the codes often represented an ideal of justice: principles that should apply in the formulation of contracts or that only applied in absence of express contractual clauses to the contrary. At most, they might represent the equitable discretion of the court (especially the royal prerogative) to strike down or modify bargains that offended the principles of social justice.[3] Particularly indicative of the

3. This is not the much-debated issue of whether the cuneiform law codes were prescriptive or descriptive. Even if the law codes were not a source of law, the law that they described, whether from custom, decree or judgment, was still valid, and the relationship between the principles that it embodied and the provisions of contracts needs to be established. A systematic study of that relationship has yet to

royal prerogative are LH 117, which declares an automatic release of debt slaves after three years' service, and LH 171, mentioned above, which does the same for a slave concubine (and her children) on the master's death. They usurp the language and overlap the functions of debt release decrees, which were declared intermittently by the king at his discretion.[4]

Consequently, it is not surprising to find contracts with express provisions that contradict the law codes. Paradoxically, they may be evidence of the validity of the principles expressed by the law codes, if not of the formalistic application of their provisions in the manner of a modern statute, since a contracting party would not normally bother to insert special clauses into the contract merely in order to establish rights that he had anyway, in the absence of contract. How far a contract might modify the principles of social justice without running foul of the equitable discretion of the courts is impossible to tell.

In the light of these considerations, the following express provisions in an Old Assyrian marriage contract should perhaps be read as designed to overcome a restraint similar to the one in LH 146-47.[5]

> If within two years she (the wife) has not provided him (the husband) with offspring, she will purchase a slave-woman, and after she (the slave) shall have provided him with a child by him, he/she may sell her wherever he/she pleases.

Contractual terms depend on the bargaining power of the parties, which could vary, even when the contract concerned slavery. Accordingly, special terms did not always restrict a slave's rights; they could equally be used to extend those rights beyond the customary limits of protection. Another Old Assyrian contract expressly protects a concu-

be undertaken (cf. R. Westbrook, 'Slave and Master in Ancient Near Eastern Law', *Chicago–Kent Law Review* 70 [1995], pp. 1631-76, esp. p. 1657). The range of possibilities may be illustrated by an example from modern legal systems. The general law often implies certain clauses in a contract of sale. Those clauses may sometimes be excluded by an express clause inserted by the parties, but sometimes (e.g. in the realm of consumer protection) they may not.

4. See Westbrook, 'Slave and Master', pp. 1656-58. As regards LH 171, the parallel provision in LL 25, discussed below, assumes that release of the slave concubine is purely a matter of her master's choice.

5. ICK I 3.7-16 (B. Hrozny [ed.], 'Über eine unveröffentlichte Urkunde vom Kültepe', in *Symbolae Koschaker* [Studia et Documenta ad Iura Orientis Antiqui Pertinentia, 2; Leiden: E.J. Brill, 1939], pp. 108-11).

bine who did not yet have the advantage of motherhood.[6]

> Shalim-beli, who has taken Kitidi (as a concubine), shall not cause her to enter the house of Amur-Ashur (his patron?). He may lead her where he wishes. Neither Amur-Ashur nor his sons nor Shalim-beli shall sell her or cause her to enter. If anyone sells her, Shalim- beli shall pay one mina of silver to Shat-ili.

We do not know the background to this enigmatic document, but it would appear that Kitidi has been given into slave concubinage by Shat-ili (her mother?) to Shalim-beli, who is in some condition of dependence upon Amur-Ashur. The contract protects the concubine from exploitation by the patron or from sale by the patron, his heirs, or his client, the immediate owner.

Motherhood could lead to another form of protection for the slave concubine, as LH 119 provides:

> If a debt has seized a man, and he sells his slave-woman who has borne him children, the owner of the slave-woman may pay the silver that the merchant paid and redeem his slave woman.

The right of redemption was widespread in the ancient Near East. It was a measure of social justice, for the benefit of native citizens, whereby a sale under pressure of debt was treated as if it were a pledge. The right appears to have been limited principally to two cases: family land and members of the family sold into slavery.[7] The slave concubine fell into neither category, but where she had borne children, a special rule was formulated in her regard, which neatly illustrates the type of compromise that resulted from the conflict between the rules of family law and property law. She was sufficiently regarded as a member of the family to benefit from the privilege of redemption, but whereas a free wife or a son sold into slavery would on redemption by the husband or father regain their former free status, the slave concubine merely returned to her former master as a slave, in the manner of family land that had been redeemed.

6. KTS 47a (G. Eisser and J. Lewy [eds.], *Die altassyrischen Rechtsurkunden vom Kültepe* [MVAG, 33; Leipzig, 1930], no. 2).

7. On the question of social justice and redemption of land, see R. Westbrook, *Property and the Family in Biblical Law* (JSOTSup, 113; Sheffield: JSOT Press 1991), pp. 15-16, 90-117; on redemption of family members, see R. Yaron, 'Redemption of Persons in the Ancient Near East', *RIDA* (3rd) 6 (1959), pp. 155-76; and Westbrook, 'Slave and Master', pp. 1651-56.

In other circumstances, concubinage could vitiate the right of redemption. Exodus 21.7-11 reads:

> If a man sells his daughter as a slave-woman, she shall not go free as the male slaves go free. If she displeases her master who assigned her to himself (/who has not assigned her), he shall let her be redeemed; he shall not have authority to sell her to a foreign people, in breach of faith with her. If he assigns her to his son, he shall treat her according to the status of daughters. If he takes another for himself, he shall not reduce her food, clothing and oil.[8] If he does not provide her with these three, she shall go free without payment of silver.

A preliminary question is whether this text concerns concubinage at all. Most commentators assume that a form of marriage is being regulated by the law, but there is nothing in the terminology to suggest that marriage is meant.[9] As we shall see, when ancient Near Eastern sources wished to indicate that a female slave was a wife, they did so explicitly, both in the language of formation and dissolution. Here, the slave is assigned and taken, but never specifically as a wife, and the relationship is ended by sale or manumission, not by divorce.

Confusion as to the slave's status has been caused in part by Mendelsohn, who compared this law with the institution of 'daughtership and daughter-in-lawship (*mārtūtu u kallatūtu*)' at Nuzi.[10] The latter was a commercial transaction in which the adopter (usually a woman) acquired a girl from her parents as a daughter, with the explicit right to give the girl in marriage and receive her betrothal payment. According to Mendelsohn, it was a 'scheme whereby certain sales into slavery of young free-born girls assumed a semblance of legitimate marriage, i.e., conditional sales whereby the giving into marriage of the slave girl was made obligatory upon her purchaser'.[11] This is incorrect. It may well be that in social terms the girls' condition was little more than slavery, but

8. The meaning 'oil' for the *hapax 'nh* was established by S. Paul ('Exod. 21.10 a Threefold Maintenance Clause', *JNES* 28 [1969], pp. 48-53). It is astonishing that this simple identification, supported by copious evidence of a banal formula found throughout the ancient Near East, has still not been universally accepted by scholars.

9. The scholarship on this law is reviewed by G. Chirichigno, who assumes that the transaction is a form of marriage (*Debt-Slavery in Israel and the Ancient Near East* [JSOTSup, 141; Sheffield: JSOT Press, 1993], pp. 24-55).

10. I. Mendelsohn, 'The Conditional Sale into Slavery of Free-born Daughters in Nuzi and the Law of Ex. 21.7-11', *JAOS* 55 (1935), pp. 190-95.

11. Mendelsohn, 'Conditional Sale', p. 191.

in law the distinction was maintained. The terminology of neither slavery nor sale is employed in the texts; there is nothing to suggest that they were anything but a transaction involving the adoption and marriage of a free woman. Mendelsohn systematically mistranslated the operative verb 'gave' (into daughtership, etc.) as 'sold', without a shred of justification.[12] The Nuzi texts do not furnish a legal model for the law in Exodus. Confusion has also been caused because the difference between concubinage and marriage has not been directly discussed in the context of this law. We shall see, however, that the distinction is of vital importance, with implications both for the consequences of the law's provisions and for the jurisprudential coherence of the legal status of female slaves as a whole.

For the moment I am concerned with the first part of the law, which deals with the question of redemption. The woman's situation differs from that of the female slave in LH 119 in that she is a free woman who has been sold by her father into debt-slavery, as the reference to redemption reveals. The father would normally have the right to redeem his daughter, but that right is lost because her enslavement is for the purpose of concubinage. The right of redemption revives only if the purchaser fails to abide by the special purpose of the contract—if he fails either to consummate the assignment himself (*qere*) or to assign her for concubinage altogether (*ketib*).[13] In either case, the purchaser has treated the contract as one of ordinary servitude, not concubinage, and has denied the slave-woman the possibility of gaining the protection available to a concubine through motherhood. In those circumstances, it is logical that the ordinary right of redemption should apply notwithstanding the fact that the slave is female.[14]

Verse 8 provides a second measure of protection. Her master "shall not have authority to sell her to a foreign people (*'am nokrî*). To understand the purpose of this prohibition, it should first be pointed out that

12. The Akkadian for 'to sell' is 'to give for silver' (*ana kaspim nadānum*).

13. In order to have legal consequences, his displeasure must have some external manifestation and a concrete act (or omission). Accordingly, the provision is unlikely to refer to a change of attitude after consummation. This eventuality is covered by v. 10, where he takes another concubine in preference to her. It is possible, however, that his displeasure could be manifested through an attempt to sell her to a third party, which again would contravene the purpose of a concubinage contract.

14. Deut. 15.12 makes it clear that a female debt-slave in a non-concubinage arrangement has exactly the same status as a male.

alienability is not the opposite of redeemability. The two concepts should not be confused.[15] A right of redemption does not make a slave inalienable, because it can always be exercised against a subsequent purchaser—the seller cannot transfer a more absolute ownership than he has.[16] In the present law, therefore, there was no danger that the mere act of selling the woman to a third party would make her irredeemable. On the contrary, because such an act treated the contract as one of ordinary servitude, in breach of the concubinage clause, it would automatically turn her into a slave who was redeemable from her new owner. In one circumstance only would the woman's redeemability be irretrievably lost: if she were sold abroad. She would then be a foreign slave for her purchaser, who would not see himself obliged to respect her rights under Israelite law. For this reason, I prefer to translate the term *'am nokrî* as 'foreign people' rather than 'outsiders', 'other clan' or the like, which would imply a total prohibition on alienation.[17]

Status of the Offspring

Because she could bear children, the female slave was a special economic asset. A child born to an unmarried slave-woman was a house-born slave.[18] The child was reckoned to be the offspring of its mother; it had no father. Like its mother, the child would be the property of her owner, no different from the offspring of the owner's herds. If her master himself took his slave-woman as a concubine, his rights over the issue of the union would be those of an owner, not of a father.

The difference can be seen clearly in an Old Assyrian document. In TuM I 22a, four brothers divide the estate of their father.[19] The agreement stipulates:

15. As does, for example, A. Schenker ('Affranchissement d'une esclave selon Ex.21,7-11', *Bib* 69 [1988], pp. 547-56, esp. p. 547).

16. Yaron, 'Redemption of Persons', pp. 158-59.

17. See Chirichigno for the contrary view (*Debt-Slavery*, p. 249). Support for my interpretation is provided by MAL C+G 2-3, which punish the sale abroad of an Assyrian taken in pledge, who might otherwise be redeemed (Westbrook, 'Slave and Master', pp. 1660-62).

18. Akkadian: *wilid bītim* (Old Babylonian period), *dušmu* (later periods); Hebrew: *yᵉlîd bayit* (Gen. 17.13, 23).

19. Eisser and Lewy (eds.), *Die altassyrischen Rechtsurkunden vom Kültepe*, no. 287; cf. B. Kienast, *Das altassyrische Kaufvertragsrecht* (Stuttgart: Franz Steiner Verlag, 1984), pp. 92-93 (3e), 98 (20).

> 18-22. As for the residue (of the estate), whether wheat or slave-woman or slave or (other) share, they shall take according to their father's testament...
> 25-32. Agi'a either here or in the city of Assur may take a slave-woman for his(!) concubinage[20] and is free of claims; Asu, Puzur- sadu and Alahum may take one each from the slave women whom they have known sexually (*lamdū*), but she shall be deducted from their share. They (the brothers) will make their (the slave-women's) offspring equal (*lillissina šunu umta[ḫḫurū]*).

The *Chicago Assyrian Dictionary* translates the last phrase: 'they will assign equal rank to their [the women's] offspring'.[21] These are fine sentiments, but misconstrue the situation. It is a matter of indifference in a division of inheritance what status the individual brothers will assign to the children of their slaves once they have received their inheritance. The problem was a mathematical one: for example, if the three brothers had slept with three slaves who had borne one, two and three children respectively, should each brother receive the children born to the slave-woman whom he took as his inheritance or should all receive an equal number, that is, two each? The agreement prefers the second solution, irrespective of who was the father.

The same considerations lead to exclusion of relations with a slave-woman from the ambit of certain sexual taboos. According to HL:

> 191. If a free man has intercourse with free maternal sisters and their mother—one in one country and one in another—it is not an offence. If it is in one place and he knows, it is an abomination.
> 194. If a free man has intercourse with slave maternal sisters and their mother, it is not an offence. If brothers sleep with a free woman, it is not an offence. If a father and his son sleep with a slave-woman or a prostitute, it is not an offence.

These provisions do not mean that in Hittite law sexual taboos never applied to relations with a female slave: HL 196 forsees the possibility of a male and female slave committing a sexual act together that amounts to an abomination. The Hittite prohibitions as regards family members cover a wider range of relationships than pure incest (that is, relatives having sexual relations with each other) because their rationale is also to prevent confusion in relations of parentage. In the examples given in the paragraphs above, would the sons of a mother and

20. *ana ištariūtīšūnu ilaqqe*. See *CAD* I-J, p. 271, '*ištariūtu*'.
21. *CAD* L, pp. 55-56, '*lamādu* 3'.

daughter by the same man be brothers or uncle and nephew? Would the daughters of a woman by a father and son be sisters or aunt and niece? The problems for the family tree, family worship, and inheritance are evident. It is not a problem, however, in certain special cases:

1. Where family ties are no more than theoretical, due to geographical (and perhaps jurisdictional) separation.
2. Where two brothers have offspring by the same woman, because the vertical family lineages are not affected. The offspring will be half-brothers or half-sisters, and it is of no great consequence that they are also cousins.
3. Where a father and son sleep with a prostitute, because the offspring of a prostitute have no paternity. The same applies to a slave concubine: in law, her offspring have no father; they only have an owner. Thus uncertainty as to whether her offspring are by the father or his son could at most lead to a property dispute. For the same reason, the offspring of a slave mother and daughter are not related in law, even if they have the same father in fact.

The law codes emphasize that slave concubinage cannot confer legitimacy on the offspring, even if both mother and child are freed. LL 25 reads:

> If a man married a wife and she bore him a child and that child is living, and a slave also bore a child for her master but the father granted freedom to the slave and her children, the child of the slave shall not divide the estate with the child of the master.

Likewise LH 170-71, which order that the children of a slave concubine be freed on the father's death, nonetheless bar them from sharing the inheritance with the legitimate children, unless the father had adopted them in his lifetime.

There is nothing surprising in these provisions; indeed, it is strange that they should have been deemed necessary. It is in the nature of concubinage that it cannot have the prime consequence of a legitimate marriage, namely the creation of legitimate heirs to the father's estate. Hence the offspring of a free concubine had no better right to inherit than the offspring of a slave concubine. On the other hand, if a man died without legitimate heirs, natural or adopted, the law codes do make provision for his illegitimate children to be recognized as his heirs. The examples that they give, however, all concern the offspring of a union with a free woman: his child by a prostitute in LL 27 or by a free concubine in MAL A 41. Whether the freed children of a slave concubine were equally entitled in those circumstances, or whether a distinction was being drawn between slave and free concubines, cannot be determined.

Position of Third Parties

Ownership implied the exclusive right to exploit the sexuality of a female slave. Accordingly, the law protected her owner against unauthorized use of her by a third party. The penalty was a relatively small payment, which appears to represent compensation for economic loss. The penalty for the wrongful defloration of another's female slave is set at 5 shekels of silver in LU 8, 20 shekels in LE 31, and 30 shekels in an Old Babylonian report of a trial from Nippur.[22] LE 31 adds: '... and the female slave remains her owner's'. The purpose of this clause was to distinguish the case from that of the defloration of a free maiden, where the penalty imposed represented a betrothal payment and might lead to marriage (e.g. MAL A 55; Exod. 22.15-16; Deut. 22.28-29). It was an emphatic statement that the principles of property law, not family law, applied in this instance.

Marriage

It is a salient feature of ancient Near Eastern law that, unlike Roman law, it recognized as legitimate the marriage of slaves, whether with other slaves or with free persons. With one exception which I shall discuss below, marriage and slavery were not legally incompatible, although their different rules led to conflicts.

The marriage of slaves can be divided into three categories: marriage between slaves, marriage with a third party who was free, and marriage with one's own master.

Between Slaves

The slave law of Exod. 21.2-6 is emblematic of the conflict between the principles of family law and property law that resulted from recognition of slave marriage. The law distinguishes between marriage prior to enslavement and marriage during slavery. If a married couple enter into

22. J. Finkelstein, 'Sex Offenses in Sumerian Laws', *JAOS* 86 (1966), pp. 355-72, esp. pp. 359-60.

debt-slavery, then release of the husband after six years' service automatically includes release of his wife. There is no theoretical difficulty in this case, since the debt for which they both were enslaved is deemed extinguished. If, on the other hand, the master gave a female slave of his own in marriage to the debt-slave, the latter's release has no effect on his wife's status. The master's property rights take precedence over the husband's marital rights.

The ambiguous language of LU 4 is best interpreted as reflecting the same rule. Following Yaron, the subject of the apodosis should be understood as the wife, not the husband.[23]

> If a slave marries a slave-woman whom he loves and that slave is freed, she shall not go out from the house.

Free Person and Slave

Marriage between free persons and slaves could arise from the enslavement of one of the partners to an existing marriage or by the voluntary marriage of a free person with a slave. In the first instance, enslavement did not affect the validity of the marriage or the husband's exclusive sexual rights over his wife, although it might limit his remedies.[24] In the second instance, two situations are covered by the sources: the general case where there is no material family relationship between slave owner and free spouse, and a special case where a family relationship between the two is the essence of the arrangement.

1. In the general case, most of the evidence relates to the marriage of a free woman with a male slave. LH 175-76 lay down the principle that

23. R. Yaron, 'Quelques remarques sur les nouveaux fragments des Lois d'Ur-Nammu', *Revue historique de droit français et étranger* 63 (1985), pp. 131-42, esp. pp. 138-39. Contra the original editor, F. Yildiz, 'A Tablet of Codex Ur-Nammu from Sippar', *Or* 50 (1981), p. 96. A Nuzi contract is cited by Yaron in support of his interpretation (JEN VI 610, M. Greenberg [ed.], *The Ḫab/piru* [New Haven: Yale University Press, 1955], no. 64, cited by Yaron as no. 65), but the situation there is somewhat more complicated. B enters into slavery with A for A's lifetime and is given a wife by A. The contract further obliges B to serve A's son, C, and imposes a penalty upon him for breach of this provision which includes forfeiture of his wife and children. It is not clear that the relationship between B and C is one of slavery or contractual in nature, and in any case forfeiture of the wife is an express penalty for breach, not the natural consequence of the end of B's slavery.

24. A reading of Lev. 19.20-22 in this sense has already been proposed and argued at length by me (*Studies in Biblical and Cuneiform Law* [CahRB, 26; Paris: J. Gabalda, 1988], pp. 101-109.

both the woman and her offspring remain free; the slave owner has no claim to either. LU 5 assumes the same principle as regards the woman, but requires one male child of the marriage to be placed at the owner's disposal.[25]

The Hittite Laws, on the other hand, appear to call into question the freedom of a woman who marries a slave, but the terms of the relevant provisions are very obscure. HL 34-35 read:

> If a slave brings a betrothal payment for a woman and takes her as his wife, no one shall release her.[26]
> If a steward or a herdsman causes a free woman to run [=elopes with/abducts?] and does not bring a betrothal payment for her, she shall become a slave in [/for?] three years.

The juxtaposition of the two paragraphs would suggest that making a betrothal payment changes the woman's status immediately, whereas in

25. In my interpretation, that child is not a slave. I translate as follows: 'If a slave marries a free woman, he/she shall place one son at the disposal of his master. The son who was placed at the disposal of his master will [divide] half the property of his father's house, the wall, the house [...] The free woman's son is not [...] with the master; he shall not cause him to enter into slavery'.

Other translations assume that this final provision relates to the other children of the marriage, although not explicitly indicated, either by the wording or the grammar (Yildiz, 'A Tablet of Codex Ur-Nammu', p. 96; Roth, *Law Collections*, p. 17; W. Römer, *Texte aus der Umwelt des Alten Testaments*. I. *Rechtsbücher* [Gütersloh: Gerd Mohn, 1982], p. 20). The couple have to supply the master with one son, who will work for him. Far from being a slave, however, after his father's death that son apparently gets the half of his estate that the master must forego, as in LH 175-76. (Any other children will have to content themselves with their mother's dowry, it seems.) The master cannot claim the son as a slave in place of his father.

26. There have been numerous attempts to translate the final verb in a way that spares the unfortunate bride from slavery. The latest is the *Chicago Hittite Dictionary*, which translates, 'no one will hand her over [to a slave master]' (P/2, p. 125, '*para tarna*' 6a 6′a′). Since the normal meaning of *para tarna* is 'to let go, release, set free, let out' (see p. 115, meaning 1 vv.), it is proposed as a special use ('legal idiom') on the basis of E. von Schuler's translation of passages in the Edict of Tudhaliya ('Hethitische Königserlässe als Quellen der Rechtsfindung und ihr Verhältnis zum kodifizierten Recht', in R. von Kienle [ed.], *Festschrift Johannes Friedrich* [Heidelberg: Carl Winter, 1959], pp. 446-48). Not cited by the Dictionary is an article in which the law of the relevant passage of the Edict was completely reinterpreted, so as to validate the normal meaning of the verb (Westbrook and R. Woodard, 'The Edict of Tudhaliya IV', *JAOS* 110 [1990], pp. 641-59, esp. pp. 643, 653-57).

its absence, three years must elapse. In the absence of any background to these laws, it is impossible to do more than speculate as to their rationale, or the parties or interests involved. The purpose might be to distinguish a betrothal payment from a loan, which would allow the recipient (her father?) a right of redemption. Another possibility is to regard the release as being from the marriage, not from slavery. In Yamada's view, these paragraphs mean that a slave cannot take a free woman to wife without paying the brideprice; if he dares to do so, it changes her status to that of a slave.[27]

As for the offspring of a marriage between a slave and a free woman, the principle of freedom expressed in the Mesopotamian law codes was frequently overridden by express clauses in marriage contracts (to which the owner was a necessary party), which assigned some or all of them to slavery.[28] There is insufficient evidence to determine whether the same principles applied where it was the wife who was a slave. Children of the marriage are mentioned in only one source: a series of legal documents from Elephantine recording the changing relationships over a period of years between an owner, his female slave and her husband.[29] In the first document (Kraeling 2) the master gives his slave in

27. M. Yamada, 'The Hittite Social Concept of "Free" in the Light of the Emar Texts', *Altorientalische Forschungen* 22 (1995), pp. 301-16 (311).

28. CT 48 53 (Westbrook [ed.] in *Old Babylonian Marriage Law* [AfO Beiheft, 23; [Horn: Berger, 1988], p. 123; JEN 2 120 (A. Saarisalo [ed.] in *New Kirkuk Documents Relating to Slaves* [Helsinki: Societas Orientalis Fennica, 1934], no. 25. On the other hand, circumstances, especially love and affection, might make the contractual terms as generous as those of the law codes. Two Middle Assyrian documents record a remarkable arrangement. In the first, a slave redeems a woman from slavery with a third party, presumably with his master's silver, and frees her (KAJ 167). In the second, while remaining a slave, he marries her (KAJ 70.2-10, 20-29): '(m)Ilima-iriba slave of Amurru-natsir redeemed (f)Asuat-Idiglat from the house of Ashur-retsuia son of Ibassi-ilu and, with Asuat-Idiglat's consent, Ilima-iriba cleansed her of her slave status and established her as his wife. Ilima-iriba is her husband and Asuat-Idiglat is his wife... Asuat-Idiglat and her children shall be villagers (*alaiū*) of Amurru-natsir and his children. They shall do village-service (*alaiūtu*) for Amurru-natsir and his children. But Amurru-natsir and his children shall not seize Asuat-Idiglat and her children for slavery...'

29. B. Porten and A. Yardeni (eds.), *Textbook of Aramaic Documents from Ancient Egypt* (Jerusalem: Hebrew University Press, 1989), II, pp. 60-63, 72-73. In an analysis of Kraeling 2, Porten and Szubin argue that not only the conditions of the wife's marriage contract, but her very slave status, is subtly altered by successive revisions of the document, and by later documents, so that she gradually

marriage to a free man. In a later document (Kraeling 5), the aged master frees the slave and her daughter who has been born in the meantime. The master refers to the daughter as 'your daughter whom you bore me' (ll.4-5). It is clear, however, that the daughter is the biological child of the husband. The phrase can only refer to the master's ownership of the daughter, which he is now relinquishing. It is not known, however, whether his ownership was based upon the general law or upon another contractual arrangement which has not been preserved in the archive.[30]

The only provision in the law codes that considers the case of a slave-woman married to a free man is HL 31, which makes equitable arrangements in case of divorce:

> If a free man and a slave-woman are in love(?) and they enter and he takes her as his wife and they make a house and children for themselves but afterwards they either become bad or separate, they shall divide the house equally. The man will take the children for himself; the woman will take one child for herself.

It is important to note that the wife receives only one child because she is a slave, not because she is a woman. In HL 32, where it is the husband who is a slave, and in HL 33, where both are slaves, the husband receives only a single child.[31]

moves from a status of slavery to one of emancipation (B. Porten and H. Szubin, 'The Status of the Handmaid Tamet', *Israel Law Review* 29 (1995), pp. 43-64). I disagree with their analysis on two grounds: (1) the concept of a gradual emancipation is legally incoherent, leaving the rights and duties of the parties uncertain at any one time. The ambiguities noted by Porten and Szubin may be readily accounted for by the division of the slave's legal personality between her master and her husband (see further below). (2) as Porten and Szubin themselves point out, the marriage contract is ancillary to the status of marriage, not determinative of it (pp. 44-45). Changes in the contract can ameliorate the slave's status, but they cannot alter it.

30. In Kraeling 2.13-14, it emerges that there was already a son of the couple prior to the marriage. The master reserves the right to reclaim that son for himself in the event of a divorce. If he was the issue of concubinage and not marriage, the son would in principle have had no paternity and hence no right to freedom. Porten and Szubin appear to confuse, or at least to conflate, him with the later daughter, attributing the phrase 'whom you bore to me' in Kraeling 5.8 to the son ('The Status of the Handmaid Tamet', p. 59).

31. In HL 32 the key words are restored, but the restoration is compelling in the light of HL 33. See the edition of J. Friedrich (*Die Hethitischen Gesetze* [Leiden: E.J. Brill, 1971], p. 26 n. 6, p. 27 n. 4).

2. The special case (where a family relationship between slave owner and free spouse is the essence of the arrangement) is best exemplified by the practice of a first wife giving her female slave in marriage to her husband as a second wife. Once again, the legal personality of the slave was split. As the Old Babylonian contracts express it: 'To H, W2 is a wife; to W1, she is a slave'.[32] It is necessary that the slave achieve the status of wife and not merely concubine, because the purpose is to provide legitimate offspring, primarily for the husband and secondarily for the first wife. This is made clear by the examples given in Genesis. Sarah, Rachel and Leah all give a slave to their husbands *as a wife*, with the express purpose of acquiring offspring for their husbands and themselves. Gen. 16.1-3 reads:

> Sarai, Abram's wife, had not borne children to him, but she had an Egyptian slave-woman by the name of Hagar. Sarah said to Abram, 'Behold, God has prevented me from giving birth. Come in to my slave—perhaps I shall be established through her'. Abram listened to the words of Sarai. Sarai, the wife of Abram took Hagar the Egyptian, her slave... and gave her to her husband Abram as a wife to him.

What then were the rights of the first wife over the slave and her offspring? The law is complicated by the fact that the first wife is subordinate to her husband within the household; she cannot assert against her husband the rights of a slave owner as she would against an outsider. Accordingly, her ownership rights become residual, both as regards the slave and her offspring. This is illustrated in Genesis by the actions of Sarah. When she wishes to punish Hagar for impudence, she first has to seek permission from her husband (16.5-6). And later, when Sarah bears a son herself and wishes to prevent Hagar's son from sharing Abram's inheritance, she cannot act directly by expelling her own slave; she must prevail upon Abraham to divorce Hagar (21.10).

In the same way, the Old Babylonian contracts, in their use of express terms, demonstrate that the first wife could no longer rely on her bare ownership to assert her rights.[33] According to CT 48 48:

32. CT 4 39a; 8 22b; 48 48; TIM 4 49 (see Westbrook, *Old Babylonian Marriage Law*, p. 104); CT 45 119 (ed. C. Wilcke, 'CT 45,119: Ein Fall legaler Bigamie', *ZA* 74 [1984], pp. 170-80).

33. There are further complicating factors in these contracts, namely adoption and sisterhood, which do not concern us here. For a full discussion, see Westbrook, *Old Babylonian Marriage Law*, pp. 104-107, and Wilcke, 'CT 45,119', pp. 171-75.

> Ahassunu has adopted Sabitum daughter of Ahushina and Ahatani from her father Ahushina and her mother Ahatani. Sabitum is a slave to Ahassunu, a wife to Warad-Sin: with whom she is hostile, she will be hostile; with whom she is friendly, she will be friendly.[34] The day she distresses Ahassunu, she will shave her and sell her.

However sweeping the first wife's powers appear, they are the result of an express contractual clause, not of her normal rights as an owner.

It will be recalled that in LH 146 the wife was forbidden to sell her slave that she had given to her husband as a concubine when the latter had borne children. In the light of the above examples, that provision may be seen as an attempt to extend to a slave concubine some of the natural protection afforded a slave by marriage.

There remains the question of the relationship between offspring of the marriage and the first wife. If her ownership rights over them are limited, does her status as owner at least make them her legitimate heirs? The latter possibility is suggested by a clause in an Old Babylonian contract that asserts: 'If she (W2) bears ten children, they are the children of W1'.[35] At the same time, its appearance in an express clause suggests that this was not the automatic result of the relative status of the two women, but that some further process was necessary.

The same appears true for the cases in Genesis. Rachel declares to Jacob (30.3): 'Here is my slave Bilhah, come in to her and she shall give birth on my knees and I too will be established through her'. Both Rachel and Leah also name the children that their slaves bear to Jacob (30.5-13). It may therefore be that, as has been often suggested, some form of adoption was involved, whereby ownership rights were turned into filiation.[36]

Slave and Master

In my view, marriage of a female slave to her own master is the one situation where marriage and slavery are altogether incompatible: a man cannot be a master and a husband of the same woman at the same

34. Correcting my translation of this phrase in *Old Babylonian Marriage Law*, p. 109 ('whenever she is angry, she will be angry; whenever she is friendly, she will be friendly') in the light of the parallels with international treaties drawn by M. Weinfeld, 'The Covenant of Grant in the Old Testament and in the Ancient Near East', *JAOS* 90 (1970), pp. 184-203, esp. p. 194.

35. CT 48 67, but see the discussion in *Old Babylonian Marriage Law*, p. 106.

36. See e.g., J. Skinner, *Genesis* (ICC; Edinburgh: T. & T. Clark, 2nd edn, 1930), pp. 386-87.

time. The reasons derive from the logic of the two institutions. Before expounding them, however, it is necessary to consider a preliminary problem of terminology. In a small number of texts, a married woman is called the slave of her husband. The texts are concentrated in three widely separated clusters of sources, altogether different in genre and in the context in which the term appears.[37]

1. Lipiński has drawn attention to first millenium West Semitic seals and tomb inscriptions where in each case the woman named is referred to as the slave (*'mt/'mh*) of a man who from the context appears to be her husband.[38] As Lipiński points out, however, the context also makes it clear that these are free women, indeed, that they are of high status. One is even a queen![39] The explanation most probably lies in the semantic relativity of slavery terminology. As has often been noted, the term for slave, male or female, was used indiscriminately in ancient Near Eastern languages to refer to any hierarchical inferior, for example, a subject before a sovereign, a king before an emperor, or an emperor before a god, without necessarily implying the strict legal relationship of ownership of the former by the latter.[40] In introducing oneself, the expression 'Your slave' was commonly used as a formula of polite self-abasement. In the sources under discussion, therefore, it would appear to have served the purposes of euphemismistic modesty rather than legal classification.[41]

2. Among the Old Assyrian tablets that document the affairs of Assyrian merchants in Anatolia there are several instances collected by Kienast where the standard Akkadian term for female slave, *amtum*, appears to refer to a wife.[42] While some of them might fall under the

37. My statement in an earlier study that wives are never referred to as slaves of the head of household is therefore incorrect, having failed to take into account the following, albeit marginal, instances ('Slave and Master', p. 1635).

38. E. Lipiński, 'Kinship Terminology in 1 Sam 25.40-42', *ZAH* 7 (1994), pp. 12-16.

39. Queen Gahimat, who is qualified as *'amat* of the *mukarrib* of Saba in a South-Arabian inscription (Lipiński, 'Kinship Terminology', p. 14).

40. A good discussion of this phenomenon may be found in Yamada ('Hittite Social Concept', pp. 301-16).

41. This is its purpose in 1 Sam. 25.41 and 1 Kgs 1.17, where the phrase is 'your slave' in direct speech. Lipiński is therefore wrong in attributing the meaning 'wife' to the term in these passages, which no more indicate marriage than they do slavery ('Kinship Terminology', pp. 12-15).

42. Kienast, *Das altassyrische Kaufvertragsrecht*, pp. 94-95, 100.

category of euphemistic modesty, as above,[43] there are two marriage documents which suggest that the term *amtum* refers to a definite legal status.[44] ICK 1 32 states that one Pilah-ishtar divorced 'his slave-woman' (*amassu*) and paid her a divorce settlement in the presence of her mother and brothers.[45] The second, I 490, is a marriage document according to which.[46]

> Puzur-ishtar took (*ēḫuz*) Ishtar-lamassi, daughter of Ashur-nada 'for female slavery' (*ana amtūtim*). He will take her with him to Purushhaddum or to Hattum or wherever he journeys, and will bring her back to Kanish with him. If he divorces her, he will pay 5 mina of silver; if she divorces him, she will pay 5 mina. Besides his wife (*aššitīšu*) in the city of Assur, he shall not take (*eḫḫaz*) another. If Ishtar-lamassi does not see a child within 3 years, he may buy a slave-woman (*amtam*) and take (*eḫḫaz*) her. Ashur-nemedi, Anina and her mother gave her.

The verb 'to take' (*aḫāzum*) in principle requires further specification in order to refer to marriage: 'to take a wife/to take for marriage'. It can be abbreviated, but the context would have to be unambiguous. Otherwise, when used alone, it refers to concubinage.[47] Hence the second occurence here indicates marriage, but the third, concubinage. On the other hand, Ishtar-lamassi herself, although taken 'for female slavery', cannot have become thereby a slave. The decisive reason is the penalty clause, which obliges her to pay her husband upon divorce. A slave, being owned, could not own property separately from his or her mas-

43. Especially a wife's letter to her husband, listed by Kienast as no. 1f (=ATHE 44.25-28a), in which the following statement is found: 'Today, have I not done well for you like a slave-woman "with a beaten head", so that you should measure out the rations to the slave-woman (i.e. me)'? (*Das altassyrische Kaufvertragsrecht*, p. 95).

44. A third marriage document is cited by Kienast, but the key term is written over an erasure and needs to be restored; hence it cannot serve as evidence (no. 1b = ICK 1 3; *Das altassyrische Kaufvertragsrecht*, p. 94). Kienast restores it as GEMÉ (the Sumerogram for *amtum*); *CAD* restores it as DAM (wife) (A/1 p. 175).

45. Edited by J. Lewy, in 'Old Assyrian Institutions', *HUCA* 27 (1956), pp. 3-6.

46. Published only in transliteration (Lewy, 'Old Assyrian', p. 6).

47. For a full discussion of *aḫāzum*, on the basis of Old Babylonian sources, see Westbrook, *Old Babylonian Marriage Law*, pp. 10-16. Old Assyrian examples are: KTS 47a (*aḫāzum* alone = concubinage); Eisser and Levy, *Die altassyrischen Rechtsurkunden*, no.1 (*aššatam aḫāzum* = marriage; see also *CAD* Vol. A/1 p. 175 *sub aḫāzu* 2a)1'); L. Matouš, 'Beiträge zum Eherecht der anatolischen Bevölkerung im 2. Jhdts. u. Z.', *ArOr* 41 (1973), p. 312 (*aḫāzum* alone = marriage, but in preamble to divorce document).

ter.[48] Hence the 'female slavery' of Ishtar-lamassi was legitimate marriage as a free woman.

The question remains why this particular terminology was employed. The reason would appear to lie in the unusual bigamous practices of the Assyrian merchants, who maintained one household at home in the city of Assur and another in the trading colony in Anatolia. It is the latter that is documented in these records. Lewy conjectured that the Assyrian merchants 'did not and could not accord to their wives the title *aššatum* [wife] whenever they were married to an *aššatum* residing elsewhere—for instance in the city of Assur—or wished to retain the right to marry another woman whom they intended to make their *aššatum*'.[49] Lewy does not explain why both wives could not bear the same title, a practice that is well attested elsewhere, but in support of his view, some legal fiction would definitely have been necessary if, for example, the merchant did not want the children of his Anatolian marriage to share his estate in Assur with his Assyrian children, or if his marriage contract with his Assyrian wife prohibited him from taking a second wife. The term *amtum* avoided difficulties that might arise from an overt admission of bigamy, even if it was understood under local law that the Anatolian partner was a free person and a legitimate wife.

3. There are two verses in Genesis where the slaves given by Sarah, Leah and Rachel as wives to their husbands Abraham and Jacob respectively are referred to as the slaves of their husbands. In 21.12 God reassures Abraham, who does not wish to send Hagar away: 'Do not be perturbed on account of the boy and of your slave-woman (*'ᵃmātekā*)'. In 32.23 Jacob 'took his two wives and his two female slaves (*šipḥōtâw*), and his eleven children and crossed the ford of the Jabbok'.[50]

This sudden shift to calling Hagar, Bilhah and Zilpah the slaves of

48. It is true that a slave in the ancient Near East might have a *peculium*, a fund allocated by the master with which the slave could transact independently, and even make payments to the master. But ultimately a *peculium* remained the master's property. In a confrontation between master and slave there would be no point in forcing the slave to pay a penalty to the master with funds that belonged to the master anyway. See M. Dandamaev, *Slavery in Babylonia* (DeKalb: Northern Illinois University Press, 1984), pp. 384-97.

49. Lewy, 'Old Assyrian Institutions', p. 4.

50. It is unnecessary for the purposes of this study to distinguish between *'āmâ* and *šipḥâ* in Biblical Hebrew. Whatever else they mean, they certainly both mean female slave.

the husband rather than of the wife, although in a narrative, cannot be dismissed simply as euphemistic modesty, especially in the second passage, where it is explicitly contrasted with the term 'wives'.[51] Nor would any comparison with the very special situation in the Old Assyrian documents be appropriate. I suggest (albeit reluctantly) that the explanation lies in an inconsistent narrative rather than in the nature of the law. Either there was some confusion in the tradition as to whether they had been given as concubines or wives, or the author of these passages was concerned to maximise the status of the primary wives at the expense of the secondary wives. Support for the latter view comes from 35.22, where the same Bilhah is called the 'free concubine' (*pîlegeš*) of Jacob, a designation that is totally inappropriate. The narrator's motive is obvious—to spare Reuben, Jacob's son, whose crime in sleeping with Bilhah would have been far more heinous if she were Jacob's wife. On the other hand, as we have seen in the Hittite laws, if Bilhah were merely Jacob's slave concubine, there would have been no breach of a sexual taboo at all. The narrator's main goal was to impose an appropriate level of moral opprobrium, in pursuit of which he was prepared to sacrifice legal or narrative consistency.

Notwithstanding the above evidence, I consider that in ancient Near Eastern law a man could not be master and husband at the same time, because of the conflicting logic of the two institutions. The purpose of marriage is to produce legitimate offspring who can inherit from their father, if there is anything to inherit. Children begotten upon a slave are the fruits of their father's property. As such, they are not capable of inheriting from him; rather, they are part of his estate, to be inherited by his legitimate heirs.[52] Even if it were conceded that by a special rule the children were free while their mother was not, the logic of the law

51. Lipiński argues that *'āmâ* is an honorific title in Gen. 21.9-13, where Hagar is presented as an Arabian queen ('Kinship Terminology', p. 14). But at that point she is still far from becoming a queen, and when Sarah uses the same term of Hagar in v. 10, it is anything but an honorific title.

52. LH 171, in decreeing the release of a slave concubine and her children by her master on the master's death, seeks to avoid the unseemly but logical consequence of the law, namely that the legitimate heirs will acquire their own siblings as slaves. It specifically (and unnecessarily) adds that the master's legitimate children are not to claim his children by the slave concubine as slaves. Nonetheless, the concern of LH does not appear to be reflected in its parallel provision in LL 25, which assumes that release of his children by a slave concubine is purely a matter of the master's choice.

would still produce absurd consequences: on the father's death, the children would inherit their own mother as a slave.

Further difficulties arising from the logic of the two institutions are illustrated by an Old Babylonian document:[53]

> Mar-ertsetim son of Ayatia has taken Atkal-ana-belti, her [Ayatia's] slave for marriage. If Atkal-ana-belti says to her mistress Ayatia, 'You are not my mistress', she will shave her and sell her. Everything that Ayatia has acquired and will acquire belongs to Mar-ertsetim. As long as she [Ayatia] lives, both of them shall support [her].

A woman has given her slave-woman to her son as a wife, but has not freed her.[54] If slavery and marriage were compatible in this instance, the husband would, on his mother's death, inherit his wife as a slave. It seems to me more reasonable to suppose that the slave's personality is split. She is a free woman as regards her husband and a slave as regards her mistress. The mistress's ownership rights as regards her slave are limited, and therefore have to be restored in part by express contractual clauses, as we have seen above—in this case a penalty clause and a support clause. On her mistress's death, any inheritance rights that her husband might have had in her will be stultified by his status as her husband.

Accordingly, marriage to one's own slave will nullify or at least suspend her slave status, as regards her husband. An Old Babylonian polygamy document makes this consequence clear.[55]

> Bunene-abi and Belessunu have purchased Shamash-nuri daughter of Ibbi-Shahan from her father Ibbi-Shahan. To Bunene-abu she is a wife, to Belessunu she is a slave. The day that Shamash-nuri says to her mistress Belessunu, 'You are not my mistress', she will shave her and sell her. He/she has paid 5 shekels of silver for her full purchase-price. He has caused her to climb over the pestle, the transaction is complete, his heart is satisfied.

As in the previous document, the slave's legal personality is split between her mistress and her husband. In this case, however, she was

53. CT 6 37a *Old Babylonian Marriage Law*, p. 117).

54. The background to this arrangement is almost certainly that the 'son' is adopted, possibly a slave whom she has manumitted. The tell-tale sign is the duty of support which falls on the son as much as upon his wife. See P. Obermark, 'Adoption in the Old Babylonian Period' (PhD dissertation, Hebrew Union College and Jewish Institute of Religion [Ohio], 1992), pp. 45-47, 83-94.

55. CT 8 22b *Old Babylonian Marriage Law*, p. 119).

originally the property of her husband, who purchased her jointly with his wife. He then married his newly acquired slave, although the document does not inform us of this directly. It is drafted for the benefit of the first wife, to show that she retains some of her rights of ownership, even though the husband has lost his through marriage.

I now propose to analyze two biblical laws in the light of my understanding of the law of slavery and marriage. The first is Deut. 21.10-14:

> When you go out to war against your enemies and God has given them into your hand and you have taken captives, and you see among the captives a beautiful woman and you desire to take her for yourself as a wife: you shall bring her into your house and she shall shave her head and pare her nails and remove her captive's garb and sit in your house and mourn her father and mother for a period of one month, and afterwards you may come in to her and take her, and she shall become your wife. If it comes about that you do not want her, you shall divorce her to herself; you shall not sell her for silver. You shall not trade in her, because you degraded her.

There is no question of slave concubinage here; the text explicitly refers to the formation of marriage and to its termination by divorce. The Hebrew verb *šlḥ* usually translated 'release' or the like, is also a technical term for divorcing a wife, as in Deut. 24.1, 3. In my analysis, the captive woman is initially a slave, marriage makes her a free person, but subsequent termination of the marriage revives her previous status: her husband becomes her master again, and therefore can in principle sell her as a slave. The law forbids him to do so; instead, he must divorce her 'to herself' (*lᵉnapšâh*).[56] This curious and seemingly redundant expression is another facet of splitting the juridical personality. The woman is reunited with herself, that is, she receives back the ownership of herself that was ceded to her captor when she became a slave, regained during marriage, but lost again to him following her divorce.

The second law is Exod. 21.7-11, which I have identified as regulating a situation where a slave-woman is the concubine, not the wife, of her master. The opening provisions have already been discussed. We are now concerned with the second part of the law, which deals with her rights if she remains within the family of the purchaser:

> If he assigns her to his son, he shall treat her according to the status of daughters. If he takes another for himself, he shall not reduce her food,

56. See *HALAT* (3rd edn), p. 673a, '*npš* 6b'.

> clothing and oil. If he does not provide her with these three, she shall go free without payment of silver.

Two situations are envisaged:

1. She is assigned to a son of the purchaser. Many commentators (including myself), have assumed that the 'status of daughters' is an oblique reference to marriage with the son.[57] In the light of my earlier discussion of this law, I now consider it more likely that the provision is designed to counter another attempt by the purchaser to subvert the purpose of the contract. Assignment points to future consummation, which gives the purchaser the opportunity to temporize regarding the female slave's position while she waits for his son to come of age. The law insists that her master must in the interim give her the standing of a daughter within the household, not a servant, because the purpose of the contract is that she provide sexual and reproductive services, not labour.

2. The master takes her himself but subsequently takes a second concubine. Since he has fulfilled the purpose of the contract (and presumably taken the woman's virginity), unravelling it by redemption is not an appropriate solution to his failure to provide her with proper sustenance, which in any case was a more serious breach. It was a form of physical abuse, not merely a loss of rights in the abstract, and accordingly it annulled not just the contract of concubinage but the underlying debt.[58]

The mention of rations provides a final indication that this law was regulating concubinage, not marriage. The duty of a husband to provide his wife with sustenance was so self-evident that it went virtually unmentioned in ancient Near Eastern sources. Only where the husband is missing abroad, does the issue come to light. The law codes consider the inadequacy of his property for providing sustenance sufficient grounds for his wife to marry another (LH 134; MAL A 36). Rations

57. Westbrook, *Studies*, p. 61.

58. The same principle may be reflected in MAL A 39. The protasis describes a complicated and obscure situation in which a girl is pledged for her father's debt and then apparently becomes the object of rival claims between the pledgee, another creditor of her father, and a man to whom she has been given in marriage (apparently by the plegdee). Our concern is with yet another contingency (ll. 34-5): 'if she is badly provided for, she is free of claims, in favour of the one who sustains her', following the interpretation of K. Veenhof ('An Ancient Anatolian Money-Lender', *Festschrift Lubor Matouš* [ed. B. Hruška; Budapest: Eötvös Lorand Tudomanyegyetem, 1978], pp. 292-95); not of *CAD* (L, p. 249, '*lumnu* 3').

are the stuff of servants and dependants, not wives. Were the slave-woman married to her master, she could have relied on the protection given by her status as wife to ensure her sustenance, and would not have required special measures.

Summary and Conclusions

In the legal systems of the ancient Near East, the female slave, no less than her male counterpart, was property. The special features of her gender were property interests of her owner, to be exploited or disposed of as the latter saw fit. Thus the owner's interest in her sexuality was protected against interference by outsiders through the rules of property law, just as the integrity of any asset might be protected. By the same token, offspring of the slave, even when fathered by her owner, were in principle subject to the rules of property law, like the fruits of any asset.

At the same time, however, the female slave's sexuality and reproductive capacity brought into play the rules of family law, either through special applications of the principles of social justice, which tempered the condition of slaves in general, or directly through the status of marriage. In certain circumstances occasioned by the exercise of her sexual and reproductive functions, the principles of social justice could override the owner's property rights to render her inalienable, redeemable, or protected from physical abuse. The status of marriage, if with the owner himself, altogether excluded the application of property law to her person.

The question of which régime—property law or family law—was to prevail varied according to circumstances, and sometimes was resolved by compromise. For example, the principles of social justice could be avoided by express contractual provisions. Presumably such provisions could not override the equitable jurisdiction of the courts altogether, but they were employed so widely as to leave little doubt as to their efficacy, the limits of which cannot be ascertained. Similarly, where marriage was to a third party, there was a wide range of possibilities. If the slave was married to another slave of her owner, the owner's property rights prevailed, but if to a free person, the slave and her offspring enjoyed some of the consequences of a free marriage.

Finally, mention should be made of the special legal mechanism employed to regulate the status of a female slave. Where the property and family interests in her person were located in different persons, the law employed a subtle jurisprudential device: her legal personality was split between them, the two parts being governed by property and family law respectively. No better symbol could have been devised for the conflicting attitudes of the law towards the female slave.

INDEXES

INDEX OF REFERENCES

Index of Ancient Near Eastern Texts

Index of Authors

JOURNAL FOR THE STUDY OF THE OLD TESTAMENT
SUPPLEMENT SERIES

133 Roger Syrén, *The Forsaken Firstborn: A Study of a Recurrent Motif in the Patriarchal Narratives*
134 Gordon Mitchell, *Together in the Land: A Reading of the Book of Joshua*
135 Gordon F. Davies, *Israel in Egypt: Reading Exodus 1–2*
136 Paul Morris & Deborah Sawyer (eds.), *A Walk in the Garden: Biblical, Iconographical and Literary Images of Eden*
137 Henning Graf Reventlow & Yair Hoffman (eds.), *Justice and Righteousness: Biblical Themes and their Influence*
138 R.P. Carroll (ed.), *Text as Pretext: Essays in Honour of Robert Davidson*
139 James W. Watts, *Psalm and Story: Inset Hymns in Hebrew Narrative*
140 Walter Houston, *Purity and Monotheism: Clean and Unclean Animals in Biblical Law*
141 Gregory C. Chirichigno, *Debt-Slavery in Israel and the Ancient Near East*
142 Frederick H. Cryer, *Divination in Ancient Israel and its Near Eastern Environment: A Socio-Historical Investigation*
143 J. Cheryl Exum & David J.A. Clines (eds.), *The New Literary Criticism and the Hebrew Bible*
144 Philip R. Davies & David J.A. Clines (eds.), *Among the Prophets: Language, Imagery and Structure in the Prophetic Writings*
145 Charles S. Shaw, *The Speeches of Micah: A Rhetorical-Historical Analysis*
146 Gösta W. Ahlström, *The History of Ancient Palestine from the Palaeolithic Period to Alexander's Conquest* (ed. D. Edelman, with a contribution by G.O. Rollefson)
147 Tony W. Cartledge, *Vows in the Hebrew Bible and the Ancient Near East*
148 Philip R. Davies, *In Search of 'Ancient Israel'*
149 Eugene Ulrich, John W. Wright, Robert P. Carroll & Philip R. Davies (eds.), *Priests, Prophets and Scribes: Essays on the Formation and Heritage of Second Temple Judaism in Honour of Joseph Blenkinsopp*
150 Janet E. Tollington, *Tradition and Innovation in Haggai and Zechariah 1–8*
151 Joel Weinberg, *The Citizen–Temple Community* (trans. Daniel L. Smith Christopher)
152 A. Graeme Auld (ed.), *Understanding Poets and Prophets: Essays in Honour of George Wishart Anderson*
153 Donald K. Berry, *The Psalms and their Readers: Interpretive Strategies for Psalm 18*
154 Marc Brettler & Michael Fishbane (eds.), *Min'ah le-Na'um: Biblical and Other Studies Presented to Nahum M. Sarna in Honour of his 70th Birthday*
155 Jeffrey A. Fager, *Land Tenure and the Biblical Jubilee: Uncovering Hebrew Ethics through the Sociology of Knowledge*

156 John W. Kleinig, *The Lord's Song: The Basis, Function and Significance of Choral Music in Chronicles*
157 Gordon R. Clark, *The Word Ḥesed in the Hebrew Bible*
158 Mary Douglas, *In the Wilderness: The Doctrine of Defilement in the Book of Numbers*
159 J. Clinton McCann (ed.), *The Shape and Shaping of the Psalter*
160 William Riley, *King and Cultus in Chronicles: Worship and the Reinterpretation of History*
161 George W. Coats, *The Moses Tradition*
162 Heather A. McKay & David J.A. Clines (eds.), *Of Prophets' Visions and the Wisdom of Sages: Essays in Honour of R. Norman Whybray on his Seventieth Birthday*
163 J. Cheryl Exum, *Fragmented Women: Feminist (Sub)versions of Biblical Narratives*
164 Lyle Eslinger, *House of God or House of David: The Rhetoric of 2 Samuel 7*
166 D.R.G. Beattie & M.J. McNamara (eds.), *The Aramaic Bible: Targums in their Historical Context*
167 Raymond F. Person, *Second Zechariah and the Deuteronomic School*
168 R.N. Whybray, *The Composition of the Book of Proverbs*
169 Bert Dicou, *Edom, Israel's Brother and Antagonist: The Role of Edom in Biblical Prophecy and Story*
170 Wilfred G.E. Watson, *Traditional Techniques in Classical Hebrew Verse*
171 Henning Graf Reventlow, Yair Hoffman & Benjamin Uffenheimer (eds.), *Politics and Theopolitics in the Bible and Postbiblical Literature*
172 Volkmar Fritz, *An Introduction to Biblical Archaeology*
173 M. Patrick Graham, William P. Brown & Jeffrey K. Kuan (eds.), *History and Interpretation: Essays in Honour of John H. Hayes*
174 Joe M. Sprinkle, *'The Book of the Covenant': A Literary Approach*
175 Tamara C. Eskenazi & Kent H. Richards (eds.), *Second Temple Studies*. II. *Temple and Community in the Persian Period*
176 Gershon Brin, *Studies in Biblical Law: From the Hebrew Bible to the Dead Sea Scrolls*
177 David Allan Dawson, *Text-Linguistics and Biblical Hebrew*
178 Martin Ravndal Hauge, *Between Sheol and Temple: Motif Structure and Function in the I-Psalms*
179 J.G. McConville & J.G. Millar, *Time and Place in Deuteronomy*
180 Richard L. Schultz, *The Search for Quotation: Verbal Parallels in the Prophets*
181 Bernard M. Levinson (ed.), *Theory and Method in Biblical and Cuneiform Law: Revision, Interpolation and Development*
182 Steven L. McKenzie & M. Patrick Graham (eds.), *The History of Israel's Traditions: The Heritage of Martin Noth*
183 John Day (ed.), *Lectures on the Religion of the Semites (Second and Third Series) by William Robertson Smith*

184 John C. Reeves & John Kampen (eds.), *Pursuing the Text: Studies in Honor of Ben Zion Wacholder on the Occasion of his Seventieth Birthday*
185 Seth Daniel Kunin, *The Logic of Incest: A Structuralist Analysis of Hebrew Mythology*
186 Linda Day, *Three Faces of a Queen: Characterization in the Books of Esther*
187 Charles V. Dorothy, *The Books of Esther: Structure, Genre and Textual Integrity*
188 Robert H. O'Connell, *Concentricity and Continuity: The Literary Structure of Isaiah*
189 William Johnstone (ed.), *William Robertson Smith: Essays in Reassessment*
190 Steven W. Holloway & Lowell K. Handy (eds.), *The Pitcher is Broken: Memorial Essays for Gösta W. Ahlström*
192 Henning Graf Reventlow & William Farmer (eds.), *Biblical Studies and the Shifting of Paradigms, 1850–1914*
193 Brooks Schramm, *The Opponents of Third Isaiah: Reconstructing the Cultic History of the Restoration*
194 Else Kragelund Holt, *Prophesying the Past: The Use of Israel's History in the Book of Hosea*
195 Jon Davies, Graham Harvey & Wilfred G.E. Watson (eds.), *Words Remembered, Texts Renewed: Essays in Honour of John F.A. Sawyer*
196 Joel S. Kaminsky, *Corporate Responsibility in the Hebrew Bible*
197 William M. Schniedewind, *The Word of God in Transition: From Prophet to Exegete in the Second Temple Period*
198 T.J. Meadowcroft, *Aramaic Daniel and Greek Daniel: A Literary Comparison*
199 J.H. Eaton, *Psalms of the Way and the Kingdom: A Conference with the Commentators*
200 Mark Daniel Carroll R., David J.A. Clines & Philip R. Davies (eds.), *The Bible in Human Society: Essays in Honour of John Rogerson*
201 John W. Rogerson, *The Bible and Criticism in Victorian Britain: Profiles of F.D. Maurice and William Robertson Smith*
202 Nanette Stahl, *Law and Liminality in the Bible*
203 Jill M. Munro, *Spikenard and Saffron: The Imagery of the Song of Songs*
204 Philip R. Davies, *Whose Bible Is It Anyway?*
205 David J.A. Clines, *Interested Parties: The Ideology of Writers and Readers of the Hebrew Bible*
206 Møgens Müller, *The First Bible of the Church: A Plea for the Septuagint*
207 John W. Rogerson, Margaret Davies & Mark Daniel Carroll R. (eds.), *The Bible in Ethics: The Second Sheffield Colloquium*
208 Beverly J. Stratton, *Out of Eden: Reading, Rhetoric, and Ideology in Genesis 2–3*
209 Patricia Dutcher-Walls, *Narrative Art, Political Rhetoric: The Case of Athaliah and Joash*
210 Jacques Berlinerblau, *The Vow and the 'Popular Religious Groups' of Ancient Israel: A Philological and Sociological Inquiry*
211 Brian E. Kelly, *Retribution and Eschatology in Chronicles*

212 Yvonne Sherwood, *The Prostitute and the Prophet: Hosea's Marriage in Literary-Theoretical Perspective*
213 Yair Hoffman, *A Blemished Perfection: The Book of Job in Context*
214 Roy F. Melugin & Marvin A. Sweeney (eds.), *New Visions of Isaiah*
215 J. Cheryl Exum, *Plotted, Shot and Painted: Cultural Representations of Biblical Women*
216 Judith E. McKinlay, *Gendering Wisdom the Host: Biblical Invitations to Eat and Drink*
217 Jerome F.D. Creach, *Yahweh as Refuge and the Editing of the Hebrew Psalter*
218 Gregory Glazov, *The Bridling of the Tongue and the Opening of the Mouth in Biblical Prophecy*
219 Gerald Morris, *Prophecy, Poetry and Hosea*
220 Raymond F. Person, Jr, *In Conversation with Jonah: Conversation Analysis, Literary Criticism, and the Book of Jonah*
221 Gillian Keys, *The Wages of Sin: A Reappraisal of the 'Succession Narrative'*
222 R.N. Whybray, *Reading the Psalms as a Book*
223 Scott B. Noegel, *Janus Parallelism in the Book of Job*
224 Paul J. Kissling, *Reliable Characters in the Primary History: Profiles of Moses, Joshua, Elijah and Elisha*
225 Richard D. Weis & David M. Carr (eds.), *A Gift of God in Due Season: Essays on Scripture and Community in Honor of James A. Sanders*
226 Lori L. Rowlett, *Joshua and the Rhetoric of Violence: A New Historicist Analysis*
227 John F.A. Sawyer (ed.), *Reading Leviticus: Responses to Mary Douglas*
228 Volkmar Fritz and Philip R. Davies (eds.), *The Origins of the Ancient Israelite States*
229 Stephen Breck Reid (ed.), *Prophets and Paradigms: Essays in Honor of Gene M. Tucker*
230 Kevin J. Cathcart and Michael Maher (eds.), *Targumic and Cognate Studies: Essays in Honour of Martin McNamara*
231 Weston W. Fields, *Sodom and Gomorrah: History and Motif in Biblical Narrative*
232 Tilde Binger, *Asherah: Goddesses in Ugarit, Israel and the Old Testament*
233 Michael D. Goulder, *The Psalms of Asaph and the Pentateuch: Studies in the Psalter, III*
234 Ken Stone, *Sex, Honor, and Power in the Deuteronomistic History*
235 James W. Watts and Paul House (eds.), *Forming Prophetic Literature: Essays on Isaiah and the Twelve in Honor of John D.W. Watts*
236 Thomas M. Bolin, *Freedom beyond Forgiveness: The Book of Jonah Re-Examined*
237 Neil Asher Silberman and David B. Small (eds.), *The Archaeology of Israel: Constructing the Past, Interpreting the Present*
238 M. Patrick Graham, Kenneth G. Hoglund and Steven L. McKenzie (eds.), *The Chronicler as Historian*

239 Mark S. Smith, *The Pilgrimage Pattern in Exodus* (with contributions by Elizabeth M. Bloch-Smith)
240 Eugene E. Carpenter (ed.), *A Biblical Itinerary: In Search of Method, Form and Content. Essays in Honor of George W. Coats*
241 Robert Karl Gnuse, *No Other Gods: Emergent Monotheism in Israel*
242 K.L. Noll, *The Faces of David*
243 Henning Graf Reventlow, *Eschatology in the Bible and in Jewish and Christian Tradition*
244 Walter E. Aufrecht, Neil A. Mirau and Steven W. Gauley (eds.), *Aspects of Urbanism in Antiquity: From Mesopotamia to Crete*
245 Lester L. Grabbe, *Can a 'History of Israel' Be Written?*
246 Gillian M. Bediako, *Primal Religion and the Bible: William Robertson Smith and his Heritage*
248 Etienne Nodet, *A Search for the Origins of Judaism: From Joshua to the Mishnah*
249 William Paul Griffin, *The God of the Prophets: An Analysis of Divine Action*
250 Josette Elayi and Jean Sapin (eds.), *Beyond the River: New Perspectives on Transeuphratene*
251 Flemming A.J. Nielsen, *The Tragedy in History: Herodotus and the Deuteronomistic History*
252 David C. Mitchell, *The Message of the Psalter: An Eschatological Programme in the Book of Psalms*
253 William Johnstone, *1 and 2 Chronicles, Vol. 1: 1 Chronicles 1–2 Chronicles 9: Israel's Place among the Nations*
254 William Johnstone, *1 and 2 Chronicles, Vol. 2: 2 Chronicles 10–36: Guilt and Atonement*
255 Larry L. Lyke, *King David with the Wise Woman of Tekoa: The Resonance of Tradition in Parabolic Narrative*
256 Roland Meynet, *Rhetorical Analysis: An Introduction to Biblical Rhetoric* translated by Luc Racaut
257 Philip R. Davies and David J.A. Clines (eds.), *The World of Genesis: Persons, Places, Perspectives*
258 Michael D. Goulder, *The Psalms of the Return (Book V, Psalms 107–150): Studies in the Psalter, IV*
259 Allen Rosengren Petersen, *The Royal God: Enthronement Festivals in Ancient Israel and Ugarit?*
262 Victor H. Matthews, Bernard M. Levinson and Tikva Frymer-Kensky (eds.), *Gender and Law in the Hebrew Bible and the Ancient Near East*
269 David J.A. Clines and Stephen D. Moore (eds.), *Auguries: The Jubilee Volume of the Sheffield Department of Biblical Studies*
272 James Richard Linville, *Israel in the Book of Kings: The Past as a Project of Social Identity*

www.ingramcontent.com/pod-product-compliance
Ingram Content Group UK Ltd.
Pitfield, Milton Keynes, MK11 3LW, UK
UKHW020138290926
15471UKWH00003B/559